PEDIGREE
AND
PROGRESS

Essays in the genealogical interpretation
of history

Pedigree
and
Progress

Essays in the
genealogical interpretation of history

by
Anthony Wagner
K.C.V.O., D.Litt., M.A.

PHILLIMORE

1975

Published by

PHILLIMORE & CO. LTD.

London and Chichester

Head Office: Shopwyke Hall,
Chichester, Sussex, England

© Sir Anthony Wagner, 1975

ISBN 0 85033 198 6

Text set in 11 pt. Baskerville
Made and printed by
Unwin Brothers Limited
Gresham Press, Old Woking, Surrey

CONTENTS

Pedigrees   *Notes*

Chapter II (apart from paragraph 2 on page 43) was delivered as the Seton Memorial Lecture at University College, London, in October 1970.

Chapter VI was delivered as a lecture at Queen Mary College, London, in 1965.

Chapter VII was delivered as the Society of Genealogists' Jubilee Lecture in the Meeting Room of the Society of Antiquaries at Burlington House on 15 December 1961.

PREFACE

In the essays which make up this book I have explored new ways in which genealogy — and heraldry — may, as I hope, throw light on history. I have attempted this less as an historian than as a herald and genealogist whose concern with history has been enlarged by the requirements of his own discipline. In the process of relating history to genealogy and heraldry I have come to feel that these latter have far more potentially to tell historians than historians in these days ask or expect of them.

Modern scientific genealogy originated in the sixteenth and following centuries mainly in the criticism of pedigrees designed to establish rights of property and nobility. Because of this, in the eyes of many historians and others critical genealogy itself is tarred with the brush of feudal and dynastic attitudes and it is assumed almost without a thought that its utility is confined to that context. Part of my purpose has therefore been to show that, great as its value indeed is in that special field, its possible application is far wider. I have tried to show that the related assumption, that the pedigrees of the non-noble cannot be traced or do not matter, has, to an unascertained extent, distorted history. If this is so, it is because, where scholarship is not attempted, uncritical assumptions — in this case uncritical assumptions of non-genealogical historians about the genealogies of the greater part of mankind — have been made.

All history is biased by accidents of documentation, the accident of whether evidence survives or not and the personal bias of those who have written things down. To detect this bias in the narrative and other documentary sources by calling in the evidence of archaeology, economics, demography, and material evidence in general has been a major concern of recent historians. It is therefore the more surprising that the vast field of factual detail which genealogical sources offer has remained so largely untilled.

Part of the trouble is that the process, in its early stages especially, is technical and immensely laborious. The records from which pedigrees may be extracted are for the most part in manuscript and may be hard to read, technical in form, occasional, unindexed and even uncalendared. Even when in print their correct interpretation calls for knowledge, judgment and experience. At the end of an earlier book having surveyed this ground in some detail, I asked and tried to answer the question how, 'if a wealthy foundation or a welfare state put astronomical funds at our disposal for providing all its citizens with pedigrees', we should spend them to the best advantage.[1] The present book tries to hint at the kind of historical illumination we might hope to find or try to look for, if this work, or much of it, had first been done.

In a book of this kind little space can be given to discussion of the evidence for the pedigrees used. I have therefore, where I could, used material for which the evidence and, where necessary, discussion of it have been printed, and I have said where this may be found. My pedigrees are, of course, mere extracts, designed to illustrate particular points, and though by printing them I express acceptance of what I print, I ought to say that I by no means always accept the whole of the pedigrees referred to, from which the parts I print are taken. It also goes without saying that in many places (e.g. in Chapter II) I have simply taken the views of those whom I believe to be good authorities.

1 *English genealogy*, Oxford, 1960 ed., p. 371, 1972 ed. p. 420.

CHAPTER I

PEDIGREE AND PROGRESS

I have an Anglo-Saxon fondness for alliteration, and *Pride and Prejudice, Progress and Poverty, Peerage and Pedigree,* floating in my head, have combined to suggest *Pedigree and Progress* as a title for what I want here to say. At first I rejected it as possibly misleading. But the more I thought of it, the more it seemed to me that discussion of the ambiguities of the words, so far from clouding, should illuminate the distinctions I wished to draw.

The reader's first thought may well be that the author is a genealogical snob setting out to argue that national progress depends on the talent of selected stocks, the creative few, the men of pedigree in the sense of pedigree dogs or cattle. To these readers, let me first say that their interpretation assumes limited, local definitions both of progress and of pedigree, and that these need clarification before such views can be intelligibly asserted, let alone proved.

Pedigree, then, is *pied de gru*, the foot of a crane, and alludes to a form in which genealogies were set out in the Middle Ages. Hence the word came to mean no more nor less than a genealogy, a schematic record of family descent. In the eighteenth century, however, new arts of stockbreeding led to records being kept of the pedigrees of race horses and prize cattle. These thus came to be called pedigreed horses, pedigreed cattle, as against the common sort whose pedigrees noone knew. Thus the word pedigree acquired overtones of superiority which the word genealogy has never had. I, however, use it here not in that way but simply as a synonym for genealogy, and I do so because it is shorter and begins with P.

I do not, naturally, overlook that the snobbish meaning of pedigree fed on the fact that noble families must know their pedigrees, while others need not. One of the meanings of noble is one whose pedigree is known; and here it is the word *known* that holds the overtones — known to royal courts, known to the world, known to the heralds. But this attitude to pedigrees and to nobility belongs to certain times and places only. It is far from primaeval, far from universal.

In the kind of society we call tribal the claims of kinship were and are paramount, for rich and poor alike. The unity of the kindred, whether expressed in the blood feud, in the rules of inheritance or exogamy, or in whatever way, was a fact of life which made it necessary for each to know who he was, so that children, from Tartary to Polynesia, from Judaea to Ireland, were taught in childhood to recite their pedigrees, or else a bardic class was maintained, among whose duties it was to preserve the pedigrees of all the tribe. When the aged Maori chief Tamarau appeared before the New Zealand land commission, he supported his people's claim to certain lands by reciting for more than three days pedigrees and ramifications comprising thirty four generations and more than fourteen hundred names.

Mrs. Bridget Fitzgerald who lived in the barony of Barrymore and County of Cork and died aged ninety in 1808, was another such repository of tradition, being known as Brighid na Senchas, Bridget of the Histories. Lord Barrymore asked her why she held his descent less honourable than that of some other Barries and, when she told him, deprived her of her farm, saying 'Have the honour, but I'll have the land'. The slight related to the bigamy of his ancestor James Barryroe of Ibawne in the fifteenth century.

The Welsh genealogists, whom the English heralds made their deputies in Wales in the sixteenth and seventeenth centuries, wrote down long, orally transmitted pedigrees, for many of which documentary confirmation has since been found. Similarly pedigrees of Polynesian chieftains, written down from oral tradition in modern times in islands scattered at thousand mile intervals across the Pacific Ocean, are confirmed by the correspondence in their early generations between lines believed to have lost contact for perhaps five centuries.

The pedigrees of the chieftains were the histories and the title deeds of their tribes or nations. Lesser lines, sometimes truly, sometimes falsely, were deduced from cadets of greater lines and these from those of the greatest. It is said that three quarters of the whole Welsh people were *bonheddig,* men of free descent capable of holding land — in English, gentlemen — the rest being sprung from slaves.

It was not for knowing anything of heraldry that Lord Carlisle as Deputy Earl Marshal nominated Sir John Vanbrugh to be Carlisle Herald in 1703 and Clarenceux King of Arms in 1704. It was merely because he had designed for him a great house, Castle Howard, and he was a witty, agreeable man of genius. Yet Vanbrugh had observed something of genealogists and had, to his new colleagues' chagrin, made a comic herald a character in one of his plays. 'Your father, Sir, ha, ha,' says Quaint, the herald, 'I know every Man's Father, Sir, and every Man's Grand-father, and every Man's Great-Grand-father. Why, Sir, I'm a Herald by Nature, my Mother was a *Welch Woman.*' '*A Welch*

Woman? prithee of what Country's that?' 'That, Sir, is a Country in the World's back-side, where every Man is born a Gentleman, and a Genealogist.'

When a king of Welsh descent, Henry VIII, did what no Norman or English conqueror had done and abolished gavelkind in Wales in 1542, the root of the tribal system there was cut and it began slowly to die. The many poor, proud gentlemen with tiny estates, subdivided in successive generations, gave place by stages to a half-Anglicized gentry, whose estates now grew by purchase, marriage and primogeniture, while Wales set out upon a course on which England was set before the Norman Conquest.

Resistance to such changes can be powerful and long drawn out. To find tribal attitudes surviving in Wales or the Scottish Highlands is not surprising. To encounter them in modern England is astonishing, yet such astonishment not long ago came my way.[1] It is the duty of Garter King of Arms to interview each newly designated peer and settle his title. In 1964 Mr. Hervey Rhodes, Labour Member of Parliament for Ashton-under-Lyne since 1945, was to be made a Life Peer — in the event becoming Lord Rhodes. When he came to see me I asked a question about his family. His ancestors, he told me, were yeomen, clothiers and handloom weavers, living in the Pennine valleys about Saddleworth on the Yorkshire-Lancashire border. They were among the many in those parts whom the Industrial Revolution ground down to the status of factory hands. But they remembered who they were and he as a child was taught to say that he was 'Hervey of Jack's of Bill's of Jack's of Joe's of John's of Thomas's of Dean Head', a seven generation pedigree. Dean Head was a clothier's house at the head of a valley, where Thomas Rhodes had lived about 1700.

When he first stood for Parliament in 1945 Lord Rhodes had occasion to speak in a part of the constituency where he was not well known. Dean Head was not far off and he introduced himself, like a Homeric hero, by reciting the pedigree he had been taught as a child. No sooner had he done so than an old, white bearded man stood up at the back of the hall and put him right, saying that Thomas was not of

---

1. I should have been less astonished if I had at that time read Sabine Baring-Gould's *Old Country Life,* 1890, p. 298, where he writes that 'To this day in the western hills of Yorkshire, separating that county from Lancashire, persons are known by their pedigrees, and very often their surnames are generally unknown. Tom is not Tom Greenwood, but Tom o' Jakes, that is, Tom the son of Jack; and if there be two Toms in a parish both sons of Jack, then one is distinguished from the other by carrying the pedigree further back a stage. One is Tom o' Jakes o' Will's and the other is Tom o' Jakes o' Harry's'. All the same Lord Rhodes' pedigree goes far beyond this.

Dean Head but of Dean Head Clough. Now Dean Head Clough was the smaller of two ancient family houses standing close together.

Sociologists and local historians should combine to throw light on this surprising survival in the industrialized twentieth century Pennines of a custom which one would not look to find nearer than in seventeenth century rural Wales. Three factors might be looked at. We are here in the Danelaw, where free tenures of land still survived in the Middle Ages, which the Anglo-Saxons of the South had lost, and with them perhaps other Viking customs. Certainly in sixteenth century South Lancashire parish registers it is not uncommon to find children described at baptism as John Thomasson Smith or Mary Thomas-daughter Taylor, as if they were Icelanders.

And not only are we in the North but in the Highlands. We remember Wordsworth's *Ode to Liberty*.

> *Two voices are there, one is of the Sea,*
> *One of the mountains, each a mighty voice:*
> *In both from age to age, thou didst rejoice.*
> *They were thy chosen music, Liberty.*

In 1869, when poverty had long overtaken the region, the people of these upland weaving villages still kept attitudes the valley people had lost. From these latter they kept apart and 'teawn's folk' they despised.[2] Yet it is said that their social conservatism had played an important part in their downfall. They had been handloom weavers, aristocrats of labour, and the last decade of the eighteenth century had been their golden age. When following years brought technological change their wages were progressively reduced so that, adhering to their old ways, they were ground down by degrees into abject poverty. It is said that by the 1830s theirs was a doomed occupation.[3] Perhaps, then, the consciousness that they were other than their neighbours and had known glories now departed, drove them even in the changed climate of this century to maintain the record of whence they came.

One could draw different morals from this story. To a genealogist the outstanding point is that to know who one is and whence one comes is a part of human dignity and self respect which men will hold to longer than one would think likely, to save themselves from total prole-tarianization — reduction, that is, to the status of human cattle, reckoned in the nation's scale by their numbers and the number of their children only.

And in what sense is the change from tribalism to industry to be called progress? Progress is a word among the branches of whose many meanings philosophers and politicians love to sport. It is, therefore, a

2 Edwin Waugh, *Lancashire Studies*, 1869, p. 128.
3 E. P. Thompson, *The making of the English Working Class*, 1963, p. 308.

word which, like democracy or public interest, no honest man should use without first saying in which of the possible senses he means to use it, and he should not, if he can help it, surreptitiously shift from that sense to others in the course of his argument. We have two questions to ask the progressives; what it is they mean by progress; and whose progress they are concerned with.

To progress is to move forward, which implies a defined objective and a fixed direction. To say that between 1850 and 1900 in England the rate of infant mortality declined is to say something clear, significant and verifiable. To say, however, that in the same time and place the sum of human happiness was increased, is to say something certainly unverifiable and probably meaningless. This, none the less, is the kind of thing many people have since the eighteenth century wished to be able to say. I suppose that neither antiquity nor the Middle Ages would have dreamed of such a concept as the sum of human happiness. But the success of scientific thought from Bacon to Newton and onwards in clarifying the world, made philosophers and legislators long, in Halévy's phrase, for a moral Newtonianism, such as for a time seemed to be provided by Bentham's felicific calculus — the test of producing or tending to produce the greatest happiness of the greatest number.

Since one could calculate mathematically the effect of particular projects which promoted happiness — the reduction of disease by sanitary measures, the improvement of nutrition, the speeding of transport and so forth — it seemed reasonable to hope that, in time and by scientific analysis, some way might be found of combining all such calculations into one grand calculus to promote the total felicity of mankind. Thus the world embarked on an age of statistics, returns, blue books, commissions and legislation, beneath the banner of reform and the umbrella name of Progress.

This bias towards the mechanical, the measurable, the quantitative, brought happiness to some but misery to others, great improvements in some of the arts of life, but decay of others, since what could not be measured was often ignored or assumed not to exist, yet continued to affect human happiness immeasurably. The preceding decades had seen a startling growth in population, never yet fully explained, and the numbers pressed on the means of subsistence. Provisions of the Poor Law indeed saved many from starvation, though not from great miseries. But a new phase now ensued. The development of factories in industrial towns gave an opening, for life if not for happiness, to great numbers of the surplus poor of the countryside. Much smaller, yet by no means small numbers from all classes meanwhile grew rich by directing this growth of industry or by indirect profit from it.

For how many of these great numbers whose lives were changed by the mechanical and industrial revolution was the change one to greater happiness? If we could take each life and see what, in its depths, it was

before and after, we should still not know what it would have been had
the world gone otherwise. But, even if we knew that, could we
confidently say that one kind of life was happier or better in itself — as
opposed to its accidents — than another, quite different kind of life? If
the depressed weavers of South Yorkshire in 1840 could, with clear
sight, have looked on the one hand back to the lives of their ancestors
in 1790 or on the other forward to those of their descendants in 1970,
which would they have chosen? They would surely not all have chosen
alike, and even if we knew the answers, how much more should we
know of the reality or unreality of progress?

If we could surmount these difficulties of fact and theory, still
another, of deep principle, would remain, namely that of valuing life
against life and period against period. Each individual, let us suppose, is
to count as a unit of happiness, while his personal happiness will be
measured as a percentage of the total happiness possible to him. On this
reckoning one thousand million people, each five per cent happy,
would be preferable to one million people, each completely happy.

But if this way of doing the sum does not appeal, we may reckon
rather by a happiness quotient. We may aim, that is, not for the highest
total of happiness, but for the highest average percentage of it. On that
footing one entirely happy man would be better than a thousand
million half happy.

> *Two paradises are in one*
> *To live in paradise alone.*

Some quibblers still might argue, that some men and their happiness
should be valued at a higher rate than others — for instance because
their lives are more beneficial. A Beethoven's happiness might weigh
heavier in the scale than that of a Titus Oates. But can we be sure that
the happiness given to others by Beethoven's music was not increased
by his own unhappiness driving him to supreme expression? Or that a
happier Titus Oates might not have been a power for good?

The *reductio ad absurdum* which these examples constitute, may
suggest to others, as it does to me, that the notion of estimating
progress by a calculation of increase in the quantity of human
happiness would be ridiculous if it were not meaningless and meaningless if not ridiculous. If we are to talk of people progressing we must be
more limited and more specific. Reduction in infant mortality, increase
in speed of travel and many more specific achievements we can tabulate
and boast. But how are these to be weighed against loss of confidence,
of contentment and of creative power?

We come now to our second question to the progressives — whose
progress are they concerned with? Not much I think with that of
persons of my age, for we shall not be here to share much if anything of
their plans' fruition — and with the *Progress of the Soul* they are little
concerned. Let us not, however, complain of that if it is our children

and grandchildren who are to benefit. But that is not so clear either. We are told that we must be prepared for our own grandchildren to go down so that those of people now *deprived* may come up.

This ideal will still engage some of us, if the unit, for whose progress we and ours are to live or die, can be acceptably defined — for instance as our nation. But that will hardly do in a nation whose current decline progressives cheer. *Wider still and wider* we have therefore to look. We must not be mere tribalist progressives. Who cares what became of the Caribs or the Tasmanians? Why, then, should we not think a century progressive in which the English name vanished and survivors of the English stock were dispersed and merged in others like the lost tribes of Israel?

Even so, the wider unit, whose progress is to be our aim, remains to be defined. Is it to be the human race and are our kindred stocks of the animal and vegetable kingdoms to be excluded, or treated but as means to our ends? That might do for genealogists, but not for those to whom *racialist* is a term of abuse. For what could be more racialist than a plan to subjugate other races than one's own — to the point of killing and eating them (just as one does now)? We conclude then that progressives must be genealogists or nothing. Their object must be the survival and success of some one group as against others. And how can any future group of living beings be defined unless genealogically — as the progeny of some group existing now?

The effect of concentrating on quantitative, measurable kinds of progress has naturally been to promote these at the expense of those other kinds which are disbelieved in by the moral Newtonians because they cannot be measured. If our age produces no Chartres, no Sistine Chapel, no Shakespeare, no Bach, is it not because the desires of those, who dispose of resources and direct activities, are set on the domination of nature, rather than on the elevation and expansion of the spirit? Despite or through the natural protest and reaction against this outlook the symptoms of this view of the world are all about us, in functionalist and abstract art and architecture, in welfare politics, in godless religion and in general frustration. May a genealogist, therefore, now briefly set out his own view of history, as a preface to a still briefer exposition of his view of progress?

To a genealogist history is a tournament of combining or competing families, whose subtle interplay and manoeuvres, never wholly to be understood, we can only begin to grasp by first analysing and clarifying their genealogies. All history is full of myth. Men see in it what they need to see and distort truth to support themselves. This is as true yesterday and today, with Whig or economic or sociological interpretations of history, as it was when mankind was derived from Adam and Eve, the kings of Rome from Troy, or Odin from a son of Noah. Witness the still flourishing seventeenth century cult of Magna Carta as the root of our liberties and the cult of the English Parliament which has produced such strange attempts to transplant that unique growth to alien soils. Each kind of history has tied to its tail its own special kind of liability to falsehood.

Claims to unsurpassed nobility and antiquity are the natural foible of genealogists. Among the Teutonic tribes which broke the barriers of the Roman Empire and resettled Western Europe from the fourth century onwards were numerous petty royal families whose claim to rule was expressed in their claims to divine descent. Conversion to Christianity undermined such claims and with them might undermine the dynasties, unless new descents of equal grandeur could be furnished, as in some instances they were, to replace these. Hence the gorgeous biblical and classical origins, provided by monkish chroniclers for convert kings from Ireland to Armenia to replace the divine origins. Among them was the basis of that British history which Geoffrey of Monmouth later turned to such advantage, and which still gratifies the British Israelites. Among them also was the descent from King David ascribed to the Bagratid kings of Georgia and Armenia — who more probably descend from Cyrus and Artaxerxes and might even possess a true descent from Jewish kings, though not the one ascribed. Possibly also among these replacement pedigrees was the Solomonic descent of the Ethiopian kings.

No less powerful than these in its own historical context was the quite different myth to which I was brought up, which treats social classes as distinct, self perpetuating hereditary corporations. I have called this the conspiracy of the conservatives and the revolutionaries to pretend that social mobility has been much less in the past than in fact it always was. The conservatives wished to believe that the same families had always been noble, which showed their merit; while the revolutionaries wished to believe that the same families had always been poor, which showed that their poverty was their oppressors' fault and not their own. Even the middle classes, whose social movement up or down was often rapid enough to be visible to the naked eye, did their best to hide this movement in the anonymity of city life.

I was first awakened from my slumbrous acceptance of all this by the raucous genealogical strictures of Horace Round. His exposures of false claims to lofty origins were funnier for the reader than for the victims, though the latter were sometimes able to raise a smile. Lord Denbigh may not have been best pleased when in 1901 Round exploded the Elizabethan tale that his thirteenth century Feilding ancestors were Counts of Rheinfelden, exiled Hapsburgs. The present family, however, appears content with its descent from fifteenth century esquires and has named the earlier ghosts Perhapsburgs.

Earl Spencer accepts with so much equanimity deprivation at the hands of Round of medieval Despencer ancestors that he actually celebrated the anniversary of the once despised grant of arms made in 1504 to his sheepowning ancestor; thereby recalling his later ancestor's retort to the Earl of Arundel in 1621 that when the Spencers were keeping sheep, (with which that Earl had reproached him), Arundel's ancestors were plotting treason.

Horace Round, though a great scholar, was not always right, nor (perhaps excused by ill health) always kind. My friend Wilfrid Hemp once, long ago, asked the porter of the Society of Antiquaries, whose was the figure crossing Burlington House courtyard. 'That's Mr. Round, Sir. He hates everybody and everybody hates him and he hates himself most of all'. A young American scholar once asked Round to comment on the proofs of his forthcoming book. He sent them back without a word, but later, reviewing the book, fell upon errors, which had been in the proofs but, unobserved by him, had been corrected in the published text. 'Could you have held up your head after that?' said Oswald Barron, who told me the story. Yet Sir Frank Stenton recalled that Round could be very generous to the work of young scholars.

From Round genealogical scholarship acquired a new critical attitude, but far more work than he had time for was, and still is, needed before we can place all in a new and just perspective. His concern was mainly with noble families and the Middle Ages and even in this field he left much for his successors to do. The group of these who produced the new *Complete Peerage* have drawn a larger picture, but still far from a comprehensive one. Indeed both their subject matter and the precise and critical nature of their scholarship have held them back from attempting such a panorama. Their business has been to verify specific facts, not to generalize.

They have, however, now established enough clear and firm examples to give both social historians and genealogists some basis for painting wider pictures. All such pictures are liable to error, but between the errors of the historians on one side and those of the genealogists on the other an important distinction may be drawn. Those of the historian are more likely to rebound on others; those of the genealogist on himself. The reason is that, whereas the historian is seeking to instruct others, the genealogist is merely trying to construct a working tool for his own use. By building up a picture of what is usual he hopes to be better able to solve his own next problem. It may be said that, if his picture errs, it will merely lead him to a false solution which noone will detect. That might have been so once — but not since Round. Critics are now armed and detection will follow, soon or later.

In my youth I think most people believed without question the agreed fable of the conservatives and the revolutionaries that social classes were in the main continuous in their family membership. New men, *nouveaux riches,* indeed appeared from time to time. But they were conspicuous by their rarity and they and their progeny remained distinguishable from the old rich, sometimes for generations. Conversely there were known, though hushed up, failures, ne'er-do-weels, exiles from their class and if possible from their country. They too were dramatic exceptions who proved the rule.

What one did not grasp was the normality and frequency of fairly close links between rich and poor arising not from these sharp dramatic social movements, but from an accumulation of small ones. I was born into a middle class, professional family and the relations on both sides whom I came to know were of similar occupations and standing. The summary pedigrees, which were shown me, recorded substantial mercantile antecedents but nothing *lower*. Before I had left school, however, my researches had ferreted out relationships of greater variety and interest — on certain sides rather higher in the social scale than had been expected, on others decidedly lower. It surprised me that near kinsmen, whose lines in two or three not very great steps had moved some way apart socially, should be not merely estranged but wholly unknown to each other. I wondered if my own family pattern was in this respect unusual. Experience as a genealogist has long since convinced me that it is not.

A not uncommon type of such a case was noted in 1874 by Francis Kilvert, the diarist, when he met at the entrance to Malmesbury 'a fine, handsome old man with a white beard, a labouring man with a spade over his shoulders'. Kilvert asked him how the Vicar, Mr. Pitt, was. 'Very ill,' he said, adding, 'His Father and my father were brothers' children, but one family has gone up and the other down.' Kilvert asked if the Vicar recognised him. 'No,' he said, adding that he had been footman at Cole Park 'pointing to the tops of the elms in the rookery avenue, leading to the house.'[4]

Doubtless the population growth and social changes and movements of the nineteenth century broke up family links and patterns with especial speed and force. Yet social movement on a considerable scale was nothing new in England. A. L. Reade discovered the piquant

---

4 Reference is made to surprising nineteenth century marriage links and relationships between rich and poor and of the various, but generally critical, attitudes taken towards them, by Derek Hudson, *Munby Man of Two Worlds: the Life and Diaries of Arthur J. Munby 1828-1910*, John Murray, 1972, pp. 51, 54-5, 72, 145, 148, 167-8 and *passim*. E.g. the second marriage in 1862 of Lord Robert Montagu (1825-1902), second son of the sixth Duke of Manchester, to Elizabeth Catherine (Betsy) Wade, a housemaid in Westbourne Grove, whom he first saw walking in Kensington Gardens. There were several children and are numerous descendants of this marriage. A 'maid of all work' with a right hand 'strong and coarse as that of a six foot bricklayer', admitted with strange confusion to Munby, in a railway train to the Crystal Palace in 1860, that her father had been *Curate to the Vicar of Grantham*. "I turned to her in amazement . . . "Impossible." I said: "Your father a *clergyman*. You do not know what you are saying", "Yes I do", she answered quietly' (p. 72). Alexander Macmillan (1818-96), founder with his brother of the great publishing firm, had some conversation with Munby in 1864 'on the word *gentleman* — wherein he told me that his father was a small farmer near Glasgow, and his mother a typical Scotch peasant woman — and that he himself began life as a shopman at thirty pounds a year, and was afterwards usher in a little school' (p 148).

connection between Samuel Johnson and Lord Chesterfield, the very types of poor scholar and disdainful patron. Ambrose Crowley, a humbly born, successful Quaker ironmaster of Stourbridge, who died in 1713, became Sheriff of London and a knight. His stepsister married Parson Ford, Johnson's first cousin, while his granddaughter married Sir William Stanhope, Chesterfield's brother.

I have printed further such cases later in this book[5] and elsewhere but will here mention one other. The Paston family of Norfolk rose from relatively humble station to wealth and local eminence by its enterprise and successive marriages to heiresses in the fifteenth century and thereafter. It was said by his enemies that William Paston was the grandson of a husbandman and a bondwoman. Certainly the pedigree deriving him from Wulstan Paston who 'came out of France three years after the Conquest' deserves no credit. About 1469 William achieved the glory of a semi-royal marriage to Ann Beaufort, a great-grand-daughter of John of Gaunt. I apply the word semi-royal here to an anomalous situation. In the lifetime of his second wife Constance, in right of whom he claimed the kingdom of Castile, John of Gaunt, Duke of Lancaster, son of King Edward III, had three sons and a daughter by his children's governess, Katherine Swynford, the widow of a knight. Not long after Constance died in 1396 John of Gaunt married Katherine and their children (who were surnamed Beaufort) were legitimated by Act of Parliament for all purposes save succession to the throne — a limitation which did not stop Henry VII claiming that throne through his mother Margaret Beaufort. Ann Paston's father, Edmund Duke of Somerset, was a Beaufort grandson of John of Gaunt.

About the time when William Paston was thus advancing his family, in 1469, his niece Margery was so thoughtless as to marry one Richard Calle, the family bailiff. He was a good bailiff and in a small way a rising man like his employers, having come to them recommended by no less a patron than the Duke of Norfolk. He would hardly, however, rank as a gentleman and it seems ran a chandler's shop as a sideline, for William's nephew John wrote that Calle 'should never have my good will for to make my sister to sell mustard and candle in Framlingham.'

One wonders whether such a family conjunction could have occurred in France,[6] where already by 1300, the families of the knights had established themselves as a nobility, a closed caste with legal privilege, so continuing till the French Revolution. Much the same thing occurred in Germany, Italy and Spain. But England, unlike most of Europe, has never had a nobility in this sense and this fact is an element in English history which perhaps deserves more emphasis and explanation than it gets. It does not mean that the great noblemen were less great in England nor that class distinctions were less marked. Its essence lies in

5 pp. 80, 84-97, 100-101, 106-111, 115, 128, 129.

6 See also p. 35 infra.

an absence of impassable social barriers and sharp dividing lines. Each class shades into the next through an indeterminate penumbra. Perhaps it was no easier here than elsewhere for a man to rise or fall in society. But when this occurred no legal barrier barred the corresponding social recognition. The descendants of impoverished gentry who relinquished their old way of life were fully assimilated to a lower class, while newly rich men or their offspring were accepted among the nobility or gentry as soon as they adopted their outlook and manner of living.

To show how far back this goes it may be mentioned here that in 1315 the great-grandson of a Northamptonshire villein, whom his lord made free about 1200, was a knight. In 1261 the son of the lord of a manor in Surrey married the daughter of one of his father's villeins — a real life Bailiff's daughter of Islington. Conversely some of the knights who rebelled with Simon de Montfort in 1264 seem to have lost everything so that their descendants sank into the ranks of the yeomen or villeins.[7]

My point is not that these transitions were commoner in England than on the continent — though they may have been — but that the mechanism for accepting them was simpler and easier. In France nobility meant on the one hand exemption from taxes and on the other restriction to a narrow range of occupations. Its conferment also was, at least in theory, within the king's absolute discretion. No doubt the rich could sometimes leap this barrier or circumvent it by subterfuge. Unlike Indian caste barriers it did not wholly prevent, though it limited and discouraged, marriage between noble and non-noble. Impoverished petty noblemen, indeed, sometimes married their daughters *bourgeoisement* so as not to have to find them dowries. Nevertheless the legal privilege of *noblesse* created economic and social barriers to which England was a stranger.

Our history books have little to say about the reasons for this extraordinary and far reaching difference of social structure between England and her neighbours, to which we owe what Sir Lewis Namier called the 'peculiar character of English society, civilian and plutocratic, though imbued with feudal habits and traditions'. Bloch saw hints of this divergence in Anglo-Saxon times, as in a reference made by Alcuin about 800 to an armed band attached to the Archbishop of York's household as including both noble and non-noble warriors. But if one predominant cause is to be picked out, it can only be the Norman Conquest, working in two ways; on the one hand giving the king of England a dominance over his subjects which no mediaeval king of France had; on the other introducing, through the changing relations of Englishman and Norman, a creative factor of uncertainty in the social order, from which France was free.

The roots of such a difference go so deep that one could begin the

7 EG (II), p. 61.

story before the dawn of human history. One could carry back the origin of class divisions to the relationship of leader to led, and this not merely to the chief in stone age societies but to the principle of the pecking order and the position of the father of the family in the higher animal kingdom. One might theorize about the effects of producing food beyond immediate needs, of a neolithic revolution in way of life from hunting to agriculture, and of the founding of cities. One might next marshal vast evidence as to social classes in antiquity, fighting men and cultivators, kings, priests and slaves.

Our present question, however, relates less to origins than to the changes in an old pattern which new circumstances can bring about, and to answer this we may lower our chronological sights to a time nearer our own, the Dark Age of Europe which divides Roman Antiquity from the civilisation of the High Middle Ages. In 732 the great Frankish king Charles Martel, the grandfather of Charlemagne, turned back, by his victory at Tours, the Islamic tide which had entered Europe through Spain. It is known that he confiscated lands from the Church and with these endowed his knights. Mr. Lynn White, in an argument[8] which has been widely accepted attributes this to the arrival in Western Europe at this time of the use of the stirrup, spreading westward from China, and giving rise to a new technique of mounted shock combat with the lance at rest, far more effective than what went before. Charles Martel, Mr. White argues, saw the possibilities of this new way of fighting and saw also that the body of elaborately armed and trained horsemen, which it called for, could be brought into existence only by creating and endowing a new class. The members of this class were the Knights, their endowment came from the Church lands and the new social system thus established was Feudalism.

Mr. White does not discuss who the knights were or where they came from and it may be that they came largely, though not exclusively from a class already existing. Marc Bloch thought that, though many lines of lords of manors were at some date derived from adventurers risen from nothing, the contrast between the lords and their tenants may yet represent one of the oldest lines of cleavage in Western Society.[9] The cleavage would be deepened when a lord of old inheritance was supplanted or replaced by a newcomer, whether a fighting adventurer, a Norman conqueror or a merchant purchaser from the city. Its origin, all the same, may go back to such village chieftains as are found in primitive societies.

What, on this view, the knightly and feudal revolution did, was to bring together on a new footing, with a new ethos and aspiration, men largely sprung from an old existing class but augmented by men of

8 Lynn White, Jr., *Medieval Technology and Social Change*, 1962, Ch.I.
9 *Feudal Society*, p. 289.

other origins and special quality. The knights were warriors, bound by the strongest ties of fealty to their feudal lords. Their moral code, the code of chivalry, was based on the warlike virtues but softened by a Christian injunction to protect the weak and by the code of manners called Courtesy, based on the Provençal cult of courtly love.

A second invention, for which claims of historical influence are made, similar to those made for the stirrup, is the heavy plough. The earlier scratch plough could be used effectively by single families in small fields. But the heavy plough, it has been argued, while far more productive, called for communal use over larger areas and so led, where it was adopted, to that organization of village councils of peasants on which in the early Middle Ages the manorial economy of northern Europe rested. This plough came, perhaps, to the Rhineland in the sixth or seventh century, to Scandinavia in the eighth and to England and Normandy with the Norsemen in the ninth.[10] That it had its greatest use in heavy lowland soils, and little value on steep hillsides, could be one among other factors differentiating upland from lowland social patterns.

It is argued that, where it came, this communal use of heavy ploughs produced, under the lord of the manor, a largely self governing village community. Within such communities there were two main classes; that of the substantial peasants, owning ploughs and plough teams and holding substantial lands; and that of the smallholders, whose livelihood depended mainly on their work because their holdings of lands were too small to make more than a small addition to what they earned by work on the land of others. Since this division also goes back beyond record, one can only guess how the smallholder class was first recruited. It seems likely, however, that, where primogeniture prevailed, it sprang largely from the younger, or less favoured or least effective sons of the poorer peasants. Through the greater part of England the prevailing inheritance custom gave substantially all a father's land to one of his sons only, usually the eldest, leaving the others to stay at home and work for the elder brother, or the lord of the manor, or a neighbour, or — if circumstances allowed — to seek fortune elsewhere. This had the advantage of keeping agriculture in viable units and tended to keep the population down to what the land would support. The number of the smallholders descended from the disinherited younger sons would thus tend to grow, but only slowly.

In some parts, however, there was another system whereby the father's land was shared or divided equally among the sons. It has been suggested[11] that the mediaeval hall houses of Kent were homes where extended family communities, which had grown up through this system of gavelkind, lived together in common. Such arrangements

10 Lynn White, op.cit. Ch.II.
11 By H. M. Colvin in *Medieval England*, Oxford, 1958, p. 91.

seem often to have led to overpopulation and poverty, as in Ireland before the famine of 1845. Legislation which followed that famine led to restriction of Irish land inheritance to one son. This in turn led to late marriage and, with emigration, to decline in population.[12]

Professor G. C. Homans has suggested that a similar custom in mediaeval East Anglia may have led, through increase of the population, to the early development of the clothing industry there as a way of escape from resulting poverty.[13] Immigration from the Low Countries, so long a feature of East Anglian life, was probably another factor. The clothiers, there and elsewhere, were often Puritans, as if their breach with tradition in way of living were reflected in a corresponding religious change. Their well known litigiousness belongs to the same character. In two of the clothing districts, the West Country and East Anglia, it is of interest that the earlier dissenting views of the Lollards had made conspicuous headway in the late fourteenth and fifteenth centuries.[14] When bad times came, opposition to established government was apt to follow, as the Roundheads showed. The links thus established between manufacture, dissent and radical politics have lasted to our own day, though subject to later complicating factors. The Puritan East Anglian element was strongly represented in the settlement of Massachusetts in 1620s and 1630s and set a mark upon the ethos of that Commonwealth which played some part in the American Revolution of 1770s, though by that time the descendants of the former outcasts were on their way to becoming an aristocracy.

A process of class formation which can be seen more clearly, because it is fairly recent and because those concerned were relatively few and were literate, is that of the professional middle class. It appears to me that, though official and legal families did exist in the Middle Ages, the effective origin of this class was the permission to the clergy to marry, given in 1548, withdrawn by Mary and given back by Elizabeth in 1559. The earlier rule of clerical celibacy had not always been observed with the strictness hoped for, but the breaches of it had been more or less surreptitious. From this time on, however, the children of the parsonages of England made a great and acknowledged contribution to the services and professions of the country and a tendency of the class thus formed to marry within itself can soon be noted.

The origins of the members of this rising class range from sons of the minor gentry, through those of officials, merchants, and yeomen, to the occasional son of a small tradesman, servant or labourer favoured by patronage or chance. The endowment of schools and colleges for the

12 C. M. Arensberg & S. T. Kimball, *Family and Community in Ireland*, Harvard U.C., 1941.
13 *Sentiments and Activities*, 1962, p. 152.
14 G. M. Trevelyan, *England in the Age of Wycliffe*, 1929, Ch.VIII.

benefit of the natives of particular localities was an important means of recruitment from the sixteenth century on. So too was the patronage of individuals and institutions. William Kent (?1685-1748), the great architect, was a coachpainter's apprentice but 'had the good fortune to find, some Gentlemen . . . to promote his studies', who 'raised a contribution and recommended him to proper persons in London to direct him to Italy'.

George III's bishops for the most part either were noblemen's relations, or had been noblemen's chaplains or noblemen's sons' tutors. In a day when public schools were not exclusive, as they became in the nineteenth century, a schoolboy friendship between a nobleman's son and a boy of humble origin often led to the latter's appointment as a tutor and thence to a career in Church or State.

It has been said that the families of such men associated and intermarried because from the point of view of other classes they were neither flesh nor fowl — more than tradesmen or mechanics, yet not quite gentlemen. That, however, is necessarily the position of a new class on the way to establishing itself and is a part of the process by which it does so. As the professional class, the upper middle class, grew larger and more powerful, in the years between about 1770 and 1840, it established by degrees its own exclusiveness, to be seen perhaps as clearly as anywhere in the changed character of the Public Schools.

These 'in the opening of the nineteenth century' have been called 'heathenish at the best, at the worst nurseries of vice'. 'A famous headmaster of those days indignantly answered a parental question as to the Christian character of his boys by pointing out that he was there in order to teach Greek, not morals. "C'est le meilleur que j'ai jamais vu, et c'est abominable", said Talleyrand on being shown over Eton.'[15] Among the factors which had led to this perhaps not the least important was the general eighteenth century dislike of religious enthusiasm. This was itself a reaction from the intolerant zeal which had plunged the two preceding centuries so deep and often into religious war and persecution.

But, though enthusiasm was at a discount in Georgian England, revival came with Wesley and attained power at the century's end with the Evangelical movement — a movement strengthened by the solid unity of such intermarried Evangelical families as Thornton, Wilberforce, Bird, Sumner, Abel Smith, Elliott, Venn and Macaulay. Robert Smith, the first financier to be made a peer (as Lord Carrington in 1796), was a first cousin of William Wilberforce; while a first cousin of them both, a London alderman's daughter, had a son who became Bishop of Winchester in 1827 and another who was made Archbishop of Canterbury in 1848.[16]

15 W. Tuckwell, *Pre-Tractarian Oxford*, 1909 p.103.
16 Charles Richard Sumner and John Bird Sumner, pp. 129, 249.

Criticism of the Public Schools was to be looked for from the Evangelicals. Wilberforce and others echoed the strictures of Cowper's *Tirocinium* (1785). By the middle of the nineteenth century Thomas Arnold and others had changed the old schools and started new ones to a model which met not only the demand of the new middle class for Christian education but their demand for social recognition also, by making the Public Schools factories of gentlemen. This manufacture had to start early in life, for the new approach replaced patronage by competitive examination, which meant, for example, that from 1841 Eton scholars were unlikely to include those clever country boys or sons of Eton and Windsor tradesmen who before that date were sometimes nominated through patrons' favour or perception of their promise. The raising of intellectual standards meant greater social exclusiveness, as we understand from the contrary movement in our own day.

Just as the knights were formed into a new hereditary class of nobility between the eighth century and the thirteenth; just as the professional class was formed between the sixteenth century and the nineteenth; so, it has been argued, the years between 1790 and 1830 saw the formation, by the traumatic experience of the Industrial Revolution, of a new and unified Working Class, which did not exist before. (Ch. VI, *infra.*)

This view adopts and expands the myth of the *Two Nations* of the rich and the poor, to which Disraeli's potent phrase gave currency. But Disraeli was writing of a strictly local and temporary contrast, that which arose in the manufacturing districts of South Lancashire and the adjoining West Riding and part of Derbyshire; between the great manufacturers and the segregated, crowded, brutalized human products of their new work discipline. Here indeed was a great new gulf and a sharp contrast. But in Birmingham, where the artisan aspired to become a small master, in London, where the range of classes and conditions described by Mayhew and Booth derives visibly from the eighteenth and earlier centuries, above all in rural parts and country towns where ancient ways lasted among the poor into our own times, the social profile is not a newly formed ravine but a long, ancient slope. We object, as did Francis Place, the radical, in 1834, to see 'the working people . . . all, jumbled together as the "lower orders", the most skilled and the most prudent workmen, with the most ignorant and imprudent labourers and paupers'. What differences could persist even in the very home of the two nations the tale of Lord Rhodes's pedigree has shown us.

The impact of these years on a London suburban industrial community may show how circumstances alter cases. Of some forty to fifty thousand French protestant refugees who fled to England in or about 1685 some fifteen thousand are thought to have settled in London, where their two largest colonies were to the west of the City in Soho and to the east in Spitalfields. Soho drew the silversmiths, jewellers, clockmakers and other skilled craftsmen who worked for the Court. Spitalfields, where there had been nonconformists and silkweavers before, became a community of silkweavers. Despite their skill, falling prices hit this community hard in the middle eighteenth century. There were distress and rioting. Price regulation, begun in 1773, helped them, but the war with France and other factors renewed their troubles. In the second half of the eighteenth century the Spitalfields Huguenots by degrees became Anglicized, though services in French continued in one of their chapels almost till 1840. In the same years the community spread from Spitalfields into neighbouring Bethnal Green, where thousands of poor weavers lived, overcrowded and working at home for the master weavers in Spitalfields.

In 1742 the petition of overcrowded Bethnal Green to be made a separate parish had been granted and its government was vested in an electorate with a property qualification low enough to let in thousands of poor journeymen weavers, living three or four families in a house. These in due course confided their destinies to a ruler of a surprising kind yet evidently congenial to them.

Joseph Merceron was born in 1764 of a lower middle class Huguenot family from Poitou. From clerk to a lottery office keeper he became assistant to a Poor Rate collector and brought business method and administrative skill to the management of the enlarging parish finances. From 1787, when his name first appears in the Minutes, he gained the confidence of the Vestry meetings, was put on all the Committees, worked hard at parish business without salary, got himself appointed permanent treasurer of several funds and at length was so well viewed by the central government as to be placed on the local tax and sewer commissions and made a Justice of the Peace. He put friends and dependents into the other parish offices and used his power with such skill that by 1800 he was a parish dictator.

He acquired public houses and cottages and through these, through parish funds and jurisdiction and, as a Justice of the Peace, was able to assist his friends and thwart his enemies. When his parish accounts were questioned he brought some hundreds of weavers and labourers to support him with riot and clamour at public meetings. Opposition to him first appeared in 1804 and grew active under a new Rector of the parish in 1809. A long struggle ensued and at length in 1818 Merceron was convicted of embezzling £925 of parish funds to pay his law expenses and was fined and imprisoned for eighteen months.

To please his followers he had permitted Sunday dog fighting and duck hunting and weekday bullock hunting through the streets and had allowed the public houses to become 'nurseries of depravity and vice' despite the protests of the Rector and the respectable. All this and his parish despotism were now ended — until his emergence from prison and the incompetence of his successors enabled him to turn the tables.

This he had done by 1820 and for nearly twenty more years with a growing aura of respectability he and his party ruled Bethnal Green.

Sidney and Beatrice Webb, who rediscovered this history, wrote that Merceron's family had after his death bought up and destroyed the scarce reports of his trial and that the parish tradition was that he had been an active and public spirited administrator whom malignant enemies harshly attacked.[17] When he died in 1839 the *Gentleman's Magazine*[18] recorded that 'he was supposed to be worth about 300,000*l*. though he always appeared to be in poor circumstances. He was followed to his grave in the parish churchyard by Mr. Byng, M.P. and Mr. Musgrove, M.P. besides the churchwardens and all the parochial officers, the children of the poor school (of which he was governor), and of the workhouse. Nearly 20,000 persons were present'. One wonders whether later and more violent doings in Bethnal Green have owed anything to this nineteenth century foundation. One would also like to know how much Joseph Merceron's achievement owed to his own special qualities and how much to those of the people over whom he ruled. Among the progeny of the Mercerons have been several distinguished officers of the British and Indian armies and it is not hard to believe that Joseph, had his lot so fallen, might have won that kind of distinction. On the other hand he may have had an understanding of the psychology of hard pressed, fourth generation Huguenots, which the respectable party lacked. Are immigrant communities in great cities especially open to Boss rule? Does democracy at times lead naturally to tyranny? Closer study of the whole strange episode might prove instructive.

It is said that a drop of Huguenot blood is worth £10,000 a year to its possessor. As the possessor of two drops I doubt the figure though I admit the principle. The Huguenots, and not least those of them who came to England, were a selected stock. When persecution came the weaker conformed, at least outwardly, while of those who would not it must have been the boldest and most adaptable who successfully faced the challenge of migration to a foreign land. Those who did so had to make a choice of destination and in this they were guided largely by what they knew of the opportunities. To the farmers and farm labourers England had little to offer. They preferred Germany, America, South Africa. To England came some persons of quality, ministers, lawyers, financiers and merchants, and a great number of tradesmen and skilled craftsmen.

As in other migrations social distinctions were largely, though not wholly, maintained, but there seems detectable a tendency for Huguenots to rise by their abilities. This, however, in general meant

17 Sidney & Beatrice Webb, *English Local Government from the Revolution to the Municipal Corporation Act,* 1906, pp. 79-90.
18 1839, Pt. II p. 21.

leaving their own community and becoming fully assimilated and it is notable that, whereas most Huguenots married Huguenot women for the first generation or two, the successful seldom did so after that. Professor Darlington indeed, attributes the distinction of the English Huguenots' descendants specifically to this 'outbreeding' — that is to the genetic combination — and not to the Huguenot element simply. Sixty five Huguenot Members of Parliament have been counted out of the 5,034 Members between 1734 and 1832. Such names as Bosanquet, Courtauld, Garrick, Labouchere, Lamerie, Layard, Martineau, Romilly, suggest the varied range of ability.

A selected stock comparable to the English Huguenots is that of the early settlers from England in New England. The number of those arriving in the fifteen years from 1628 to 1643 was estimated to be 21,200. They kept excellent records and their group self-consciousness led them to carry out extensive genealogical work in the century after about 1840; while their special part in building the United States, its institutions and prosperity, has been a theme of American historians.

Two things were needed to secure settlement of this rocky wilderness, considerable financial outlay to meet the costs of voyages and a powerful motive to induce settlers to brave the hardships. The finance of the first two expeditions, that of the *Mayflower* Pilgrims of 1620 and that of the Rev. John White's Massachusetts Bay settlement of 1624, came from London merchants with an interest in fishing and the fur trade. The settlers' motives were various but a large minority among the earliest were men of strong religious views, on the puritan wing of dissent, whose position at home was unhappy. When the 1624 settlement was in difficulties, White, who was a Puritan and Rector of Holy Trinity, Dorchester, Dorset, conceived the plan of promoting settlement in Massachusetts as a refuge for the righteous and 'a bulwark against the Kingdom of Antichrist which the Jesuits labour to rear up in all quarters of the world'. White had influence with the Earls of Warwick and Lincoln and other powerful Puritans. In 1629 by their help the Massachusetts Bay Company received a grant of land and charter of incorporation and made the drastic decision to transfer its members, property and activities from England to Massachusetts.

John Winthrop was the squire of Groton in Suffolk, a former manor of the Abbey of Bury St. Edmunds, which his grandfather, a Lavenham clothier, had bought. Because of his puritanism he had lost a profitable legal office and this decided him to leave England. In October 1629 he was chosen governor of the Massachusetts Bay Company and in 1630 sailed with a fleet of eleven ships carrying freight, livestock and some seven hundred passengers of whom perhaps a quarter came from within ten miles of Groton.

Of the thousands who sailed to join his settlement in the next twelve years a large proportion came also from Suffolk and Essex. Winthrop's personal prestige, the prevalence of Puritanism in East Anglia and the decline of the once great clothing industry there were interconnected influences all working the same way. Some would see both as expressions of the discontent which local population pressure often produces, especially when prosperity declines. But though Puritanism was in the ascendant in Massachusetts it has been pointed out that only one adult male in five valued it enough to become a church member and no doubt the hunger for land and independence were important motives. Or again the disgruntlement which in England had produced Puritanism may here have been mollified or given other outlets by migration. Whatever their motive, however, those who freely left home and crossed the sea to settle in the wilderness, while it was still a wilderness, were people of exceptional determination.

Group settlement led by ministers was important and it seems that this Great Migration was drawn largely from the middle classes, ranging from the gentry and substantial yeomen and merchants to shopkeepers and craftsmen. As with the Huguenots the social distinctions of the land of origin were largely maintained in the land of settlement. It has been reckoned that one in fourteen of the freemen of Massachusetts before 1649 was esteemed a gentleman and addressed as Master.

After 1640 the brighter prospects for Puritans 'caused all men to stay in England in expectation of a new world'. Migration to Massachusetts almost ceased and some settlers returned thence to England. When settlement was resumed it had a different character. Substantial merchants, craftsmen and tradesmen came in relatively small numbers and a number of indentured labourers and pauper children were imported. The descendants of the original settlers, however, remained predominant and were not outnumbered as were those of Virginia, for example, by a later influx of settlers of a different sort, including transported felons. The claim of the New Englanders to have played a special part in their country's history has been supported by reference to their part in the Revolution of the 1770s and in the nineteenth century settlement of the West and industrialization of the East.

Is it fanciful to see analogies between the coming together of these selected — or self selecting — stocks, the Huguenots in England, the Puritans in New England, on the one hand, and the birth of new social classes on the other? Both are syntheses of the like minded from diverse sources but with shared aspirations. A new class is born when a group, which has become self conscious, feels that it needs a name. The name embodies an aspiration and in turn helps to mould the group. Thus the yeomen in the sixteenth century came to be thought of as a class in which membership was a matter for pride, 'an estate of people almost peculiar to England living in the temperate zone betwixt greatness and want'. They developed a folklore. Their ancestors were the archers who fought at Crécy and Poitiers. Those below them aspired to join them and many aspired no higher. 'A man may find sundry yeomen although otherwise for wealth comparable with the gentle sort that will not yet for all that change their condition nor desire to be apparelled with the titles of gentry.'

If we look but a little earlier we find the gentry in the same case. In the fourteenth century *gentil homme* or gentleman was not a specific class name but a general description for a man of family from barons down to landless junior scions of knightly houses. In the fifteenth century, however, a flattering name was needed for the numerous emerging class of those, not themselves knights or esquires, nor even always of knightly descent, who were nevertheless now discharging many of the knights' former functions and acquiring a comparable social status. These were the first to use the name gentleman as a class description.

The process continues and nomenclature today plays as important a part in it as ever. We read of the new middle class, by which seems to be meant a section of the former lower or 'working' class which has adopted what are thought of as middle class ways of living. But why the special name, when the middle classes have been absorbing recruits from below time out of mind? Presumably because this is not just individual recruitment but the emergence of a new class, which must find a name, whether this or another, in order to find an identity.

A similar exercise in nomenclature is the current use of the word 'classless'. A classless accent is one which mingles older class accents into something new — the accent, perhaps, of a new class. I read a few years since that many emigrants to Australia were attracted by the idea of a 'classless society' there 'in which their children would find it easier to move up the social and work scale than in Britain'.[19] A classless society in the usual sense would not have a social scale, so that here too the word must have a new sense.

This brings us round again to English social fluidity and the ambiguity of class description which goes with it. A conspicuous case of this is our use of 'middle class' and 'working class' as if they were correlative and mutually exclusive terms, whereas the true correlative to 'middle class' is 'lower class' and the true correlative to 'working class' is 'rentier class'. The middle class no doubt includes rentiers but certainly comprises many more who work. Why then is the lower class called the working class? Is it a mere euphemism to escape the pejorative sense of 'lower'? Or does it mean the class of *manual* workers? But many of the middle class work with their hands. Or does it mean what used to be called the labouring poor (with 'poor' left out)? But that excludes the idle poor, or beggars, who decidedly belong to the lower class.

There is certainly an English feeling, born of English experience, that some blurring of the niceties of social gradation will make things go more easily. But this feeling has to contend with the no less urgent

19 *The Times,* 20 May 1963.

feeling that some distinctions are too important to be blurred. Anthony Trollope, than whom our social scene has had no shrewder observer, gives the classic picture of the difficulty in describing Miss Thorne's *fête champètre*.

'In the first place there was a dreadful line to be drawn. Who were to dispose themselves within the ha-ha, and who without? To this the unthinking will give an off-hand answer, as they will to every ponderous question. Oh, the bishop and such-like within the ha-ha; and Farmer Greenacre and such like without. True, my unthinking friend; but who shall define these such-likes? It is in such definitions that the whole difficulty of society consists. To seat the bishop on an armchair on the lawn and place Farmer Greenacre at the end of a long table in the paddock is easy enough; but where will you put Mrs. Lookaloft, whose husband though a tenant on the estate hunts in a red coat, whose daughters go to a fashionable seminary in Barchester, who calls her farmhouse Rosebank, and who has a piano forte in her drawing-room? The Misses Lookaloft, as they call themselves, won't sit contented among the bumpkins. Mrs. Lookaloft won't squeeze her fine clothes on a bench and talk familiarly about cream and ducklings to good Mrs. Greenacre. And yet Mrs. Lookaloft is no fit companion and never has been the associate of the Thornes and the Grantlys. And if Mrs. Lookaloft be admitted within the sanctum of fashionable life, if she be allowed with her three daughters to leap the ha-ha, why not the wives and daughters of other families also? Mrs. Greenacre is at present well contented with the paddock, but she might cease to be so if she saw Mrs. Lookaloft on the lawn. And thus poor Miss Thorne had a hard time of it.'

A hundred years later, despite the efforts of levellers, feelings no less shocking to egalitarians than those of Mrs. Lookaloft are still much with us. Indeed I would argue that recent policies — as opposed to exhortations — have stoked rather than quenched the fires of ambition and competition. This is because neither those who lead the way in levelling nor those who follow behind them have been made to realize that a part of its price is abandonment of the Cult of Progress. I do not mean by this abandonment of the belief that we can and should try to improve the conditions of human life for our children and descendants. I mean the belief that we can do this in double quick time by means of a moral Newtonianism, by concentrating on the measurable things, and especially by technology and industrialism.

By concentrating on these things, to the exclusion of some others which our ancestors valued more, we propel ourselves in a particular direction, we *progress,* if one likes, in that direction. But progress of this kind, at this speed, depends, I would argue, on society having or acquiring a certain form, a streamlined, stratified, arrowhead form, the very form of which egalitarians complain.

This view will encounter resistance. Many who agree that class stratification is not diminishing will find other explanations for this. Some of these — looking at England and ignoring parallels elsewhere — blame the tenacity of our aristocracy and such institutions as the House of Lords and the Public Schools, through which, they think, this tenacity operates to preserve an antiquated class structure. Could they believe this if their view of the world were wider in time and place and their knowledge of genealogical history greater?

Our aristocracy are, indeed, tenacious, yet they fall quite often from their perches. There are, moreover, permanent factors in the English social structure which make for a steady, if slow, turnover of families in the seats of wealth and power. But the permanence of the structural form does not depend on the perpetuity of its materials, which can be renewed. What gives a society a stratified or any other form is not so much the drive of one class against others (though this does affect the upshot) as a drive of the whole body in a direction which the particular form helps it to attain. It is a question of streamlining. If the body politic or social organism is to move at a certain speed in a certain direction, it must have or by such movement acquire an edge and form adapted thereto.

It may be true that the needs and demands which brought into existence first a military, feudal nobility and later a political aristocracy, have themselves passed away, while vestiges of the social forms they brought into existence are still with us. There are three factors here, however, which make this picture not quite what it seems. First, the time scale we are dealing with is a long one. Patterns built up over generations do not vanish in a few years. The wash of a boat still disturbs the river when the boat itself has passed out of sight. Secondly, the economy of nature often finds new uses for existing material, so that old classes and institutions may seem to retain their identity, when what has really happened is that the old forms have acquired new functions and new substance.

Third and of special relevance to our own situation is the fact that, while older forces tending to make society hierarchical may have weakened in recent centuries, powerful new forces have sprung up to take their place. Chief of these are the cult of progress, which has gained since the eighteenth century so strong a hold on men's minds, and the simultaneous mechanical and scientific developments, which have fed and been fed by this cult. If the pace of progress has always to be maintained or increased, that army, which the few whose capacities can secure this are to lead, must be marshalled in arrowhead formation, with these few in the van and ever more numerous ranks of ever less skilled majorities in their rear. Simultaneously the complexities of technology have demanded an organization in which degrees of skill and knowledge are graded and marshalled in ever longer sequence. With this inevitably comes loss of independence.

Tawney, the apostle of Equality, thus described one aspect of this process. 'The growth in the size of the business unit necessarily accelerates the process by which ever larger bodies of wage-earners are brigaded under the direction of a comparatively small staff of entrepreneurs. The movement towards combination and amalgamation which is advancing so rapidly today in Great Britain, does the same. The emergence, side by side with questions of wages and control, is one symptom of the more definite horizontal cleavage which that centralization of economic command has tended to produce.'[20]

The concentration of power in a small group of like minded men is an important part of the mechanism of rapid change or progress. The members of such a group may begin as proscribed conspirators and revolutionaries. But, if their revolution succeeds, they or their successors will end as a governing group — what is now called an *establishment.* This by the effluxion of time and influence of family feeling will tend to turn into a hereditary class, no matter what safeguards may be devised to prevent this. It may be remarked in passing that this influence of family feeling has been known to turn the spirit of tyranny, which infects revolutions, by degrees into something less barbarous. It is by what one may call *the levelling trick* that politicians often persuade their supporters that they are establishing equality, when what they are really doing is to clear away an old ruling group, so that they themselves and their friends may step into its shoes and form a new one. Indeed it might be said that historically speaking this is the normal purpose and upshot of egalitarianism.

The replacement of ruling classes is an old phenomenon. Let us come back to the newer one we were approaching, the apparent tendency of the cult of Progress to renew or extend class stratification. This arises from the organization its nature calls for, with long chains of command and emphasis on leadership. Without leadership the common people may well not change at all — certainly will not change rapidly. Those in the different ranges which such organization produces naturally tend to live and intermarry with those of their own kind rather than the others. There are countervailing tendencies at work also, religious, educational, political, social, sexual, which may modify or soften the rigidities of stratification to a greater or lesser degree. Yet if we look at the most industrialized countries, even those which profess social and political egalitarianism, we shall find it hard to deny the existence of distinct social classes with endogamous tendencies, closely related to the industrial division of labour. This endogamy, this marriage within the class, continued long enough, spreads the genetic characters existing within it ever more evenly and so reinforces the class character. All this would fit the widely held belief, that industrialization contains in itself a tendency to make the rich richer and the poor poorer.

It could be argued that the nearest approaches to general social

20 R. H. Tawney, *Equality,* 1931, p. 86.

equality have existed in the static societies, where man has been
content for long periods to accept unaltered a particular equilibrium
with his natural environment. If our quest is for classlessness in action
we may find something more like it among the Bushmen or the Eskimo
than in the lands of high technology, however progressive or
democratic. We recall again Wordsworth's two voices of the sea and the
mountains and link the liberty they foster with this enduring
equilibrium. The hierarchies of the great empires built up in the
continental plains afford the extreme contrast.

Class division as a system has been unjustly associated with extremes
of wealth and poverty. These may go with it or may not, and I would
argue that their usual 'cause is the impact on a class system of a
population problem. In a crowded time and place like ours it is hard to
realize how easily overpopulation could once be remedied — even if it
did not seem easy then. In the earlier Middle Ages most English villages
were islands of cultivation in a sea of primaeval forest. If the labour of
generations had raised the fertility of the settlement to its apex, but the
number of its inhabitants yet grew by natural increase, it was only
necessary to fell more trees and cultivate the waste. Only after 1500,
when the waste was nearly all gone and the colonization completed,
were other remedies strictly necessary.

Three main such remedies existed, movement into towns, development of industry and migration overseas. But three more may be
mentioned — the forces, vagrancy and crime. Towns came into existence
to serve two purposes, as strong places of defence and as central
markets of exchange. The second purpose, which has survived the first,
provided employment for the surplus population of the countryside.
Indeed even before there was such a surplus, the needs of the towns for
men made them refuges to which the discontented of the villages could
and did flee. Some who fled to the towns sank to the bottom there.
Others made their fortunes and put it about that the streets were paved
with gold. If we knew their genealogies, we might, I think, find that the
early town rich also were a selected stock of unusually enterprising and
capable people. But as the balance of motive for migration to the towns
changed from the drawing power of town opportunities to the pressure
of numbers in the countryside, so, one must suppose, would the
proportion of the inert and helpless among the migrants grow.

Industry at first meant forges in the forests and cloth mills by the
streams in a few places where materials and human enterprise and skill
were in the right balance. Slow growth through the Middle Ages
received an acceleration in the sixteenth century and another, and
much greater, in the late eighteenth and early nineteenth. This latter
had behind it the pressure of a great population increase and possessed
an intrinsic, pervasive character of grime, ugliness and intensive work
discipline, with a proliferation of monotonous, limited forms of
employment.

Between the thirteenth century and the twentieth industry has swung from town to country, from country to town and a little way back again. Cloth was manufactured first in the towns. Then about 1300 the development of the watermill removed it to the country, as great churches in the Cotswolds and East Anglia, built by wealthy clothiers, remind us. Freedom there from the tightening guild restrictions of the cities helped to keep the manufacture in the small towns and villages. Cottage handloom weaving suited the country too and still in the 1760s the first factories of the new technology were planted in country places. As they grew in size, however, the labour needs of factories either brought them into towns or caused towns to grow round them. Only in our own day, when factory workers can come to their work in motor cars and on motor bicycles from villages within a large radius, has the trend begun to reverse again.

Mediaeval towns were spaciously laid out, often with long gardens behind the houses. As population grew, however, so did pressure upon space so that most such gardens were in time built over. There were rich and poor in the towns and therefore large and small houses, often mingled close together. But as the towns and their population grew, so did segregation of rich and poor and of their housing, though not quickly and not completely. Many factors then determined which districts should be sought after and beautified by the rich and which should be crowded and devalued by the poor.

In this field, as in some others, England developed an important difference from the continent. Many continental towns and most notably the great free cities of the Rhineland and North Italy were ruled by leading merchant families who formed self contained urban patriciates, different in way of life and outlook from the rural nobility. In England, with one partial exception, this did not occur. This was because it was the aspiration and the unimpeded practice of our great merchant families to purchase country manors and become assimilated to the rural gentry. The cities, therefore, were in general ruled by a succession of new families, whose heirs after perhaps three generations left for the countryside or whose heiresses conveyed their wealth to noblemen still sooner.

The partial exception to this was the close knit group of aldermanic families, FitzAilwin, Basings, Buckerel, Cornhill and others, who ruled the City of London from the early twelfth century until 1285, when, following troubles, Edward I took the City into his own hands and ended their dominance.[21] It may be thought, however, that our own day has seen some return to dynasticism in the City. If so, it is perhaps because political and economic events have made City greatness seem a surer base than the land for family continuity. Here, at all events, is a thesis for genealogical historians to explore and confirm or demolish.

21 P.87.

By 1500, and still more by 1700, London had become a sink into which the displaced surplus of the countryside was poured. By 1800 other towns shared this function. The later nineteenth and twentieth centuries have seen a vast growth of big towns with increasing geographical segregation of their rich and poor inhabitants. The political measures taken to promote health and welfare are thought by some, while ameliorating symptoms, to have exacerbated root troubles by speeding population growth among the poor, by lowering the death rate dysgenically, and by encouraging attitudes of acceptance and passivity at the cost of self help and initiative.

Among the consequences of such segregation is a form of class alienation in which the culture and *mores* forced on the poor by poverty seem to many of them the only right and proper ones, while the niceties that grow with wealth arouse their dislike and contempt. Conversely the poverty of the mean streets, spiritual as well as material, breeds inhabitants whom some of the less imaginative rich despise as mere animals.

In England, happily, there have also been powerful forces working the other way. The Royal Family, since Queen Victoria, has been one of them. Our social profile, with its gentle, steady slope and absence of clifflike breaks is a second. The concomitant social movement pattern, with constant risings, fallings and intermarriages is a third. Building bridges between classes has been a social and political ideal often achieved. There is, however, a risk that some of the keenest exponents of this ideal may mistake its nature, may see it as a step towards the abolition of class distinctions and in consequence may misapply it.

The danger of this is that they may defeat their purpose by arousing expectations, which cannot be fulfilled, because they are self contradictory, and may thus bring their promoters into discredit. I am, as Ruskin called himself, a Tory of the school of Homer and Walter Scott — but not untinctured with the Socialism of William Morris, who believed that Art is man's expression of his joy in labour and that for society to compel most men to labour without pleasure is among the most hideous injustices inflicted by man on man.

There is a theory that at the end of our present tunnel an Eden lies waiting for us, where all the hard work will be done by machines, while men will be made happy by cultivating the use of leisure. I do not believe, but if I believed should dread this. Yet the possibility must be considered, and the first step to its consideration is to work out what eugenic controls of human mating and what political controls of social organization would be needed to give mankind, so long adapted and genetically selected on clean contrary lines, a twist this way. For the genealogical progressives, the promoters of our own kind's future — which more of us than admit it are — it will be an interesting question what support we should give to a plan for the promotion of a limited interest among our fellows to the exclusion of the rest of us. This question has engaged the Utopiasts' attention and will engage it further.

Having thus rashly entered on the realm of teleology, the discussion of the purposes of life, I must briefly indicate an attitude. Our age, strong in scientific and technological competence, is weak precisely in those spiritual and aesthetic aptitudes in which some ages, which have lacked our special competence, have been strong. It is difficult to look all ways and cultivate all aptitudes at once. The conclusion, which with more humility we should accept more readily, is that progress on some fronts has been balanced by regress on others.

An ideology is a poor man's — or a blind man's — religion. One may have to make do with it, but had better be clear that it is and can be no more than a second rate substitute. Traditions coming down from ages of sharper spiritual perception might be a better guide to right and wrong — if there be such things — than any ideology.

The cult of progress I see as a self contradictory attempt to universalize the hereditary principle. I mean by the hereditary principle the impulse in us to prefer our own children, kinsmen and descendants to other people's and to do the best we can for them. When Sir Robert Walpole conferred public offices or sinecures on his kinsmen and supporters, and, where he could, made these hereditary, he was acting on this principle and thereby building up a party which gave his country a time of much needed stability. When the great Whig lords of his day built their Palladian mansions, formed their splendid collections and landscaped their parks, they identified themselves with their successors in blood, title and estate and wrought for this continuing entity.

So successful were their efforts, so splendid their achievements, that to their descendants who enjoyed the fruits, the later philanthropic Whigs, the contrast of what they themselves had but others lacked became a stimulus to spread the benefits more widely — with a misplaced confidence that their generosity, however great, could never undermine the base from which it sprang and worked. This was not the view of those who, moved by envy, made plans or theories to promote the poor by pulling down the rich. Progress for them meant revolution, a turning of society upside down; and towards this doctrine many generous possessors were propelled or converted by a sense of guilt, while blinded still or lulled by a conviction of impregnability.

In this state of mindlessness the possessors became persuaded that they or others could lead the poor to a materialist millennium while abandoning the leadership, hierarchy and division of function through which material progress actually operated. The leaders of the dispossessed added the rider that, though hierarchy would indeed wither away at length, there were stages to come before, of which the first was that they themselves should take it over.

This is a formula for abdication and replacement, but, as those who assist the process are changed by it as they go, the question is, replacement by what? Doubtless by some new hierarchy and perhaps, at least for a time, a more rigid one, save that the theory's inner contradiction may tend to mitigate the efficiency of its practice.

As the word itself might tell us, there is no prospect that revolution will release us from the wheel to which we are bound. Individual astronauts — prophets, mystics, thinkers, saints — may strike from the circle on a radius or tangent into the empyrean or outer space, but no ark yet devised will take the multitude. The hope might be greater if historical study were less obsessed by breadth as against length. Dr. Peter Spufford has made a useful distinction between long and broad genealogies. Long genealogies are those of many descents, which fascinate genealogists and exhibit the changes and multiple influences brought by length of time and many generations. Broad genealogies bring out the links of association and ensuing marriage which at some one moment bind together a political or social group, certainly often fascinating and illuminating, but surely not to be compared in the depth of explanation they may be made to yield with the long patterns of the ages.

Yet for modern historians, we are told, the broad genealogies hold more interest than the long. This is, I suppose, because intense specialization, and especially specialization by period, is inimical to the study of long historical patterns altogether. Those who try to study them must depend more largely than the specialists on secondary sources, that is, on the work of those very specialists, and so seem to these to be engaged in less profound and serious studies. Those who attempt great syntheses are bound to fall into errors easily visible to specialists, who may therefore despise them. Furthermore synthesists may seem one sided men because they follow single threads through immense mazes. They may, therefore, while complementing, disagree with one another. Witness the opposed world views of Arnold Toynbee, C. D. Darlington, and Teilhard de Chardin. Yet are not these the prophets of our time, to whom historians of particular times and places should turn, if not for answers, at least for questions to try to answer?

The first conclusion of all this may seem a glimpse of the obvious -- that we cannot sensibly pursue progress without first specifying that which is to progress and in what direction it is to do so. For human beings, once we pass beyond the progress of individuals, the only definition of the subject of progress which seems likely to commend itself to anyone is a genealogical definition — the descendants of so and so — whether it be a Founder's progeny or kin, or a class or tribe or nation or race, and whether with or without time limit. The direction of progress sought may be narrow and precise or wide and vague.

So much seems inescapable, but there may be less wide assent to the proposition that the closer the definitions the more sense any plans for progress will make and the better chance they will have of fulfilment. The Religion of Progress, in general and in capital letters, I deplore, not merely because it insults common sense on the one hand and spiritual religion on the other, but because it cannot be intelligibly defined.

Intelligible progress, it seems to me, can only be the progress of an individual or of a group and, if the latter means a group continuing in time, it can hardly be other than genealogically defined — a hereditary group. But promotion of the progress of a hereditary group calls for guidance by hereditary principles, social, environmental and genetic, to which accordingly more attention ought to be paid by those concerned with such aims.

It need hardly be added that promotion of the progress, alike of groups and of individuals, calls for clearer definitions of ultimate purposes than are often found. Wiser men than I have always known that ultimate purposes must be spiritual purposes and that perception of them depends on spiritual insight. If other ages have had more of this than ours has, we might do worse than turn for guidance to the words of wisdom and insight they have bequeathed to us.

POSTSCRIPT A:
THE ORIGIN OF ENGLISH SOCIAL FLUIDITY

'The most striking feature' wrote A. F. Pollard (*The Evolution of Parliament,* 2nd ed. 1926, p.63) 'of English Society in the early middle ages is the confusion of classes.' The absence of the kind of legal privilege possessed by noblemen on the continent, especially in France from the tenth century or earlier, and the consequences for England of the greater consequent social mobility there, as well as its origin and reasons, have been much discussed (see pp. 5, 13, *supra*; 88, 92, 101, *infra:* &c). The Norman Conquest and its sequel, which probably gave the mediaeval Kings of England greater power over their feudal lords and vassals than any others in Europe, have been, and no doubt with reason, accorded an important part in this.

Marc Bloch, however, pointed (p. 12, *supra: Feudal Society,* 1961, p. 183) to the existence of evidence of such a difference between England and France, as early as 801, and Dr. John Morris (*The Age of Arthur,* 1973, pp. 327, 330, 332 &c.) now advances arguments for a much older origin still of this pattern.

Briefly his thesis is that the Romano-British Kings Vortigern (c. 425-459), Ambrosius Aurelianus (c. 460-475) and Arthur (c. 475-515), after some fifty years of struggle with mutinous Saxon mercenaries, 'restored the forms and institutions of Imperial Rome' in Britain and so made of it the last working vestige of the Western Roman Empire, until further Saxon invasions by degrees dissolved it into a series of warring warlord kingdoms; that the gradualness of this process did much to civilize the conquerors, while Arthur's Empire left a consciousness of Britain as a unity, which successors, and especially 'the long quiet rule of the Mercian Kings' in the seventh and eighth centuries helped to maintain. It was thus, Dr. Morris argues (p.333), that 'the English emerged as the permanent heirs to the ruins of Arthur's empire; the multiple origin of their population obliged their kings to admit infinite local and social difference, that hindered attempts to impose uniformity and enabled English administration from the beginning 'to avoid much of the arrogant ineptitude that centralised European governments inherited from Rome and the Germanic kings.'

It will be interesting to see what other historians make of this.

Dr. Morris also points out (p. 318) in another, but here relevant connection, that the Angles, from whose continental dynasty that of Mercia claimed descent, differed in their monarchical convention 'from that of most other Germans, in that the undivided succession passed to the late king's nearest adult male relative, usually to his eldest son, unless he were a child or otherwise unfitted to rule.' On the incalculable effect of differing royal succession customs see Wagner, *English Genealogy,* 2nd ed., 1972, pp. 219-20.

POSTSCRIPT B:
NOBILITY IN FRANCE

Letters from Le Comte Gérard de Puymège of Olivet (especially of 25 Jan. 1974) warn me; that, just as 'the subject of the English aristocracy . . . should not appear as such a hermetic and incomprehensible world to the French' despite its confusion, sometimes deliberate, of terminology; so the English must beware of taking wholly at face value customary statements of the rigid legal and social separateness of noblemen from the rest in France. The subject calls for fuller study, and in due course (as I hope) a book from the pen of M. de Puymège. He tells me that a recent work by Professor Meyer of Rennes University, *Noblesse et Pouvoirs dans L'Europe d' Ancien Regime* already stresses the care needed in dealing with the subject of *dérogeance*, in regard to which, despite the lawyers' assertions, actual practice differed greatly from time to time and place to place.

'For instance', M. de Puymège writes, 'in the sixteenth century a member of the Grille family is called "Damoiseau, marchand et citoyen d' Arles"; in Toulouse the members of the Puybusque family are often called "Miles et mercator" from the Middle ages to the 16th century. Another example can be also found in the system of the "Tribes" (tribus), which is peculiar to Alsace. These tribes were sorts of guilds, and each area of a town was the seat of a certain tribe. It was therefore necessary, in order to obtain citizenship, to join one of them. Therefore you find very surprising documents in which people of noble birth are described as "X . . . , knight, of the Blacksmiths' tribe", etc. Which at first sight, seems incompatible. "Also, the qualification of 'negoçiant' is not incompatible with nobility, for instance in Bordeaux "écuyer et negoçiant".

'And in the Gard younger branches of a family of ancient nobility, who were ruined, practised very modest trades (e.g. weavers), but nevertheless remained "noble".

'. . . . An inquiry like "la milice française" of the Père Daniel in the mid-18th century shows that a lot of people did not know what was their status, and apparently did not suffer from it. In more ancient times and concerning what we call "noblesse de cloche", i.e. municipal magistrates, the greatest variety can be found as it was linked to royal privileges. Hence, an alderman of Marseilles was not enrolled by his office, but the one of St. Jean d'Angely was. And furthermore this practice varied in time: Therefore the aldermen from Lyon were noble at certain times, and not their successors a short time later, and so on, and therefore this applied to their descendants.'

CHAPTER II

HERALDRY AND THE HISTORIAN

The heralds are sometimes criticized for writing so little of the history of heraldry. This is like criticizing lawyers for not being legal historians or architects for not writing histories of architecture. With all these subjects some knowledge of the history must be an element in the practice, but the searching out and writing of that history is a distinct activity with which the current practice may, but need not, be linked. The heralds, probably, are more subject than the others to this unjust criticism because the nature and extent of their current activities are less understood. These, however, I have written of elsewhere, and shall not here discuss.

A juster criticism might be that the strong appeal of heraldry to the romantic mind and consequent expositions of it by romantic writers have operated as deterrents to the more critically disposed, leading them to think that their energies would be wasted on a subject so wide open to extravagance and fantasy. Whatever the cause, the fact remains that despite useful beginnings the critical editing of heraldic source materials has not gone far, while most of the serious history which could be based on them has still to be written.

The old literature of heraldry is voluminous but the greatest part of it deals with the current practice of its time and has little to say of the history. A few exceptions must however be made, and our first honourable mention must be of William Camden, born in 1551, the publication of whose great work *Britannia* in 1586 was, as it seems, the magnet which brought together the Elizabethan Society of Antiquaries, a group of historical scholars whose discussions marked a beginning in the critical study of English History. Camden was brought into the College of Arms in 1597 as its second officer, Clarenceux King of Arms, as part of a general reformation of an institution which had fallen into some disorder. I have told the story of this reformation and its outcome elsewhere and shall not now repeat it, since we are not concerned here with changes in the practice of heraldry and the heralds as such but with something more restricted, namely the change which began with Camden from a romantic to a scientific approach alike to heraldry and to history.

In 1623, the year of Camden's death, a little volume of his *Remains concerning Britain* was printed, consisting of short essays on a number of topics which look like byproducts of the great work on the *Britannia.* They include essays on languages, names, surnames, allusions, monies, impresses, apparel, artillery, wise speeches, proverbs and epitaphs; but the one which now concerns us deals with armories and is the earliest scientific essay on heraldic history which I have seen. It begins with references to devices of more or less heraldic type among the Israelites, the ancient Greeks and Romans, Germans, Danes and Anglo-Saxons; but coming on the fourth page to heraldry proper begins it firmly with a literary reference which is still our earliest, namely the description by John of Marmoutier of the knighting in 1127 of Geoffrey Plantagenet by his father-in-law King Henry I, when boots embroidered with golden lions were drawn on his legs and a shield with golden lions thereon was hung about his neck. From this Camden passes, as we still must, to the Great Seal of King Richard I and goes on with an admirably concise and judicious selection of precise facts bearing on the early history of the subject, making the excellent point that in the thirteenth century many gentlemen began to bear arms by borrowing from their lords' arms of whom they held in fee or to whom they were most devoted, and giving instances. Later Camden notes that he has observed that crests were first appropriated to families about the time of King Edward II. We now know of one or two before that time, but how unlike Camden is to his predecessors in claiming a lesser antiquity than might be claimed for anything!

The greatness of Camden's step forward from speculation to critical history may be measured by contrasting his approach with one of the best and most remarkable of the fifteenth century treatises on armory, the third part of the book of St. Albans, printed in 1486 but probably written early in the fifteenth century; sometimes though very doubtfully attributed to one Dame Julian Barnes or Berners whom later writers have provided with a pedigree and a biography for which there seems to be no warrant. The author of this work one might say, asked all the right questions, but, as answers from authentic sources were unfortunately not forthcoming, he (or she) made them up. The first breathless sentence indicates the scope of the work. 'Here in this book following is determined the lineage of coat armours; and how gentlemen shall be known from ungentlemen: and how bondage began first in angels and after succeeded in mankind, as it is showed in process both in the childer of Adam and also of Noe, and how Noe divided the world in three parts for his three sons; also there be showed the four colours in arms figured by the four orders of angels and it is showed by the four said colours which be worthy and which be royal' — and so forth.

The writer was evidently concerned to produce a plausible answer to John Ball's question

When Adam delved and Eve span
Which was then the gentleman?

In the sons of Adam and Eve, we are told, were found both gentleman and churl. Cain became a churl, and all his offspring after him, by cursing God and his own father Adam, and Seth was made a gentleman through his father's and mother's blessing; and of the offspring of Seth Noah became a gentleman by kind. With Noah's sons the same pattern was repeated. Ham's ungentleness was found in his conduct to his father, while Japheth reproved his brother like a gentleman. Noah therefore cursed Ham and assigned to him the third part of the world which (one reads with surprise) shall be called Europe, that is to say the country of churls. Japheth had Asia with his father's blessing and Shem, to whom was assigned the inheritance of Adam's son Abel, was also made a gentleman and given Africa. One might think that things had got mixed here, especially when we read that of the offspring of the gentleman Japheth come Abraham, Moses, Aaron and the prophets and also the King, of the right line of Mary, of whom that gentleman Jesus was born, Very God and Man, King of the land of Judah and Prince of coat armour.

We are further told that knighthood existed before coat armour and Olybion was the first knight that ever was. Asterial, his father, was of the right line of that gentleman David and when his son asked his blessing smote him four times on the right shoulder and made him take the vows of knighthood, giving him a shield of arms. Our author, it will be seen, was a prehistorian in the best tradition. He asked sensible questions, used such evidence as he had to the best of his ability, and when it did not take him all the way, fell back on creative imagination.

Camden's method, by contrast, was to start from the documents. For heraldry, at least, he began where they began, and in their absence ventured no conjecture. Unlike the author of the St. Albans treatise he took the world as he found it, wasting no time on efforts to relate heraldry to the cosmos or the structure of human society. The heralds and antiquaries of his own and immediately following generations devoted great labour to the transcription and extraction of original evidence of genealogy and heraldry both from public and private records. Of such manuscript materials, in Sir Robert Cotton's and other collections, Camden was able to avail himself and it might have been hoped that such great herald scholars as Sir William Dugdale (1605-86), Francis Sandford (1630-1694) or John Anstis (1669-1744), all of whom produced extensive work within the general field of study to which heraldry belongs, might have produced such treatises upon it as Claude François Menestrier (1631-1705) did in France. Sandford did

indeed include important heraldic data in his *Genealogical History of the Kings and Queens of England* (1677), but the strictly heraldic manuscripts of Dugdale, and the important treatise *Aspilogia* by Anstis remain to this day unpublished.

I suppose the truth is that in this first great burst of English mediaeval scholarship between the reigns of Elizabeth and George I the volume of work done, and still for the most part preserved in manuscript, far outran the possibilities of publication, while the collection of raw material similarly outran its analysis and digestion. In both respects historical heraldry was at the tail of the queue and not least because the commercial market for heraldry was, as it still is, predominantly of another kind — or rather of two other kinds. On the one hand are those concerned not with heraldry in general, but with that of their own ancestors. In Victorian times, indeed, some of these burst into print, but in the seventeenth century they were content with the individual products of the herald and the herald painter. On the other hand were those whose heraldic appetite, though generalized, was not for sober history but for romance or for practical guidance on current rules and practice. For these many writers and printers catered, ranging from the sobriety of John Guillim and his successive editors to the wild extravagance of Sylvanus Morgan.

There were indeed partial exceptions. In 1654, at a moment which one might, quite wrongly, suppose to have been unfriendly to heraldry, Edward Bysshe, the Garter King of Arms intruded by the Parliament, published texts of two mediaeval heraldic treatises together with a historical treatise on heraldry, written probably in the 1580s[1] by Sir Henry Spelman (c.1564-1641), which is scholarly in classical allusions at least. Again the great work of Elias Ashmole, Windsor Herald, *The Institution, Laws and Ceremonies of the Order of the Garter,* which appeared in 1672, deals historically with matters near akin to heraldry, as does Anstis's published work on the *Knighthood of the Bath and the Order of the Garter* and his manuscript work on others of the heralds' activities from which Joseph Edmondson printed copious extracts in 1780.

However, for an informed, historical view of heraldry as such, one has to jump, so far as English scholarship goes, from Camden to the Reverend James Dallaway, whose *Inquiries into the Origin and Progress of the Science of Heraldry in England* appeared in 1793. This book is not only the first large scale history of English heraldry which attempts to relate its development to social history on the one hand and to that of art, architecture and literature on the other. It is also, so far, surprisingly the last. Dallaway's scholarship, though careful and

---

1 It is dedicated to four noblemen of the Howard family. The first three give a date between 1604 and 1614, but the fourth, Philip, Earl of Arundel was such only between 1580 and 1589, which in Bysshe's view dates the work.

judicious, naturally has the limitations of its day. But for breadth of
approach and treatment no later English writer on heraldry approaches
him till J. R. Planché and Sir William St. John Hope, and though both
of these published seminal small books on the subject, neither
attempted a comprehensive view of it on Dallaway's lines. Horace
Walpole wrote to Samuel Lysons on 19 March 1794, 'Since I left you, I
have done nothing but examine Mr. Dallaway's book, and am delighted
with it'.[2] Walpole probably enjoyed especially such passages as that
in which an analogy is traced 'between the progress of gothic architecture and heraldic ornament'.

'In the norman reigns,' Dallaway writes, 'the baronial fortresses were
massive, of square or circular form; and the implements of fortification
and war were vast and rude. The escocheons were then occupied by the
simple ordinaries. When the more minute and florid embellishments of
masonry were introduced, a greater variety of charges was borne in the
shield, and both were progressively increased, till taste originated in the
necessity of the selection'. During the fifteenth century which, we
should note, Dallaway, unlike later critics, regarded as 'the aera of both'
Gothic architecture and heraldic ornament 'in the state of the greatest
purity and perfection', 'the escocheon, enriched with numerous
quarterings, had that air of chastness and profusion at the same time,
by which those beautiful structures are distinguished. And when that
style, under the auspices of the succeeding princes, degenerated into
filligraine by the multiplication of small parts, and was made incongruous by the intermixture of the members of grecian architecture, the
idea of beauty seems to have consisted in redoubling the elements, and
loading them with the ornamental particles'. He refers to grants of
arms made in the 1520s and 1530s by Garter Wriothesley and his
successor Barker, whom he justly calls 'strong heraldic mannerists', to
the 'new order of men', who, at this time and especially upon the
dissolution of the monasteries, 'without hereditary pretensions, became
so wealthy, as to claim the rank and enjoy the luxuries of the first
stations' and 'therefore with more ardour sought for the symbols of
nobility, and endeavoured by greater pomp to conceal their original
deficiency'. As he justly observes 'Wriothesley appears to have been
eager to admit this new order of gentry', and he notes the complicating
effect on heraldic design of the need for differentiation combined with
florid taste. He instances a comment on the characteristically complex
coat, granted in 1541 to William Paget, made by the heraldic writer
Gerard Legh, who calls it 'as fayre a cote as you shall see amongst two
thousand'.[3]

2 *The Yale Edition of Horace Walpole's Correspondence*, ed. W. S. Lewis, Vol.
15, 1952, p. 249.

3 Dallaway, op.cit. pp. 173-6.

FORM AUTHORISING A BANKER TO PAY ANNUALLY / HALF-YEARLY

To_____Bank plc

Name_____
(in Block Letters)

Address_____

Address_____

_____

Account No._____

Please pay on_____19____ to the Co-operative Bank, 17

High Street, Kingston-upon-Thames, KT1 1LP (code number 08 90 34) the sum of £   :

as my annual subscription to the Fabian Society (account number 50492202) and pay

£   :   annually/half-yearly on the_____/_____thereafter

until the cancellation by me of this standing order.

Date_____   Signature_____

THIS ORDER SHOULD BE SENT TO THE GENERAL SECRETARY, FABIAN SOCIETY
11 DARTMOUTH STREET, LONDON SW1H 9BN AND NOT DIRECT TO YOUR BANKER

I wish Dallaway could have had the pleasure of noticing the reaction to simplicity in heraldic design, which ensued under Elizabeth when the new men or their sons had absorbed the notion that plain coats are noblest. Among those who were granted new and plainer coats to replace their florid Henrician arms were the second Sir Thomas Kytson of Hengrave who in 1569 was granted a simplified version of those granted to his father in 1527. The North family had two later simplified recensions of the complex coat granted to Edward North in 1527.

Dallaway's interest in all aspects of heraldry continued down to his own century; but the Victorian Gothic Revival produced a doctrine, which long prevailed, that the only heraldry worth serious attention was the heraldry of the Middle Ages. 'With the accession of the Tudors', wrote that great scholar Oswald Barron in 1910, 'armory began a rapid decadence'. He proceeded, therefore, to give to what happened to it after 1500 something less than three per cent of the space in an otherwise excellent general account of the subject.[4] Barron is not alone among historians in succumbing to the temptation of selection by predilection.

One might think, however, that on these terms the heraldry of the Middle Ages at least and its history would by now have been well analysed and worked out. Yet such is far from being the case, and the reasons, if we can discern them, may throw light on both the difficulties and the potentialities of the subject. The difficulties will begin to appear when it is explained that the basic raw material from which study of the subject has to start, is very bulky and much of it technically difficult, very little of it has been edited or printed, and of that little only a minute proportion has been done adequately.

For mediaeval heraldry, which is the foundation, what are known as the Rolls of Arms are the basic documents. More than thirty years ago a small group, of whom I am the sole survivor, started work on these. In 1950 I printed a Catalogue of them. They number about a hundred, some being long, some short, some existing in a single text only, others in many texts calling for collation. In 1967 a second volume appeared containing proper texts, with full annotation, of the three earliest Rolls, which belong to the reign of Henry III, the work of the late Mr. H. Stanford London and the late Mr. T. D. Tremlett. In the same volume I incorporated some additions to my 1950 Catalogue. In addition to these full editions texts preliminary to full editions but in various stages of completion were prepared by Mr. London for most of the other hundred mediaeval Rolls and for some of the early sixteenth century also. There are old and more or less unsatisfactory editions of some thirty of the Rolls.

From Mr. London's texts and from a few others prepared by Oswald Barron some sixty years ago card indices have been made, from which

4 *Encyclopaedia Britannica,* 11th edition.

the mediaeval part of a comprehensive Dictionary of British Arms has
been in course of preparation for thirty years under the auspices of the
Society of Antiquaries of London, which has an endowment for the
purpose. If something were to appear in the next ten years I should feel
we had not done badly. But the great need is a larger endowment.

How large a pasture we have, even by these first efforts, opened for
study is shown by a work which, in its turn, throws new light on their
subject for all heralds. This is the work of a philologist, Professor
Gerard Brault, Professor of French at the Pennsylvania State University,
published by the Clarendon Press in 1972, entitled *Early Blazon
Heraldic Terminology in the twelfth and thirteenth centuries with
special reference to Arthurian literature,* It is in form a dictionary of
the terms used in the thirteenth century blazoned Rolls of Arms and of
terms used in descriptions of arms in twelfth and thirteenth century
French romances, with an introduction in which the origins and early
development of heraldic language and thus, in a measure, of heraldry
itself are discussed. Serious heralds, who have always known how much
they had to learn from philologists, may now seriously begin to learn it,
and will be gratified to find that philologists have also something to
learn from them.

Besides the evidence of the Rolls of Arms that of Seals, which goes
back further and is in other ways supplementary, has to be used. As
Seals are among the more perishable historical documents and their
value is by no means confined to their heraldic information, one might
have expected that editions of the principal collections, such as that in
the Public Record Office, would have been printed, as they have been
in France. With the exception of Birch's unsatisfactory *Catalogue of the
British Museum Seals* and C. H. Hunter Blair's excellent *Catalogue of
the Durham Seals,* this has not occurred and, so far as I can see, is not
likely to. The heraldry on brasses and other monuments has been better
edited though still not adequately.

From the end of the Middle Ages to the present day the Heralds'
Visitation Books and the other records of the College of Arms form the
core of the source material. These have been made available to the
Society of Antiquaries for the Dictionary of British Arms and a small
beginning has been made with indexing them for that purpose. In
general they are easier to interpret than the earlier material though still
not always easy, but their bulk is many times greater.

King Henry VIII's purpose in ordering heraldic visitation was to
regulate the use and suppress the usurpation of arms and the activity of
the Court of Chivalry at the beginning and end of the seventeenth
century had largely the same purpose. History has therefore to take
account of a substantial illicit use of heraldry of which the details have
in the main to be sought outside the official records. Much manuscript
and other evidence of such use survives and calls for study if the record
is to be complete. A proportion of it may be found in print in local

histories, printed pedigrees and the like.

From all this it will appear that before general historians can make much use of heraldic evidence, it will be necessary for heraldic historians to make more progress than as yet they have in editing their raw material, and the question which may well be asked is whether the likely results afford sufficient incentive to this great labour and, if so, why more has not already been done. The two questions are intertwined and the effort to answer them will, I believe, carry us deep into problems of wider importance than one would at first sight expect.

We must first remind ourselves that heraldry has two faces, one turned in, the other outward. The inward aspect comprises the technical, artistic, symbolic and allusive elements of heraldic design, as they have developed through eight centuries in the countries of Western Europe and in the last two centuries through much of the rest of the world. The permutations imposed by geographical, social and psychological factors on this beautifully balanced and flexible system of recognition mark design, since the Normans invented it, with so much else, in the 12th century, make a fascinating and instructive study for those willing to digest its technicalities. This once done they can use it as a mirror and index of changing circumstances and attitudes. One must envisage treatment of these aspects not as it usually has been but as it might be. What an essay might, for example, be written by a commentator with sufficient knowledge and insight on the College of Arms manuscript, *The Princely Armory of India,* which records the translation into European heraldic form, for the Delhi Durbar of 1877, of emblems associated with or thought appropriate to the Indian princes then subject to the Queen Empress. Yet the art historical side of heraldry, which belongs to this inward aspect, has on the whole had fuller and better treatment than the others. We could, indeed, do with more of it and better; but as it is already the most appreciated side of the subject, I shall give it the least attention here.

I will rather turn now to the outward aspect, and here I see heraldry as, first and foremost, the fullest and most reliable tracer and indicator over many centuries of the development and composition of the upper classes. Paradoxically I believe that it is largely for this very reason that since the seventeenth century scientific history, especially in England and for the post-mediaeval period, has pretty well ignored the heraldic evidence. I have written elsewhere of what I see, to express it dramatically, as a silent conspiracy between conservatives and revolutionaries to represent the facts of social history as other than they truly are. Both, for different reasons, have liked to believe that through history the descendants of the rich have consistently remained rich and the descendants of the poor have consistently remained poor. This, I believe, is not the lesson of the genealogical evidence and would not be the lesson of the heraldic evidence if it could be fully analysed and presented.

Though heraldry appears in the second quarter of the twelfth century, it is not until about the middle of the thirteenth that the evidence of its use becomes reasonably full and substantial, with the appearance of Rolls of Arms. From this point to the reign of Edward III an important attempt has recently been made by Dr. Noel Denholm-Young to relate the heraldic evidence to history in two books, *History and Heraldry 1254 to 1310. A study of the historical value of the rolls of arms* (Oxford, 1965) and *The Country Gentry in the Fourteenth Century with special reference to the heraldic rolls of arms* (Oxford, 1969). Some of our texts were used in these to such advantage as to foreshadow what may come when more texts have been edited.

It is Dr. Denholm-Young's view that all the arms recorded in the earlier rolls are those of knights who had seen or hoped to see military action.[5] In none of those he has examined down to about 1370 are any names included of persons not identifiable as having actually been knights.[6] However in 1386 Sir Robert de Laton testified on behalf of Sir Richard Scrope, at a hearing in the cause of Scrope *versus* Grosvenor in the Court of Chivalry, that some time earlier he had made a roll at the dictation of his aged father of all the arms the latter remembered to have seen in war and at tournaments, not only of kings, princes, earls, barons, lords and knights, but also of esquires — a category who would not at earlier dates have been armigerous.[7] In 1389 Richard II actually issued letters patent declaring that he had received a man into the estate of gentleman, created him esquire and granted him arms. Furthermore surviving rolls of the late fourteenth and the fifteenth centuries do in fact give arms for many families not found in the rolls before, and of whom no members are known to have been knights.

This suggests that when the editing of the rolls, including the identification, where possible, of the persons and families named in them, has been completed, it may be possible to use them, in conjunction with other evidence, and not least that of heraldic seals, as tracers of the changing composition of the class which begins as the chivalry and ends as the gentry. What Dr. Denholm-Young has so far done is at once more and less than this. It is less because he has had available to him only part of what may in time be had from the rolls of arms. And it is more because, while using the rolls as a text, he has added to their evidence such inferences from his great knowledge of the personal background and connections of individual knights as few others could have supplied. It emerges that, while the rolls of arms of Henry III's and Edward I's reigns are in the main first hand records of arms actually seen and the great roll of about 1312, to which the name of the Parliamentary Roll has been given, is a remarkably full and

5 *History and Heraldry*, p. 2.
6 *The Country Gentry*, p. 5.
7 Wagner, *Heralds of England*, p. 32.

accurate official record, thereafter, though there are exceptions, a secondhand, retrospective element creeps more and more into these documents. Careful editing can, however, often distinguish this element.

The fifteenth and the early sixteenth centuries saw on the one hand a great incursion of new men and families into the heraldic field and on the other hand a beginning and gradual extension of official control, from the institution of the office of Garter King of Arms in 1415, down to the first issue of royal letters patent for heraldic visitation in 1530. I have set down what I know of these developments in my book *Heralds of England* (H.M.S.O. 1967). Much more, however, remains to be discovered from the editing of rolls of arms, early heraldic treatises and other texts and from the records of early grants of arms of which some hundreds were made even before 1530. The greatest brake on the work is a shortage not of material but of qualified editors.

The text of the oldest known heraldic treatise, dating perhaps from the early fourteenth century has recently been printed from a manuscript in Cambridge University Library.[8] A full edition by Professor Gerard J. Brault of Pennsylvania State University is hoped for. Some seventeen treatises of the fourteenth and fifteenth centuries, for the most part still unedited, were listed by Mr. H. Stanford London, Norfolk Herald Extraordinary, in 1953.[9] Mr. R. O. Dennys, Somerset Herald, is now in process of noting others which were unknown to Mr. London.

Heralds have from early times been conservatives and archaists. Some of their copies of earlier rolls have been such excellent facsimiles that British Museum cataloguers have paid them the compliment of mistaking a fifteenth century copy for a thirteenth century original.[10] and a seventeenth century copy for a fifteenth century original.[11] In spite of this radical changes in design and style have at certain moments been forced upon the heralds either by changes of outlook and fashion in the outer world or by the intrinsic growth of heraldry itself, as when the need to differentiate new arms from old forced the heralds to turn to new systems, patterns and charges. The remarkable difference of the developments of heraldry in the different countries of Europe is in point here. The best analysis I have seen of these differences is in the article on *Continental Heraldry,* which I persuaded that remarkable polyglot American-Swiss armorist and scholar, the late D. L. Galbreath, to write for the 1949 edition of *Chambers's Encyclopaedia.* He pointed

8 MS. Ee 4.20, by Ruth J. Dean in *Romance Studies in Memory of Edward Billings Ham,* ed. Urban Tigner Holmes, California State College Publications, No. 2, 1967.

9 'Some Medieval Treatises on English Heraldry', *The Antiquaries' Journal,* XXXII, pp. 169-183.

10 MS Add.38537, Dering Roll, CEMRA p. 15.

11 MS. Add.37340, Writhe's Garter book, CEMRA, p. 124.

out, for instance, that from an early date English heraldry runs more to a variety of linear figures and that of France and still more that of Germany to a greater variety of representations of natural objects. The differencing of arms of different branches of families, common in England, France and the Rhineland, is almost unknown in the rest of Germany. Bordures charged with small objects are markedly more frequent in Spain than elsewhere. Polish heraldry has a clan basis and makes great use of rune-like symbols. Crests were of great importance in Germany and in certain parts some families had many crests, but in Italy crests are relatively rare. Either in the realm of art or of social history reasons for some of these differences ought to be discoverable, but they have so far had little attention. The best and fullest such treatment known to me is the comparison of Scottish with English and other practice made by Sir James Balfour Paul, Lord Lyon King of Arms, in his 1898 Rhind lectures on *Heraldry in relation to Scottish history and art.*[12]

On the other side of the account certain heraldic themes have permeated European heraldry from west to east and from north to south, while heraldic traces of common historical origins have lingered long after those origins themselves have been forgotten. An example is the series of swans with golden collars and chains, borne as crests, badges and supporters between about 1300 and modern times by families including those of Bohun, Stafford, Courtenay, Beauchamp, Luttrell and Cary in England, the Counts of Boulogne and Auvergne in France, the Dukes of Cleves and Lords of Ravenstein in Germany, the Kings of Portugal[13] and the Gonzaga, Dukes of Mantua in Italy. The explanation is a descent shared by all of them from kinsmen of Godfrey of Bouillon, whom legend made the grandson of the Swan Knight.[14] Edward Stafford, Duke of Buckingham still cherished the legend in 1512, when Robert Copland translated from the French and Wynkyn

12 Edinburgh, 1900.

13 If we may infer this from the room painted with swans, the Sala dos Cisnes, which has existed in the palace at Cintra from the time of King John I (D.1433), the son in law of John of Gaunt.

14 See Pedigrees 1 to 4, *infra*; A. R. Wagner. 'The Swan Badge and the Swan Knight', *Archaeologia*, XCVII, 1959, pp. 127-138. How and why the legend came to be linked with Godfrey and his family remains mysterious. The first known mention of the legend is by William of Tyre in the ninth book of his History of the First Crusade, composed before 1173, where Godfrey's supposed descent from the Knight is mentioned but discounted. Mr. Robert L. Schurfranz, in an unpublished thesis for the University of North Carolina, makes the interesting suggestion that the association may have originated in the name of Swanehilde (d.1132) Countess of Flanders, first wife of the father of Matthew of Flanders, husband of Mary of Boulogne. Another possibility worth considering is that it may have originated from the nickname of Rainier *of the long neck*, Count of Hainault (D.973), who took part in the Diet of Nijmegen in 947, whose grandson Godfrey, Duke of Upper and Lower Lorraine, was the father of Ida, the mother of Godfrey of Bouillon.

de Worde printed, at the Duke's instigation, 'the history of the noble Helyas Knight of the Swanne'. Charles Gonzaga, Duke of Mantua, is said to have wished to re-establish a supposed Order of the Swan in 1615 and as late as 1750 a pedigree was painted for the Counts of Limburg-Styrum showing their descent from the Swan knight through the Counts of Cleves and Altena. Heraldry here illuminates the ramifications both of mediaeval noble kinship and of the romantic mediaeval mind. The golden chains links the kindred from Portugal to the Rhine and from Thornbury to Mantua.[15]

The characteristic forms and usages of Tudor and early Stuart heraldry need the less description here because they are well known. As Dallaway long ago pointed out, the pompous effigies with their many quartered shields reflect at once the love of funeral pomp, of which Professor Lawrence Stone has reminded us, and the assertion of ancestry to which a traditional but partly parvenu society attached importance. The successive cycles of heraldic visitation between 1530 and 1688 both illustrate and fit into this picture.

So much is clear, but the change in the heraldic climate, which accompanied and followed the end of the Visitations, is less well understood. Their sudden ending has been linked with the Revolution of 1688 but I suggested in *Heralds of England*[16] that the truth might be less simple.

On a wide view the whole phase of English antiquarianism between the later sixteenth and the late seventeenth centuries, with its emphasis on heraldry, genealogy and manorial rights, may be seen, among other things, as a compound of national pride with local patriotism in intense reaction against incursions by central government, whether Court or Commonwealth. In time the tide of freer movement and mercantile activity did as much as politics to wear this reaction down, so that though local pride and patriotism did not cease, their forms became milder and the assertion of rights by county leaders less. Thus in circles, where not long before it had had its strongest hold, heraldry was coming to seem a trifle old fashioned. Yet an effort by the heralds might have captured the allegiance of a whole potential new clientèle of rising men. Some of the last heralds' Visitations had in fact encountered difficulties, but so had some of the earlier ones. An application made by Norroy in 1688 for a Visitation Commission suggests that those immediately preceding had from his point of view justified themselves. Preparatory notes made by Gregory King, Lancaster Herald, in 1686-7 for a projected Visitation of Derbyshire, suggest that the father of demography saw the social changes of the time rather as an opportunity than as a deterrent. As late as 1730 the Kings of Arms were convinced that a Visitation Commission could be obtained if they could but agree

15 Pedigrees 1 to 4.
16 Pp. 312-318.

on its terms. Gregory King's failure to secure appointment as Norroy in 1693 or as Clarenceux in 1703 may have contributed to the failure, for those in charge at a difficult moment seem to have been ill equipped to deal with the difficulties.

An important element in these difficulties was the rising class of what Professor Alan Everitt has conveniently, if unkindly, called the pseudo-gentry,[17] 'that class of leisured and predominantly urban families who, by their manner of life, were commonly regarded as gentry, though they were not supported by a landed estate'; most of them originating in and after the late seventeenth century, but some earlier; some, gentry who had lost their lands; some, cadets of gentle families; others, sprung from clergy, army officers, lawyers, doctors, factors, maltsters, moneylenders, innkeepers or others who had made money. They wished to be known as gentry and to bear arms in token of their gentility. But not all of them qualified to do so and of those who were not qualified not all were willing to admit the facts by applying for grants of arms. Heraldry itself was never more popular than with them. Defoe wrote in 1726 of 'the tradesmen of *England,* as they grow wealthy, coming every day to the Heralds' Office, to search for the Coats of Arms of their ancestors, in order to paint them upon their coaches, and engrave them upon their plate, embroider them upon their furniture, or carve them upon the pediments of their new houses'.[18]

Paradoxically the power of Visitation would have enabled the heralds to gratify these wishes more easily. The heralds were told in 1730 that 'the King and Queen approved of Visitations and Sir Robert Walpole was not against it'. The Duke of Norfolk, debarred as a Catholic from personal exercise of his office of Earl Marshal, asked his Deputy, Lord Sussex, to sign the necessary warrant. But the latter told Norroy 'he could not do it. He should have all the County upon his back . . . he knew a gentleman worth several thousands a year that had no Arms. What would he say to have his Arms defaced. I replyd', says Norroy, 'I was sorry there was such a person so mean as to Usurp Arms. That he was consequently no Gentleman notwithstanding his Thousands . . . That it was a discretionary power in the Kings of Arms who for their own sakes would act therein with great Circumspection, He said it would make the County mad. I replyd the Gentlemen of my Province if I was rightly informed were mad to see so little regard shewn to ancient Familys. That it was hard to deny Justice to the Worthier part of Mankind and to a King of Arms the Rights of his Office out of

17 Everitt, 'Social Mobility in Early Modern England', *Past and Present,* No. 33, April 1966, pp. 70-2, & *Change in the Provinces: The Seventeenth Century,* Leicester Univ. Press, Department of English Local History, Occasional Papers, 2nd Series, No. 1, 1969, pp. 44-5.

18 Daniel Defoe, *The Complete English Tradesman,* 1726, p. 377.

Defference to a few ignoble Upstarts who were ashamed to own what they were and had not the honour to do for their posterity what they wisht their Fathers had done for them. That whilst such people despised Arms and nevertheless used them they exposed their pride & Folly and belied their own Consciences'.[19]

Some of these 'ignoble upstarts' have their memorial in handsome pieces of Georgian silver engraved with arms which on examination prove baseless or discrepant. Something is known of the illicit herald painters' shops from which such designs came and a study of the surviving records of their activity would contribute both to heraldic and to social history. There exists a manuscript in which an eighteenth century Norwich coach painter noted all the arms he saw on the panels of coaches and carriages, with attributions. An analysis of their authenticity and scope would contribute similarly.

Stylistically the best of the sculptors', woodcarvers' and engravers' heraldry of seventeenth and early eighteenth century England seems to me to reach great heights — comparable, if in a different vein, with the work of the High Middle Ages and far better than much intervening work. Then in the later eighteenth and the nineteenth century comes a falling away into the neat little compositions of neat little charges, so much favoured by the Victorians, which Oswald Barron used to call 'buttonmakers' heraldry'. After being spat upon by the early twentieth century revival this style has lately enjoyed some return to fashion in high art circles. It is the style of Victorian 'crested' stationery, of menservants' livery buttons, and of coronets on the flaps of envelopes.

In the mean time Romantic mediaevalism, from Horace Walpole or earlier, had set a powerful new force behind the revival and spread of heraldry in general. Like the Gothic revival in architecture it took some four generations for scholarship and taste to sift the sense from the nonsense, and bring discipline to enthusiasm. Good work was done throughout but for a long time risked submersion in a mass of bad. There is splendid herald painters' illumination of the late eighteenth and early nineteenth centuries. Pugin's heraldic decoration in the House of Lords is remarkably fine. When William Morris now and then turned to heraldry he handled it with the skill and sympathy one would expect. Such an antiquary scholar as J. G. Waller, historian and maker of monumental brasses, could produce superb heraldic enamel work, witness his restoration, probably about 1870, of the tomb of Edmund Tudor, father of Henry VII, in St. David's Cathedral, the heraldry of which is new work by Waller. In the present century there have been several first rate heraldic designers and craftsmen, working alongside others of whom the less said the better.

In this as in earlier phases of heraldic art national differences are striking. That of Germany, for instance kept through the last century a vitality which France, I fear, lost even more completely than England.

19 Wagner, *Heralds of England*, 1967, pp. 363-5.

By an unexpected but not inexplicable reversal of rôles Switzerland, the
early home of European democracy, became in the late nineteenth and
the twentieth century the headquarters of European heraldic studies,
and to a great extent remains so. The explanation I take to be that
Swiss democracy dates from a half literate time when heraldry and its
visual language were not a rarefied study but a part of the common air
men breathed. So attractive and so useful was this Norman invention
that in France and England before 1300 merchants and peasants had
ventured to depict arms of their own adoption on their seals,[20] and a
famous fourteenth century jurist Bartolus of Sassoferrato justified this
by analogy from the law of names, though he concedes that such arms
were not of equal dignity with those granted by royal authority.[21] In
monarchical countries the conclusion that arms, to be valid, must derive
from the sovereign, by and large prevailed. Switzerland, naturally,
became the home of the opposite view that legal right in any coat of
arms belonged simply to the first to adopt it *proprio motu*.

It is notable that in the Western European homelands of heraldry,
though the original Norman concept has from time to time been
changed or debased by the irruption of alien elements or by mere
accretion, there have yet been periodical attempts to return to the
splendid, logical simplicity of the original scheme. This is not, I think,
mere archaism, though that too has been powerful, but is rather a
recognition of the unique merit of the original Norman practice. It
must, however, be added that in the last two or three centuries heraldry
has been admired and more or less adopted in many countries of the
world, far beyond its early home, and in some of these has in the
process assumed forms which seem no more heraldic to us than one
fancies Chinese Chippendale seems Chinese to the Chinese. The
Saracenic heraldry which arose in the Near East by imitation of the
Crusaders is orthodox by comparison with some modern developments
in remoter regions.

It would not surprise me if some time hence the wish to return to
older models were to come upon these regions also. From time to time
recourse, suggesting such an outcome, is had to the institution which
more than any other has maintained in these affairs a continuous
tradition. As a member of that institution I view such events with
pleasure, though I see no reason actually to provoke them.

Thus I have sought to show that heraldry, with the background
which accompanies and explains it, is of greater potential interest to the
historian than his actual interest in it hitherto might suggest. But I have
also tried to make it clear that this cannot in any full sense become
actual without a prior full collection and analysis of materials, requiring
technical knowledge. This once done the way will be clear to a kind of

21 Rémi Mathieu, *Le systeme héraldique français*, 1946, pp. 40-42.
21 Wagner, *Heralds of England*, p. 30.

picture hitherto impossible of the rise and recruitment of the knightly class which became the gentry; of the thoughts which informed the symbolic system whereby that class distinguished itself from others and its members one from another; and of the ease and general enthusiasm with which that system was in time applied — though not always perfectly — to wholly different objects and social situations. If, in claiming so much for the little science of heraldry, I should seem to have gone too far, I hope a convert's enthusiasm may be pardoned, for my own interest in it was not original but a slow extension of an earlier concern with genealogy.

CHAPTER III

BRIDGES TO ANTIQUITY

The difficulty or impossibility of tracing any modern European descent from classical antiquity has been pointed to as a symptom and instance of the breach in historical continuity made by the fall of the Roman Empire. If the one phenomenon is to throw light on the other, however, closer analysis is required than has yet been given; the nature of the genealogical difficulty not being always clearly understood and the causes of the fall of Rome remaining a matter of controversy. The main use of such analysis may be to focus attention on some of the detail relevant to that controversy.

A crude but inadequate view of the genealogical gap sees it as coterminous with a Dark Age chasm between classical and mediaeval civilization — as if classical pedigrees ended in 476 with Romulus Augustulus and modern pedigrees began in 800 with Charlemagne. The truth, however, is less simple. The great comital houses of France, northern Italy and western Germany, from which so many royal houses sprang, do indeed appear with startling suddenness in the ninth and tenth centuries, and we may agree with Marc Bloch[1] that this may well be due not just to the loss of earlier record but to the families in question having been established in that period by selfmade men, to whom the conditions of the age gave opportunities and whose near successors did not know their origins. This does not mean that they were drawn from the ranks of the serfs, but more probably from those of the petty manorial lords, whose pedigrees, however, lie nearly as far below the threshold of the scanty records of that age.

These conditions belong to the lands where thoroughgoing Roman civilization had been broken down yet remained the basis of what order there was. But if we turn our eyes to lands on the fringes of the former Roman Empire, where tribal traditions remained strong, we find royal

1 *Feudal Society*, 1961, pp. 284-5.

pedigrees which modern authorities accept as historical back to the fifth or even the fourth century of our era.[2]

In Ireland — always well beyond the Roman frontier — the line of the High Kings is taken back to Niall of the Nine Hostages (d.405) and can be carried down to the present day.[3] Fergus Mor Mac Eirc who crossed the sea from Ireland to Scotland, (c.503) founded the kingdom of Dalriada there and is among our own Queen's ancestors, was derived traditionally from the same line.[4] It has been inferred that Crinan the Thane (d.1045), the father of the Scottish king Duncan, was of the kin of St. Columba (d.597) and thus of the male line of Niall of the Nine Hostages. The Earls of Dunbar and later families of Dunbar were of Crinan's male line. So possibly was the great English family of Neville.[5] Recently Mr. George S. H. L. Washington has argued plausibly that the Washingtons of Durham descend from Patric of the Hirsel, younger son of Gospatric III (d.1166), Earl of Dunbar, great grandson of Maldred, son of Crinan.[6] This would give the first President of the United States a clear male line descent from the brother of King Duncan, whom Macbeth murdered in 1040, and a possible male descent from the oldest Western European dynasty, that of the High Kings of Ireland.

A Welsh princely line, with many living descendants, can be taken back to Cunedda who came from southern Scotland to North Wales about 430 A.D. The names given by the pedigrees for Cunnedda's immediate ancestors and three of his sons have been interpreted as those of Romanized Britons. [7] H. M. Chadwick also interpreted as Romano-British the names given by the genealogies for the father and grandfather of Coroticus, perhaps king at Dumbarton and born about 400 A.D., from whom a line may be traced through the kings of Strathclyde to the Irish O'Melaghlin line and its existing progeny.[8]

An eighth century pedigree of the Kings of Mercia is though acceptable back to Wermund, King of Angel in Schleswig about 350 A.D., while the line of the Kings of Wessex, who became Kings of England, has been considered historical from about 500.[9]

---

2 Wagner, *English Genealogy*, 1st ed., 1960 and 2nd ed., 1972, hereafter cited as EG I and II, gives references to sources.

3 EG I, 22-4, II 23-8; *Burke's Peerage*, 1963, s.v. O'Neill. For a recent discussion of Niall's disputed date and on these matters generally see Francis John Byrne, *Irish Kings and High Kings*, 1973.

4 EG I, 26; II, 28.

5 EG I, 24-5, II, 26-7.

6 George S. H. L. Washington. *The Earliest Washingtons and their Anglo-Scottish connexions*, privately printed for the Author, Cambridge, 1964. His argument is accepted by Sir Charles Clay. EG II, 27.

7 *The Dictionary of Welsh Biography*, 1959, pp. 87-8. Eg., I, 27; II, 29-30. For the best recent discussion see John Morris, *The Age of Arthur*, 1973, pp. 66-8 etc.

8 H. M. Chadwick, *Early Scotland*, 1949, p.150.

9 EG I and II, 14-15. But Morris, op. cit. p. 103 & c rejects this.

Thus barbarian lines which continue to the present day can be carried back to the days of the later Roman Empire. The difficulty is to link them actually with Rome. This is not because Romans of imperial family did not intermarry with barbarians, both Romanized and external. Stilicho (d.408), whose military genius for a time upheld the Empire, was the son of a Vandal captain of auxiliaries, was married to a niece of the Emperor Theodosius the Great and married both his daughters successively to the Emperor Honorius (Ped. 25). Ricimer (d.472), the son of a Suevic chief and grandson of a Visigothic king, who played the part of a king (or emperor) maker in the last days of the Western Empire, married the daughter of the Emperor Anthemius (467-472). The sister of Ricimer (Ped. 27) married a Burgundian king and her granddaughter Clotilda, wife of Clovis the Frank was ancestress of the Kings of Kent and perhaps, through them, of the Kings of Wessex and England.[10] Galla Placidia (Ped. 25: d.c.450) whose tomb is among the glories of Ravenna, the daughter of Theodosius I and later wife of Constantius III (d.421), having fallen into the hands of Alaric the Visigoth, about the time of his sack of Rome in 410, was married in 414 to his brother-in-law and successor Ataulfus (d.415). Her step-brother the Emperor Arcadius (395-408) married the daughter of Bauto, a Frankish general in the Roman service. Eudoxia daughter of Valentinian III (425-455) was married in 456 to Huneric, King of the Vandals (Peds. 25, 27); and Juliana daughter of the Emperor Olybrius (Ped. 25: d.472) was offered in marriage by the Emperor Zeno to Theodoric, the future King of the Ostrogoths, who had lived for ten years at Constantinople, as a hostage[11] Theodoric did not accept this offer and the lady actually married Flavius Areobindus (Ped. 26: consul in 506) a descendant of German generals in the Emperor's service. A pedigree recorded by Jordanes and Cassiodorus carries the male ancestry of Theodoric himself back fourteen generations and may be historical from his ninth ancestor Ostrogotha living about 245 A.D.[12]

The difficulty is that from no such marriages as these can a pedigree be proved down to mediaeval times. Is this mere accident or can a reason be discerned? Among the possible explanations the first which seems worth exploring is that the marriages noted of Roman ladies to barbarian kings took place in or near the heart of the Empire, where the barbaric dynasties in question were soon themselves displaced by later invaders. The Ostrogothic kingdom in Italy and the Vandal kingdom in Africa were ended by the Byzantine reconquest of Justinian in the 530s. Visigothic kings went on in Spain, indeed, till the Moslem conquest of 711, but there was no continuing dynasty among them and no line sprung from Ataulfus and Galla Placidia.

10 P. 53, *infra.*

11 Thomas Hodgkin, *Italy and her invaders,* Vol.II, 1892, p. 474, citing Malchus, fragment 16. (Peds. 26, 28).

12 *Ibid.* I. 49, III. 5.

The longest enduring of the barbarian dynasties which took over directly from the Roman *imperium* was the Frankish line of the Merovingian kings in Gaul. Clovis its founder defeated the Roman Syagrius in 486 and his last male descendant, Childeric III, was relegated to the cloister in 751. But though there are[13] possible female descents from the Merovingians to the present day, none is proved beyond doubt.

Perhaps the most interesting such possibility is one propounded by Professor David H. Kelley. Before 588 Ethelbert, King of Kent, grandson of Hengist, married Bertha, daughter of the Frankish King of Paris, Charlbert I (d.567), a grandson of Clovis. Sir Frank Stenton surmises that the Frankish purpose in arranging this marriage was to strengthen the ties between those Jutes who remained in Gaul and those who had passed over into Britain and were ruled by Ethelbert. It was to Ethelbert, whose Queen was a Christian by upbringing, that Pope Gregory the Great sent Augustine upon his mission to convert England in 596[14]

From Ethelbert and Bertha the line of the Kings of Kent is clearly traceable for six generations down to Eardwulf (d.765).[15] There is no direct evidence of the place in the pedigree of his successors Egbert II (765-779) and Eadbert Praen (796-8), though they are thought to have been brothers. Professor Kelley conjectures that they were sons of Eardwulf's uncle Ethelbert II (748-762), that they had a sister who married Ealhmund of the house of Wessex, whereby the latter became a sub-king in Kent, and that the name Egbert, not previously found in the house of Wessex, thus came to be given to their son Egbert, King of Wessex (802-39), the ancestor of the Kings of England (Ped. 29).

It is true that Charlemagne (d.814), ancestor of innumerable living descendants, whose dynasty replaced the Merovingians, has been conjecturally deduced from an ancestor said to have been a kinsman of Clovis.[16] Among his possible forbears moreover, was a Duke Boso Bodegisel living about 600 A.D., who married the daughter of Gallus Magnus, Bishop of Troyes, a Gallo-Roman.[17] Professor Toynbee points out[18] that, whereas barbarians in Roman service, who had previously taken Roman names, from the middle of the fourth century retained their own, in Gaul between the late fifth and the late sixth centuries the Gallo-Romans, on the contrary adopted Frankish names, which by the eighth century were universal, so that families of Gallo-Roman descent were by then effectively disguised as Franks. A

13 EG I, 31n., 32: II, 33-4; and infra.

14 F. M. Stenton, *Anglo-Saxon England*, 1943, pp. 59, 105.

15 W. G. Searle, *Anglo-Saxon Bishops, Kings and Nobles*, 1899, pp. 258-9.

16 EG I, 31; II, 34.

17 Venantius Fortunatus, *Carmina*, Bk.VII, Nos. 5, 6; *Monumenta Germaniae Historica*, IV. 1881, p. 158.

18 A. J. Toynbee, *A study of History*, Vol.V, 1939, pp. 468, 476.

Gallo-Roman in any case is not a Roman,[19] and the Merovingians themselves have no known Roman descent. But they have, what may lead us to a fresh phase of enquiry, clear if indirect Roman marriage connections.

These come, as mentioned above, through Clotilda[20] and through the marriage of Augofleda (or Audefleda), the sister of Clovis, to Theodoric, King of the Ostrogoths (d.526), that most nearly civilized of barbarians, whose thirty three years' reign was looked back to in the black days which followed as an age of gold. He is said to have governed the two nations of the Goths and Romans as if they were one people and to have maintained the administration of Italy as it had been under the Emperors. Of his sayings which were remembered as proverbs one was that the Roman when in misery imitates the Goth and the Goth when in comfort imitates the Roman.[21]

His marriage alliances suggest a vision, in Hodgkin's words 'of a "family compact", binding together all the kingdoms of the West, from the Scheldt to Mount Atlas, in a great confederacy, filling all the new barbarian thrones with the sons, the grandsons, or the nephews of Theodoric, a matrimonial State-system surpassing (may we not say?) anything that Hapsburg or Bourbon ever succeeded in accomplishing, when they sought to make Venus instead of Mars build up their empires."[22] It lasted only a generation, then snapped under the strain of rivalry or was overwhelmed by fresh barbarian incursions. In this generation none the less matrimonial links were forged, which in however roundabout a way make clear connections between modern dynasties and those of antiquity.

Theodoric's sister married a Vandal king whose uncle had married a daughter of the Western Roman Emperor Valentian III. His niece married a Thuringian king and their daughter a Lombard king. Of his own daughters one married the king of the Burgundians and one the king of the Visigoths; and of his granddaughters one married a king of the Franks and one a nephew of the Eastern Roman Emperor Justinian (d.565).[23]

One might expect that from this great barbarian edifice, this new born concert of Europe, dynastic lines would branch outward and downward to the present day. In fact Theodoric's latest known descendants were his Byzantine great-grandson Germanus the younger

19 There were, however, fifth century Gallo-Roman senators who claimed Roman descent, cf. A. H. M. Jones, *The Later Roman Empire* 284-602, 1964, Vol.III, p. 158, n.57, quoting Sidonius Apollinaris, Ep.IV.14 for the claim of Polemius to descend from the historian Tacitus (fl. A.D. 77-117) and Ep.VIII 3 for that of Leo to descend from the orator Fronto (Consul A.D. 143).

20 P. 52, *supra*. Ped. 27.

21 *Anonymus Valesii*, quoted by Hodgkin, *op.cit*, Vol.III, pp. 262-3.

22 Ib. p. 231.

23 Ped. 28 & Hodgkin, *op.cit.* Vol.III pp. 320-1.

(b.550) and his Frankish great-great-grandson King Theudebald of Austrasia (d.555), nor, I think is this mere genealogical accident (Peds. 26-8).

The barbarian dynasties of the fifth century sought to build on Roman foundations which were still collapsing. They took over the Roman administration because they had nothing to put in its place, but their effect on it was destructive. Only after three more centuries, when the long slide had reached bottom, could the process of building up begin again. The barbarian dynasties in the Roman heart land were as unstable and short lived as their imperial predecessors. Because of this continuous descents are not traceable, for chroniclers of this disordered age tell us little of the pedigrees of lesser families. Yet, what they tell us of dynastic links and the continuity which these establish, suggests that, if we knew but a little more, there would be continuous lines of moderate eminence across the chasm, even if traceable only through females.

The links set out in Pedigree 27 pass from the Frankish kings by marriage to those of the Lombards, whose own succession passed from dynasty to dynasty by revolution more than once, and at other times through the marriage of a queen or heiress to the scion of a ducal or other noble family. We have the impression of a continuous, inter-married Lombard nobility with roots in barbaric Germany, linked by marriage in early days with the rulers of such tribes as the Heruli, Gepidae and Thuringians and both then and later with the Merovingian and perhaps with other Frankish noble families.[24]

Among these the most important links are provided by the family of the Agilolfings, of whom one line were Dukes of Bavaria and another line Dukes of Asti and Kings of the Lombards.[25] (Ped. 30). Hodgkin quotes the reasons adduced by Quitzmann for thinking that their founder Garibald I (553-595/6?) was a Salian Frank and probably akin to the Merovingians,[26] Garibald married Walderada, daughter of a Lombard king, Waccho, former wife of two Frankish kings, Theudebald of Austrasia (548-555) and Chlotochar I of Neustria (511-561).

Though no extant line is derived from the Agilolfings, they are linked with extant lines by the marriage of Charles Martel (d.741), the grandfather of Charlemagne, to Swanahild daughter of Theudebert, Duke of Bavaria (d.722). There is one unproved though probable link in the descent of Theudebert from Garibald,[27] but through the

24 Hodgkin, *op.cit.* V, 118, 121 & VI, 177 nn. where the pedigree of King Waccho (510-540) is carried back five generations and that of King Rothari (636-652) eleven; VI 62, 337, 438.

25 Hodgkin, VI 148, 300, VII, 64.

26 VII, 66n.

27 For the affiliation of Tassilo I (596-611) to Garibald I, Hodgkin, *op.cit.* VI. 67.

marriage of Swanahild's sister Guntrud to the Lombard king Liutprand (712-744) there is a clear, if roundabout, connection with Garibald through the Dukes of Benevento and the Lombard kings of the house of Arlpert.[28] From Charles Martel, though from another wife, not Swanahild, descents to the present day are innumerable and we are in the system of modern genealogy.

Having thus linked modern Europe with the late Roman Empire, we have as hard a task still to face to link that late phase of antiquity genealogically with its earlier golden age.

The marriage of the Emperor Gratian (d.383) to the daughter of Constantius II (d.361) joins us to the house of Constantine, which links us to that of Diocletian (284-305), but with his obscure origin we reach a full stop.[29] (Ped. 24).

There were indeed fifth century Roman senators who claimed descents of high antiquity. 'The temporal honours which the devout Paula inherited and despised are', in Gibbon's words, 'carefully recapitulated by Jerome, the guide of her conscience and the historian of her life. The genealogy of her father, Rogatus, which ascended as high as Agamemnon, might seem to betray a Grecian origin; but her mother Blaesilla, numbered the Scipios, Aemilius Paulus and the Gracchi, in the list of her ancestors; and Toxotius, the husband of Paula, deduced his royal lineage from Aeneas, the father of the Julian line'.[30] Professor A. H. M. Jones considered that though such pedigrees cannot be verified, 'it would be rash to deny that by adoptions or through the female line', the nucleus of ancient families in the fourth century Roman senate 'may have been able to trace some tenuous link with Republican nobility'. [31] In support or at all events in explanation of the claims of Paula it may be mentioned that Publius Scipio Aemilianus Africanus minor, Consul in 147 and 134 B.C., was a son of Lucius Aemilius Paulus, was adopted by Publius Scipio Africanus, son of the great Africanus, and married Sempronia the sister of the Gracchi; that fifty years before St. Paula's birth there was living in Rome one Lucius Cornelius Scipio Orifitus, whom Professor Jones and his fellow authors of the *Prosopography of the Later Roman Empire*[32] regard as 'evidently descended from the early empire Cornelii Scipiones' and thus of ancient and aristocratic family; while marriage links can be estab-

---

28 *Ibid*, III 64, VI 438, VI 62, VI 148.

29 The pedigree which makes the mother of Constantius Chlorus a niece of the Emperor Claudius Gothicus (268-270) is now thought 'probably fictitious', A. H. M. Jones, J. R. Martindale, J. Morris, *The Prosopography of the Later Roman Empire*, Vol.I, A. D. 260-395, p. 316.

30 Edward Gibbon, *The History of the Decline and Fall of the Roman Empire*, ed. J. B. Bury, 1897, Vol.III, pp. 289-90. *Jerome*, Epistle 108, paras 1-4.

31 A. H. M. Jones, *The Later Roman Empire 284-602*, 1964, Vol.II, pp. 545-6.

32 II. 651.

lished between Paula's family and leading aristocratic families of her day.[33]

In fuller detail, though still conjecturally, Mr. John Morris has worked out a probable line of descent leading through seventeen generations (nine men and eight women. Ped. 20) from Scribonia, the first wife of Augustus Caesar (d.14 A.D.), and her first husband Publius Cornelius Scipio to Paula (born c.400), the granddaughter of St. Paula.[34] 'That kind of exercise', he writes, 'is not too difficult'. He emphasizes, however, that he and his fellow authors of the *Prosopography* 'have been at pains in the stemmata to distinguish between guesses, shown by dotted lines, and evidenced relationships, shown by continuous lines'. The dotted line reconstructions 'are the best we can do with the faulty evidence at present available' but 'can provide future scholars with a base on which they may write articles improving on our interpretation'.[35] Unfortunately both the Anician pedigree (Peds. 21, 22) and that in which Mr. Morris derives Paula from Scribonia (Ped. 20) consist mainly of dotted lines.

Mr. Morris's comments on the former show the nature of the evidence and arguments on which such pedigrees are based. Thus 'the probable and natural explanation' of the name of Cornelia Cethegilla Aemilia Plancina, a senatorial lady of the middle first century known from an inscription, is 'that her parents were named Cornelius Cethegus and Aemilia Plancina'. We are told that 'the age of Augustus, like the fourth century, was conscious of its ancestors, and delighted in calling its children by antique names. Thus the Valerii revived the fine old names of Volesus and Potitus; but like the fourth century, they brought back into use names proper to their own gens, to which they had some semblance of a claim'. The lady's mother's name 'argues a marriage, not elsewhere recorded, between an Aemilius and a Plancina, the proper root of the name Aemilia Plancina'.

Inferences are drawn from successions to property in different provinces. In the fourth century 'the younger line of the Nummii seem, like some branches of other great families, to have retired to their provincial estates, in their case in Tarraconensis. There, in the middle of the century, one of them became Bishop of Barcelona; he may, like St. Ambrose of Milan a generation later, have been son of a Praetorian Prefect. But when the Emperor Theodosius was summoned from Spain to Constantinople, he was accompanied by the Bishop's son, Nummius Aemilianus Dexter, whose last recorded office was the Praetorian Prefecture of Italy under Honorius'.

The evidence for such persons and pedigrees comes predominantly from inscriptions from all parts of the Roman Empire, though also

33 Ped. 23.

34 Bonner Jahrbücher. Band 165, 1965, pp. 88-96, John Morris, 'Munatius Plancus Paulinus'.

35 Letter to the writer, 10 Aug. 1971.

from literary sources, laws and papyri. One may spare a moment here
to smile at the hopes of modern destroyers who justify their
destruction of monumental inscriptions graven on stone by saying that
copies have been made and lodged in public libraries.

Though inferences from the Roman system of nomenclature often
make alternative affiliations possible, they may still leave no doubt but
that *some* descent from the given line exists. Such evidence, taken
together, leaves no doubt of 'the tenacity of the noble families of the
principate, of their continuity into the fourth century and beyond. In
default of sons, property, names and tradition passed through
heiresses . . . and the fourth century nobility of western Rome, unlike
their parvenu fellows in the senate of Constantinople, were rich in
inherited lands and inherited tradition. Their jejune historical writing
shows their desperate attachment to the great days of the past, when
their ancestors had enjoyed a greater political influence. But in seeking
to revive the power and glory of the senatorial families, they were
impelled not only by a general nostalgia for the former eminence of
their class and their order, but also by the proud traditions of their
individual family ancestors'.[36] With this attitude the eminence of
some members of these families in the Christian church and their
generous endowment of it may be linked.

Of all such families continuity with the Roman past can most
confidently be attributed to the house to which the senators of that
day 'unanimously yielded the pre-eminence,' the *gens Anicia*. Their
name appears in Praeneste (the modern Palestrina) with Quintus
Anicius Gallus about B.C. 340 and Quintus Anicius Gallus Praenestinus
became curule aedile in Rome in B.C. 304.[37] Their part in early
Roman history was respectable but unimportant. 'The ambition of
those new citizens was long satisfied with the Plebeian honours of
tribunes of the people', until 'one hundred and sixty-eight years before
the Christian era, the family was ennobled by the praetorship of
Anicius, who gloriously terminated the Illyrian war by the conquest of
the nation and the captivity of their king'. Livy[38] places them at this
time below the great families of Rome, but a century later they were
linked by marriage with greater families, for Anicia, who was a cousin
(*consobrina*) of Pomponius Atticus, the friend of Cicero, married
Servius, brother of P. Sulpicius Rufus, consul in B.C.51.[39] Since
Atticus' daughter married Agrippa and their daughter was Vipsania, the
wife of the Emperor Tiberius, we have a link here with the main stream
of ancient history. (Ped. 20).

36 Morris *op.cit.*
37 Pauly-Wissowa, Real Encyclopädie, I. ii. 1894, pp. 2196-9: Joseph Aschbach,
Die Anicier und die Römische dichterin Proba, Vienna, 1870: Hodgkin, *op.cit.*, II.
474. Gibbon, (op. cit., p. 56, n.30)
38 xlv, 43.
39 Cornelius Nepos, *Atticus*, I.Ω.

For two centuries and more thereafter little is heard of the Anicii. But 'simply by living on through the wars, proscriptions and massacres of the Empire,' they become eminent in the third century and 'a large and mighty kinship in the fourth century after Christ, when so many of the great names of the Republic had gone out for ever'.[40] Thus in England have the Howards survived the Bohuns, Mortimers and Veres.

From Sextus Cocceius Anicius Faustus Paulinus, proconsul of Africa about 260 A.D., Dr. Seeck's account (in Pauly-Wissowa) gives a pedigree of twelve generations to Flavius Anicius Olybrius the younger, consul in 491, with one name missing, that of the father of Anicius Olybrius, Emperor of the West in 472. It is to be noted, however, that the descent and name within this span pass four times through females (Peds. 22-3). The authors of the *Prosopography* [41] conclude that Sextus Cocceius Anicius Faustus Paulinus will have been son of Anicius Faustus Paulinus, legate of Lower Moesia in 230, a descendant of Quintus Anicius Faustus, consul in 198, whose wife was probably Sergia Paulla, daughter of the last of six successive senators named Lucius Sergius Paullus, of Pisidian Antioch, the first of whom was the proconsul of Cyprus under Claudius to whom St. Paul preached.

The pedigrees reveal intermarriage and combination of names with such other families as the Auchenii, Petronii, Probi, Amnii, Paulini, Fausti, and Olybrii. This was common Roman practice, so that continuity of name need not imply male descent, and Anician prestige was now such that any who could claim the blood might covet the name. They also suggest the existence of close social and genealogical links between a small group of these rich, powerful and relatively old families, possessed of lands in many parts of the Empire, with which some of their members later endowed the Christian church. These links, however, did not exclude occasional alliances with families whose wealth and eminence had other origins. They in time took place, for instance, with descendants of obscure soldiers who attained the Imperial purple,[42] especially after the accession of Theodosius I in 379, when, as Mr. Peter Brown puts it, the Italian and Gallic senatorial families annexed the governmental machine to their own style of life and established a near monopoly of the highest offices.[43]

The first Anician link with the barbarian kings comes through the marriage of the Emperor Olybrius (472) with Placidia, daughter of the Emperor Valentinian III (425-455) and sister of Eudoxia, wife of Huneric King of the Vandals (477-484) whose nephew Thrasamund (496-523) married a sister of Theodoric the Ostrogoth (Ped. 25).

40 Hodgkin, *op.cit.* III. 471.
41 P.680.
42 Ped. 23.
43 *The World of late Antiquity*, 1970, p. 120.

Juliana, Olybrius' daughter, was, as we have seen, offered in marriage by the Eastern Emperor Zeno·(474-5 & 477-91) to Theodoric himself but was rejected by him and instead married Flavius Areobindus.[44] Their son Flavius Anicius Olybrius, consul in 491, married a niece of the Eastern Emperor Anastasius (491-518). Since they are said to have left only daughters, it is likely that one of these was the mother of Areobindus, eighth in descent from the Emperor Theodosius I (379-395), who married Praejecta niece of the Emperor Justinian I (527-565).[45] The last proved Anician of the name was apparently the last private consul in 541. A most distinguished Anician was the statesman and philosopher Anicius Manlius Severinus Boethius (d.524), who through his writings, and especially his *Consolation of Philosophy*, written when he was in prison, condemned to death by Theodoric, had immense influence on the thought and literature of the Middle Ages. Mr. Morris is disposed to accept[46] the suggestion that St. Benedict of Nursia (c.480-c.544), the founder of western monasticism, belonged to the Anician family and thinks possible the suggestion that the pope St. Gregory the Great (c.540-604) did so also. Gregory's father was of senatorial rank and owned large estates in Sicily and property on the Coelian hill in Rome which is thought to have been at one time in the inheritance of the Anicii. Were these the noblest Romans of them all? Unhappily the later we get 'the mistier the evidence becomes, in two stages: with many people it is possible to say that they belong to the family, not possible to say where exactly they fit; then it becomes probable or possible but not well proven that a man belongs to the family at all'.[47] What a family it would be to which all these men belonged! Such was the glory of the Anician name that the Emperor Justin I (518-527) assumed it soon after his accession without any claim unless perhaps an adoption by some member of the family arranged for the purpose. His nephew and successor Justinian (527-565) followed suit, and the marriage of his nephew Germanus (d.550) to the Ostrogothic princess Matasuentha was somewhat absurdly called by the historian Jordanes a union of the Anician and Amal races.[48] In 1613 the Abbot Seifridus von Zwettel sought to derive the Habsburgs from the Anicii![49]

By these several intermarriages a connection (though no descent) is established between imperial Rome and modern times. We may ask, however, whether the same thing — or even a descent — could not have been found more easily through Byzantium, where Roman civilization

44 P. 52, *supra.* In 512 rioters against Anastasius called for Areobindus to be made Emperor (Hodgkin III, 412).

45 Ducange, *Familiae Augustae Byzantinae*, ed. 1729, pp. 74, 75.

46 Morris, *op.cit.*

47 Morris, letter 10 Aug. 1971.

48 Aschbach, *op.cit.*, p. 49, n.1., quotes Jordanes, *De Rebus Geticis* c.60.

49 *Ibid* p. 10, n.1.

and institutions continued so long unbroken. The answer is that this cannot be, or at least has not been, done — but not because there are no modern descents from Byzantium. In the time of the Crusades several marriages in fact took place between western European families and Byzantine houses from which descents are traceable to the present day. The difficulty is that between the sixth and ninth centuries there is a breach in our record of Byzantine genealogy even more complete than we have met with in the lands of the former Western Empire.

It is unlikely that this is because no eminent lines lasted through this epoch in the Eastern Empire. Unsubstantiated claims to have done so were indeed made. The family of Doukas was alleged to descend from a cousin and colleague of Constantine the Great, who moved from Rome to Constantinople and was made *dux* of that city. The Emperor Nikephoros Botoneiates (1078-81) claimed descent from the family of Phokas, which in turn was said to be linked with Roman Fabii by way of an ancestor transplanted by Constantine the Great to Georgia. Claims, possibly more plausible, to Arsacid and Seleucid ancestry were also made by Byzantines of the later empire.[50]

The explanation of this chasm is rather to be sought partly in the social and political stresses and changes, brought about in the Eastern Empire by the pressure of the Moslem invasions in the seventh and succeeding centuries, and partly in the loss of record due to these and later vicissitudes and the Empire's final collapse in 1453. For possible genealogical continuity at this eastern end of Europe we have, as we shall see, to look towards and beyond the Empire's frontiers, to the Caucasian and sub-Caucasian lands of Armenia, Georgia and their neighbours, which struggled through long centuries with varying success to keep their independence between the Greek and Roman pressure from the West and that of Persia, Parthia, the Caliphate and the Turks from the East. From the time of the Roman victory over Mithridates of Pontus the control of Caucasia, strategically vital to both, was disputed between Rome and the successive dynasties which ruled in Persia — Parthian, Sassanid and Saracen.

The Armenian kingdom was a buffer and often a puppet state, where the opposed influences of Rome and Persia alternated or divided the country between them. Their manoeuvres were assisted by a peculiar feature of the Caucasian polity itself, going back to the kingdom of Urartu in Hittite and Assyrian times; in Prince Toumanoff's words 'the survival of a whole class, a caste in fact, of dynastic princes . . . older than kingship, which derived from them. Their principalities' he adds, 'were self-sufficient and self-determined, being territorialised tribes and clans of old. And their rights over these states were fully sovereign . . . On the international scale, they received the treatment accorded to

50 Demetrios I. Polemis, *The Doukai, A Contribution to Byzantine Prosopography*, Athlone Press, 1968, pp. 3, 4, 152, 184 and p. 66 *infra*.

minor kings. Armenia and Iberia were therefore largely federations of princely states presided over by the king'.[51]

In his *Studies in Christian Caucasian History*,[52] Prince Toumanoff shows how, while geography long protected these small polities against total absorption, the example of the neighbouring Empires of Rome and Persia impelled them constantly towards unification under one king. The upshot was an uneasy balance which for more than a thousand years preserved the princely states as recognizable entities.

No situation, perhaps, could be more favourable to the preservation of dynastic families and their pedigrees, and there is indeed evidence that both were preserved. The existence of the Bagratids whose hereditary right it was to crown the kings of Armenia, is recorded from the time of the Conversion of Armenia in 314 A.D., though their connected pedigree begins only in the sixth century or later.[53] So is that of the Mamikonids, who held the office of High Constable (sparapet)[54] and the Artsrunis[55] and the Haykids of Siunia.[56] Though there are gaps in the genealogical record of these families and others, the continuity of their existence from these dates or earlier seems clear. There is some confusion between the names, and therefore the pedigrees, of two Armenian dynasties, the Artaxiads who ruled from 188 B.C. to about 12 A.D., of whom a branch also reigned in Iberia (Eastern Georgia) from 90 to 30 B.C., and the Arsacids, members of more than one branch of the Parthian dynasty which ruled in Persia from about 250 B.C. to 229 A.D. The first Arsacids to rule in Armenia followed immediately on the Artaxiads, but continuity in a separate Armenian Arsacid line began with Vologaeses IV of Parthia and II of Armenia, who ruled the latter from 180 to 191 A.D. and whose descendants ruled there down to 428. (Ped. 35).

For the relationships of the Parthian Arsacids we depend mainly on Graeco-Roman sources which frequently fail us. To secure their own position the Arsacid kings at times eliminated their near kindred and the genealogies of the distant kinsmen who then succeeded are obscure to us. The Armenian native histories begin only in the fifth century and much of our genealogical information comes from much later writings in this category. It no doubt incorporates genuine traditions but their interpretation is made harder by discrepancies from earlier statements in Graeco-Roman sources. The succession is from time to time com-

---

51 *The Cambridge Medieval History*, Vol. IV, (1966), Ch. XIV, 'Armenia and Georgia' by C. Toumanoff, p. 596.

52 Cyril Toumanoff, *Studies in Christian Caucasian History*, (Hereafter cited as *S.C.C.H.*), (Georgetown, 1963). See also his 'Introduction to Christian Caucasian History. The Formative Centuries', *Traditio*, Vol. XV, New York 1959).

53 *S.C.C.H.*, pp. 337-354.

54 *Ibid.*, pp. 209-11. 52.

55 *Ibid.*, p. 214.

56 *Ibid.*, pp. 199 200.

plicated by the displacement by the Parthians or their Sassanid successors of Armenian kings, who were puppets or adherents of the Roman or Byzantine Empire, and conversely. Nevertheless by close analysis and comparison of the different sources Prince Toumanoff has gone far to establish the sequence, pedigrees and chronology of these dynasties.[57] Much the same applies to the linked Pharnabazid, Artaxia, Arsacid and Chosroid dynasties which ruled Iberia between about 299 B.C. and 580 A.D.[58]

Though certain links remain conjectural, probable continuous lines of descent can be shown (Ped. 33) from Zariadres, the father of Artaxias, who became king of Armenia in 188 B.C. and from Pharnabazus I, king of Iberia, thought to have been born about 326 B.C., to king Amazaspus II who perished in 189 A.D., leaving a sister married to the Arsacid Vologaeses IV of Parthia and II of Armenia, from whom descended later kings both of Armenia and Georgia.

Since the Arsacids of Parthia were linked by marriages with the Seleucid kings of Syria and the kings of Commagene, who had, in turn, connections with the Ptolemies of Egypt, with Alexander the Great and the kings of Macedon and with the Achaemenid kings of Persia; and also with the earlier Artaxiad kings of Armenia, who were linked to the same connection through the kings of Pontus; and since the later Arsacids of Armenia intermarried with the Bagratid, Siuni and Pahlavi families from whom living persons claim descent, it might seem that we are within sight of a bridge to antiquity which will bear our weight.

We shall find, however, that though probable descents, broken or conjectural at perhaps three points, can be shown from Zariadres and Pharnabazus (in the third and fourth centuries before Christ) to the present day; and though links with older dynasties can be shown and descents from these may well exist, these last cannot at present be traced.

In 314 Armenia became Christian and till 428 the patriarchate was in effect hereditary for six generations in the family of the apostle of Armenia, St. Gregory the Illuminator (d.325) a member of the noble Persian family of Suren-Pahlav (Ped. 36). A prolonged struggle, in which the feudal princes tended to the Persian and the kings to the Roman side, was at length settled by the recognition in 387 of two Armenian puppet kingdoms, one under each empire. The Roman dominated kingship, however, ceased with Arsaces III about 390, while the Persian dominated one was ended by the deposition of Artaxias IV and the deprivation of the patriarch St. Isaac in 428.[59] St. Isaac,

57 *S.C.C.H.*, *op. cit.*, and *Revue des Etudes Armeniennes*, N. S. Tom. VI, (1969), pp. 233-281, Cyrille Toumanoff, 'The Third-Century Armenian Arsacids: A Chronological and Genealogical Commentary'.

58 *Traditio*, Vol. XXV, (1969), pp. 1-33, Cyrille Toumanoff, 'Chronology of the Early Kings of Iberia'.

59 *Camb. Med. Hist.* IV. 598-9.

himself, however, was the grandson and great-grandson of Arsacid princesses (Ped. 36) and through his daughter, Sahakanoysh, wife of the Mamikonid prince, Hamazasp I, the line continued.

From this time until the establishment of the Bagratid kingdom in 885, under its Persian and Byzantine masters, the Armenian scene was dominated by the feudal dynasties and especially by two of their number; first the Mamikonids till about 600 and then the Bagratids. The genealogical evidence, naturally, is plentiful only for the dominant dynasty of the day. Thus the descent, from the ancient stem, of the Mamikonids mentioned after 600 is not entirely clear, though it can be conjectured and we reach firm ground again with the marriage of the Bagratid Prince Smbat VI (d.772) to the daughter of the Mamikonid Prince Samuel (Ped. 37). Unknown also is the pedigree of the Arsacid Prince Manuel whose daughter married the Bagratid Smbat V in 643 (Ped. 38).

Thus it comes about that we have statements for men living in the eleventh to thirteenth centuries of descent from ancestors centuries earlier, which must be taken seriously even though they lack all detail. In an inscription dated 1029 Vahram II Pahlavuni describes himself as 'of the race of Pahlavids and of the family of St. Gregory'.[60] Again in his memento in the Book of Gospels of King Hetum I (who shared his descent) his cousin Oshin I (d.1294) of Askuras and Marnish, Marshal of Armenia, describes his kinsman as 'of the race of the Pahlavids to which was united the family of the Arsacids'.[61] It will be recalled that the line of St. Gregory claimed descent from the Arsacid kings through two marriages.[62]

Prince Toumanoff points out a *prima facie* discrepancy here in that the Pahlavid family to which Vahram and Hetum belonged was that of Karin-Pahlav, whereas the family of St. Gregory, from whom Vahram is said to be descended, was the distinct line of Suren-Pahlav. He points also, however, to a probable answer. The daughter and heir of St. Isaac (d.439), the last male descendant of St. Gregory, married, as we saw, the Mamikonid prince Hamazasp I. Vartanoysh, the daughter of their son St. Vardan (d.451), married Arshavir II Kamsarakan of the Karin-Pahlav family (Ped. 37). Their descendants, the princes Kamsarakan, were also called Arsharuni from their principality of Arsharunik. In the Kamsarakan pedigree there is a gap between Narses,

60 C. Toumanoff, *Studies in Christian Caucasian History*, 1963, p. 207, n.236, quoting from K. J. Basmadjian, *Les inscriptions arméniennes d'Ani, de Bagnair et de Marmachên*, Paris, 1931, No. 212, p. 193 & transl. 196.

61 Ib. p. 208 n., quoting *Handes Amsorya* (Vienna) 1898, p. 245. He notes, however, that for 'Arsakids', Rudt-Collenberg, *The Rupenides, Hethumides and Lusignans*, 56 reads, 'Ardzouni', while Mader in *Revue des etudes arméniennes*, p. 173, reads 'Archarouni.'

62 That of Hosychius to a daughter of Tiridates IV, (d. c. 330) and that of their son Athenogenes, to her niece Bambishon (Peds. 35 6).

son of this marriage, living in 482, and a later Narses II Kamsarakan, prince of Armenia under the Byzantine Emperor and Curopalate in 690,[63] but the continuity is hard to doubt and seems to be confirmed by the statement of Matthew of Edessa[64] that Vasag the Sparapet (d.1021), ancestor of the later Karin-Pahlav line, was descended through the female line from St. Isaac. (Ped. 40).

The descent from this family of the lords of Lambron in Cilicia and the later Armenian kings of their house came through the marriage of Oshin II of Lambron to Sahandukht, sister of the Catholicos Grigor VI Apirat (d.1203) of the Karin-Pahlav line (Ped. 40). Through his grandmother, a member of the princely Artsruni family, Oshin himself probably shared the Gregorid and Mamikonid descent together with Bagratid ancestry (Ped. 39). The questions here are exactly where Khachik Artsruni, whose great-grand-daughter Oshin I of Lambron (d.1110) married, fits into the pedigree of the Artsruni kings of Vaspurakan: and exactly how Samuel the Mamikonid (d.772) was descended from the marriage of the Hamazasp to the daughter of St. Isaac. Prince Toumanoff's conjecture, based on land succession and name patterns, is shown in Peds. 39 and 37.

From about 1020 Armenia began to disintegrate under pressure from the Seljuk Turks together with domestic and Byzantine intrigue. Many Armenian princes and noblemen moved into Cappadocia and other Byzantine provinces and obtained domains there. In 1045 the Armenian king Gagik II was induced to go to Constantinople and there to abdicate. He was compensated with lands in Cappadocia and a palace in Constantinople and survived till 1080 when he fell a victim to Byzantine enmity. In 1071 the Seljuk Alp Arslan defeated the Emperor Romanus IV at the battle of Manazkert and conquered Armenia, overrunning Cappadocia in 1074. Armenian royalties and others from both Armenia and Cappadocia thereupon joined Armenians already settled in Cilicia, the only part of Asia Minor still unoccupied by the Turks. There Ruben established the kingdom of Armenia in exile, which lasted until overwhelmed by the Mamluks in 1375. Ruben is said by later historians to have been a cousin of Gagik II, and so perhaps of Bagratid descent, but this is doubted.[65] His male line ended in 1219 and was followed by that of his son in law Hetum I (d.1270), prince of Bardzrberd and Karikas of the house of Lambron, who had, as we have seen, a Karin-Pahlav descent.

---

63 (Ped. 37) Toumanoff, *Studies in Christian Caucasian History*, pp. 206-7: Ferdinand Justi, *Iranisches Namenbuch*, 1963 ed., P. 425; René Grousset, *Histoire de l'Arménie*, 1947, pp. 200, 204-5, 214, 218, 222-5, 289, 308.

64 Tr. Dulaurier, 1858, Pt.i. Ch.2, pp. 9, 10, Ch.12, p. 12, Ch.59, p. 70: Justi, *op.cit., p. 423.*

65 Vide, Count W. H. Rüdt-Collenberg, *The Rupenides Hethumides and Lusignans, The structure of the Armeno-Cilician dynasties,* Paris, 1963, p. 47.

The nearest Christian neighbour of the Armenian kingdom in Cilicia was the Crusader kingdom of Cyprus and the last kings of Armenia were Lusignan kings of Cyprus. This came about through a marriage link without blood descent, but the latest Lusignans had both Rubenid and Hetumid blood through the lords of Jebeil (Giblet) in Syria and other Crusader lords of Outre Mer who had married Armenian ladies. Hence, through the house of Savoy, the blood of the Armenian kings came to Western Europe and has flowed in the veins of the Kings of England since James I and in those of many English families through the marriage of James (Stanley), Earl of Derby (d.1651) to Charlotte de la Tremoille (Ped. 42). Thus the researches and conjectures of Prince Toumanoff, to whom my debt is immense, indicate a possible pedigree of 73 generations from Pharnabazus of Iberia, born in the time of Alexander the Great, to Queen Elizabeth II. An earlier, and therefore wider, infusion of Armenian blood was brought to Western Europe through the marriage of Baldwin II, King of Jerusalem, (d.1131) to Morfia daughter of Gabriel, Lord of Melitene (d.1103), whose descent, however, is unknown.[66] Doubtless, if surviving record were less incomplete, we should be able to trace Armenian and Georgian dynastic descents through scions who settled in the Byzantine Empire and intermarried with Imperial and other Byzantine families. Toumanoff cites the Armenian ancestry of the Heraclid and Basilid Emperors and of Leo V, Romanus Lecapenus and John Tzimisces. But in none of these cases has it yet (to my knowledge) proved possible to carry a proved line right through.[67] The Byzantine Taronitae, for instance, were Bagratids, but no extant line has been derived from them.[68] King Edward I of England, however, was a descendant of the Empress Theophano (married in 972 to the Emperor Otto II), who had probably Armenian ancestry, though this remains controversial.[69] Prince Toumanoff favours the traditional belief that she was a daughter of the Byzantine Emperor Romanus II, who was great-grandson of the Emperor Basil I (867-886), whom Adontz has, in Toumanoff's view, shown convincingly to have been almost certainly of Mamikonid descent (Ped. 43).[70]

Armenian families also fled to Georgia.[71] Bagratids were established there after 772, became hereditary presiding princes of Iberia

66 *Op. cit.* pp. 35, 78. In a letter of 19 April 1967 Count Rüdt Collenberg writes that as Gabriel succeeded Thoros it may be that Gabriel's wife was the sister of Thoros, 'but this is mere speculation.'

67 *Studies in Christian Caucasian History*, p. 13.

68 Ib. p. 202.

69 Hugo Graf Rüdt von Collenberg, war Theophano?' *Genealogisches Jahrbuch*, Zentralstelle für Deutsche Personen — und Familiengeschichte zu Berlin, 1964, pp. 49-71. (See also Ped. 43 &n. p. 258)

70 Letter, 5. Nov. 1972 and Ped. 43 &n. p. 258.

71 SCCH, pp. 270, 273.

(East Georgia) in 813 and restored the dormant kingship in 888, ruling Georgia until the Russian annexation in 1810. The Bagratids exist in several branches and as recently as 1948 the daughter of the head of one of these married a claimant to the headship of the house of Romanoff. Three Georgian noble families claimed Pahlavid descent. The Palavandishvili came to Georgia from Ani in 1184; the name of the Mkhargrjelis (= long hand) embodies a claim to descent from Artaxerxes I Longimanus, King of Persia (d.425 B.C.), doubtless through the Arsacids, who claimed an unsubstantiated descent from him, and from whom, as we have seen (p. 64), the Armenian Pahlavids in turn claimed descent from Smbat, Constable of Armenia (d.1275), brother of King Hetum I.[72] Other houses deriving from the Mamikonids are the Orbelids and the Tumanids.

Having thus established several broken but probable descents to the present day from the Arsacid dynasty which ruled Armenia from the 2nd century after Christ, we may now look back to the origins of that dynasty and its possible links, already mentioned (p. 64), with others of still older date. We have seen (p. 62) that dynastic strife and disturbance combine with the lateness of native and the incompleteness of Graeco-Roman sources to confuse and obscure for us the links, which certainly existed, between the earlier and the later Arsacids in Parthia and between the Artaxiad and Arsacid dynasties in Armenia. The Persian Empire conquered by Alexander the Great (d.323 B.C.) fell to the share of his general Seleucus. But two generations later, when Seleucus' grandson Antiochus II (d.247 B.C.) was engaged in war with Egypt, his easternmost province, Bactria, rebelled and soon after, about 250 B.C., two brothers, Arsaces (d.248 B.C.) and Tiridates (d.211 B.C.) rebelled in Parthia, to the east of the Caspian sea, and they and their successors established an Empire in the old Persian territory which had formed the eastern half of the Seleucid Empire.

From Tiridates (d.21 B.C.) a line with two doubtful links is traced through ten generations down to four sons of Phraates IV (d. 2 B.C.) who were carried off to Rome in 16 B.C. One of these, Vonones I (d. 12 A.D.) later returned to Parthia as king, but was opposed and defeated by another Arsacid, Artabanus III, King of Media Atropatene (d. c.38 A.D.). Contending claimants follow of unknown relationship. The Armenian Arsacids descend from Vologaeses IV of Parthia (191-207/8), whose place in the pedigree has not been established. Before accession to the throne of Parthia, he had been king of Armenia as Vologaeses II (180-191) and had married (p. 63) supra), the daughter of Pharasmenes III of Iberia, whose ancestry is carried back to the fourth century before Christ. Two of their sons followed him as kings of Parthia. A fourth was king of Armenia and ancestor there of

72 Toumanoff, *Studies in Christian Caucasian History*, **pp.** 202-3, 208n. 210, 352-4, 407-434.

the Arsacid of Chosroid dynasty already mentioned (p. 63, Ped. 35), while the youngest, as it would seem, became King Rev I of Iberia. From the Chosroids, as we have seen, probable descents are traceable to the present day [p. 66] [73]

Though the line of Vologaeses' descent from the earlier Arsacids has not been established, it certainly existed.

With the older Arsacids of Parthia we enter a world of intermarried dynasties (Peds. 8, 10-16) of which the greatest — the Ptolemies of Egypt and the Seleucids of Syria — were sprung from generals of Alexander the Great (d.323 B.C.) (Peds. 10-12) while the lesser were descendants of Persian satraps or local potentates who at some point in the warfare or weakness of the greater powers had established partial or complete independence. The pedigrees (10, 1-13, 16) show how a growing consciousness of royal dignity and isolation led more than one of their members — like the Pharaohs and Achaemenids before and the Caesars after — to intermarry with 'his sisters and his cousins, whom he reckons up by dozens, and his aunts'. In the second century before Christ the growing power of Rome entered the picture and spread eastward by stages until Pompey's conquest of the sixties B.C. brought Asia Minor, Syria and Palestine under Roman sway and Octavian defeating Antony at Actium in 31 B.C., conquered Egypt.

In later times descendants of Alexander's general Seleucus (d.281 B.C.), who succeeded to the eastern part of his Empire from the Mediterranean to India, claimed descent from Alexander himself by wrongly identifying Apama, Seleucus' wife, as a daughter of Alexander by Roxana, the daughter of the Persian king Darius III, whom Alexander conquered. Apama was in fact the daughter of Spitamenes, a Sogdian magnate in the Persian service, but it is thought that her mother was indeed of the Achaemenid Persian dynasty. [74]

Between the last Achaemenids and the Macedonians there were several marriage links (Ped. 6) though no continuing descent is traceable through them. Indeed the clearest descent from the Achaemenids is the one mentioned below through the Kings of Commagene (Ped. 14). Achaemenes, the eponymous ancestor, must have lived about 700 B.C. and his descendants' female ancestry is traceable also to about this date through the kings of Media and Lydia. Links with an earlier world still are dimly seen in the asserted marriage of a sister of Astyages of Media to Nebuchadnezzar king of Babylon and that of Cyrus the Great of

73 The complex and conflicting evidence of the different sources is analyzed and reconciled by Cyrille Toumanoff, 'The Third-Century Armenian Arsacids: A Chronological and Genealogical Commentary, *Revue des Etudes Armeniennes*, N.S., Tome VI, (1969), pp. 234-281. Probable descents to the present day from Rev I of Iberia through the Bagratid kings of Georgia are not here followed.

74 W. W. Tarn, *The Greeks in Bactria and India*, 2nd. ed. 1951, p. 447; and 'Queen Ptolemais and Apama'. *The Classical Quarterly*, Vol. XXIII, 1929, pp. 138-141.

Persia or his son Cambyses to Nitetis an Egyptian princess, daughter of one of the last Pharaohs of the twenty sixth dynasty.[75]

Arsinoe the mother of Ptolemy (d.283 B.C.), Alexander's general who became King of Egypt, was variously said to have been herself of Macedonian royal blood and to have been a concubine of Alexander's father, Philip of Macedon, till shortly before Ptolemy's birth and it is said to have been rumoured that Ptolemy was in fact Philip's son. Tarn, however, argues that both these stories were fictions designed to derive the Ptolemies from the ancestors of Alexander. He thought it possible, however, that Ptolemy I may have married in 323 a daughter of the last line of native Pharaohs, the thirtieth (Sebennyte) dynasty.[76]

A possible descent from the Achaemenid kings of Persia was claimed by the Kings of Pontus by the Black Sea and an accepted one by the Kings of Commagene on the upper Euphrates. This last is clarified by the genealogical inscription set up at Nimrud-dag by Antiochus I of Commagene (c.69-c.38 B.C.).[77] The first ancestor, Orontes, lived in the fifth century before Christ and his grandson and namesake (d.c.344 B.C.) married a daughter of Artaxerxes II of Persia (d.358 B.C.), who was ninth in descent from Achaemenes, living in the seventh century B.C. This Orontid dynasty (Ped. 14, 15), whose earlier members were satraps and kings of Armenia and which intermarried with Seleucids, Arsacids and the Armenian branch of the house of Herod, lasted through fourteen generations from the son in law of Artaxerxes to the extinction of the kingdom of Commagene by Rome in 72 A.D. The family then moved to Rome, where the last king's grandson, Gaius Julius Philopappus, was consul in 100 A.D.

Toumanoff argues ingeniously that the oldest accounts of the origin of the Artsruni, the Bagratids and certain other Armenian princely houses, implying descent from the god Angl-Tork', mean when properly understood that they claimed and possessed Orontid ancestry.[78] The pedigree, perhaps of the fifth century, deriving the Artsruni from Sennacherib, King of Assyria, and that of the eighth or ninth deriving the Bagratids from David, King of Israel, are in his view, substitutes for

75 Pauly-Wissowa, XVII, i. 168, unable to decide between three incompatible versions of this story, yet considers that it has a basis of truth.

76 *Journal of Hellenic Studies*, Vol.53, 1933, pp. 47-61, W. W. Tarn, 'Two notes on Ptolemaic History', *The Classical Quarterly*, Vol. XXIII, 1929, p. 138, 'Queen Ptolemais and Apama'.

77 W. Dittenberger, *Orientis graeci inscriptiones selectae*, I, Leipzig, 1903, 608, n.7: L. Jalabert & R. Mouterde, *Inscriptions grecques et latines de la Syrie*, I, *Commagene et Cyrrhestique*, Paris, 1929, p. 27.

78 Pauly-Wissowa, Supp. IV. 1924, pp. 978-990. For the conclusion that the Orontids were Kings of Armenia see C. Toumanoff, 'A note on the Orontids', *Le Muséon*, Vol. 72, Louvain, 1959, Vol. 73, 1960, and *Studies in Christian Caucasian History*, 1963, pp. 277-354.

the pagan Angl-Tork' descent which the adoption of Christianity had made no longer respectable.[79]

Another instance of the early fondness of the Armenian dynastic families for tales of exotic ancestry is the Mamikonid claim to descent from the Emperors of China. The fifth century writer Faustus of Buzanda mentions this as referred to by a fourth century Armenian king. Prince Toumanoff (who himself claims Mamikonid descent) explains it as a confusion between *cen,* meaning Chinese, and *can,* the name of an ethnic division of the proto-Georgians.[80]

Tigranes I, (d. c.54 B.C.), the leading king of the Artaxiad dynasty, which overthrew the Orontids of Armenia in the second century B.C. married Cleopatra one of the many children of the great Mithridates VI Eupator, King of Pontus (111-64 B.C.), whom Pompey at length overthrew. Through this and later marriages the house of Tigranes was linked not only with Seleucids, Arsacids and others mentioned earlier, but with two further groups, one Jewish, one Roman (Ped. 13).

The Jewish house is that of Herod the Great (d.4 B.C.) — King of Judaea — though his family was reproached with Edomite or Philistine origin. His descendants, at all events, had distinguished Jewish ancestry through Herod's marriage to Mariamne a princess of the Hasmonean or Maccabee family (Ped. 16). Submitting himself after the battle of Actium in 31 B.C. to the victorious Octavian, Herod became a client king of Rome and cultivated alliances with other such.

These vassal dynasties of the Roman Empire formed at this time, in the words of Professor Minns, 'a special class whose members from Mauretania to Bosporus and from Judaea to Thrace intermarried and were regarded as interchangeable.'[81] About 17 B.C. Herod's son Alexander married Glaphyra daughter of a certain Archelaus, who had become king of Cappadocia by favour of Mark Anthony. Glaphyra boasted of her genealogy, as deriving on her father's side from Temenus and on her mother's from Darius the son of Hystaspes.[82] She claimed, in fact, paternal descent from the Kings of Macedon and maternal descent from the Achaemenid kings of Persia. Archelaus, her father, was great-grandson of another Archelaus, a general of Mithridates Eupator of Pontus, who may well have been a cadet of the Macedonian royal house. Her mother's identity is unknown, but the fact that Glaphyra's son was named Tigranes and was made King of Armenia by the Romans about 6 A.D. as being of the royal race of Armenia,[83] suggests a possibility that her mother was an Artaxiad

79 Cf. p. 5, *supra.*

80 Cyril Toumanoff, 'The Mamikonids and the Liparids', in *Armeniaca, Mélanges d'études Armeniennes,* (1969), pp. 125-37.

81 Ellis H. Minns, *Scythians and Greeks,* 1913, p. 594.

82 Josephus, Wars of the Jews, Bk. I. c. xxiv, sec.2.

83 Tacitus, Annals, VI, 40.

princess.[84] Chronology, then, might suggest that she was a daughter or granddaughter of Tigranes the Great (d. c.54 B.C.) and, if by his marriage to the daughter of Mithridates of Pontus, the claim to Achaemenid descent would be explained (Peds. 16, 34). The nephew and namesake of this Tigranes was likewise king of Armenia under Roman auspices about 60 A.D. and married an Artaxiad princess. Their son married a daughter of the last king of Commagene.

The Roman links of these Near Eastern dynasties were primarily through Mark Antony (d. 31 B.C.), though Cleopatra, heir of the Ptolemies of Egypt, had already established a Roman link by bearing a son, Caesarion, to Julius Caesar. It was after Caesar's murder and the victory over his murderers at Philippi (42 B.C.) that Antony, turning to eastward conquest, encountered and fell to the charms of Cleopatra. She bore him three children, of whom Alexander was made King of Armenia by his father in 34 B.C. and married to a daughter of the King of Atropatene; and Cleopatra Selene, who was married to Juba (d.19-24 A.D.), King by Roman favour, of Numidia and later of Mauretania. Their daughter Drusilla appears to have married Antonius Felix, the freedman who was Roman procurator of Judaea from A.D. 52 to 60 and before whom St. Paul appeared.[85] Confusion is, however, caused by Felix's undoubted marriage to another Drusilla of the Herodian family.

Antony's connection with Cleopatra was not his only eastward genealogical link. By his second wife Antonia he had a daughter Antonia, who married an Asiatic Greek, Pythodorus of Tralles. Their daughter Pythodoris was given in marriage to Polemon, the son of another Asiatic Greek, Zeno, a rhetorician of Laodicea on the Lycus. In 39 B.C. Antony made Polemon king of a part of the former domains of Mithridates of Pontus, whose granddaughter, Dynamis, had been Polemon's first wife.

The progeny of Polemon and Pythodoris (Antony's granddaughter) include a Roman line, sprung from their son Marcus Antonius Polemon; a son Zeno, who, having been given an Armenian education by his far seeing mother, was acceptable to the Armenians when the Roman Germanicus made him their king in 18 A.D. and ruled them, as Artaxias II, till 34 A.D.; and a daughter Antonia Tryphaena, who married Kotys, King of Thrace, one of a dynasty which seems to have continued there till the 4th century A.D.[86] One of her sons, Polemon II of Pontus, married a daughter of Herod Agrippa, sister of the wife of Felix. After Polemon's death Pythodoris married, for her second husband and as

84 J. G. C. Anderson, *Cambridge Ancient History*, X, 277, thinks the wife of Archelaus in all probability a princess of the Armenian royal house.

85 *Acts 23 & 24.*

86 Pauly-Wissowa, Real encyclopädie, XXIV, 1963, p. 583. E. H. Minns, *Scythians and Greeks*, Cambridge, 1913 pp. 604-111.

his second wife, Archelaus, King of Cappodocia, the father of Glaphyra mentioned earlier (p. 70) (Ped. 19).

The conquests of Alexander, followed after two more centuries by those of Rome, opened up for a time unprecedented communication between the Iranic lands eastward to India and the Roman lands westward to the Atlantic. When Cleopatra Selene was Queen of Mauretania on the Atlantic seaboard, kinsmen of her sister in law had lately ruled on the Bactrian borders of India.[87] Genealogy throughout history illustrates thus the alternate forming and severance of such links and contacts. Small scale examples are the brief seasons of marriages between Anglo-Norman and Welsh princely families in the twelfth and thirteenth centuries and between Anglo-Norman and Scottish families in the thirteenth. Both reflect the contact, following invasion, which later events soon ended.

For the greatest, possibly, of all such linkages — and that on the continental scale — we must turn to the centuries between the thirteenth and fifteenth and to the movements, converging on the Near East, of crusading Franks from Western Europe and invading Turks, and Mongols from central and Eastern Asia. In the year 1265 a nephew of Kubla Khan, Emperor of China, married the half-sister of a Byzantine Emperor,[88] who in 1279 married the sister in law of a nephew of St. Louis IX, King of France,[89] and of Eleanor of Provence, Queen of England. Thus in five years and through only eight persons a genealogical bridge was built across the Eurasian land mass from the Pacific to the Atlantic ocean, (Ped. 44). It is unlikely that such a link had been made before, the nearest, possibly, being the Seleucid-Ptolemaic link from India to Morocco mentioned above.

Incongruous as it may seem with its cruelties, the house of Genghis Khan had at first no prejudice against Christianity. Indeed Count Rüdt-Collenberg's pedigrees[90] show in the six generations from Genghis (d.1227) to Ulajtu (d.1316) ten (polygamous) marriages

87 W. W. Tarn, *The Greeks in Bactria and India*, Pedigree at end, shows the descent of the Greek Bactrian dynasties from the Seleucids of Syria. For the Seleucid descent of the Kings of Pontus and the descent of Iotape, Queen of Armenia, the wife of Antony's son, Alexander, see Peds. 13, 34 *infra.*

88 Henry H. Howorth, *History of the Mongols*, Pt.III, 1888, p. 223. Hulagu asked Michael VIII Palaeologus for the hand of one of his daughters in marriage. He sent a natural daughter, Maria (her mother was a Diplovatatze), escorted by Theodosius of Villehardouin, archimandrite of the convent of Pantocrator and brother of the Prince of Achaia (but others say Euthymius, patriarch of Antioch). Presents she took with her included a tent of silken hangings, golden figures of saints, crosses and sacred vessels. At Caesarea she heard of Hulagu's death but went on and married Abaka.

89 Andronicus II (d.1338), son of Michael VIII, married Anna, daughter of Stephen V of Hungary and her sister Maria married Charles of Anjou (d.1285), King of Naples, nephew of St. Louis.

90 *Op.cit.* Ped. XIV (M).

between them and daughters of the Nestorian Christian house of Kherait and in the third to fifth generations from Genghis four such unions with illegitimate daughters of Byzantine Emperors.[91] Thoros and Smbat, brothers and successive Kings of Armenia of the House of Hetum, both in 1297 married Mongol princesses. In the same generation another Mongol princess married successively two Bagratid Kings of Georgia.[92]

The Palaeologi of Byzantium, the Comneni of Trebizond, the Hetumids of Armenia and the Bagratids of Georgia all made political marriages with Turkish Seljukids of Rum; while successive Ottoman Sultans, from Orchan in 1346 to Mahomed II the Conqueror to whom Byzantium fell in 1453, took into their harems Cantacuzenae, Palaeologinae and Comnenae from Byzantium and Trebizond.

Our analysis, we may hope, has in some degree clarified the question we set out to answer. What descents and genealogical links are traceable between ancient and modern history? But has it, in so doing, thrown light on history itself? There are two aspects one would like historians to consider: the kind of locality and the kind of society in which this special sort of continuity is found. What is it that places, so far separated as Gaul and Wessex from Armenia and Georgia had in common? They were near enough, I suggest, to the great centres to be literate and organized, yet far enough from the storm centres and sufficiently protected by geography to have some hope of salvaging a little of the old learning and culture from the onrush of the barbaric flood. They shared also a tenacious royalism or dynasticism strong enough to survive and surmount even the shortcomings of their dynasties. When the old dynasties failed this sentiment raised up new ones knit, if possible, to the old by marriage.

These lands shared something else, their early conversion, as antiquity collapsed, to Christianity. Toumanoff remarks how in the Caucasus, even as in Western Europe, the warrior virtues under its influence flowered into Chivalry.[93] The social structure thus formed, he adds, 'was the most perdurable and, possibly, the most decisive factor in Caucasian history'. We may compare Bloch's references to the concept, of a special virtue inherent in a predestined royal race and of how in Western Europe this enabled a new legitimacy to be built on the ruins of the old.[94] Our concern with these forces here is strictly with their first, nascent, stages only. But their strength and importance is shown by what they led to and grew into. Professor C. D.

91 Maria daughter of Michael VIII Palaeologus to Abaka the Ilkhan in 1265; Euphrosyne, another bastard of the same, to Nogai Khan c.1266-71; Maria, bastard of Andronicus II Palaeologus to Toktai Khan, c. 1300; and Maria, bastard of Michael IX Palaeologus to Ulajtu the Ilkhan (1304-1316).

92 Wakhtang II (d.1292) and David VI (d.1310).

93 SCCH, 140.

94 *Feudal Society*, p. 388.

Darlington[95] has expounded the genetic factors in the building up of that royal caste, which played so great a part in the making of mediaeval Europe, out of which in turn sprang the Renaissance and the scientific and industrial revolutions. The marriage of barbarian kings to Christian princesses and their prior or consequent conversion to Christianity was a renewal by cross breeding of royal stocks as well as cultures.[96] Clotilda and Bertha (Ped. 27, 29) are leading examples. By the tenth century the nascent feudal polity was giving rise across Western Europe to dynastic families competitively aspiring to kingship or lesser suzerainty. The growing power of the church and especially the papacy of Hildebrand, Pope Gregory VII (1073-85), affected the composition of this royal caste in two ways. Its position was at once enhanced and established by the coronation rite, which by marking off kings from subjects favoured the intermarriage of royal families as against the marriage of kings to their subjects — a tendency which grew slowly and for a long time usefully, but in the end to dangerous excess.

The other papal genetic influence was for some time a useful antidote to this danger — the prohibition, namely, of marriage within certain, widely defined, degrees of consanguinity, extending at its peak to a prohibition of marriage between nearer kin than seventh cousins. That of William Duke of Normandy, the future Conqueror of England, to Matilda of Flanders in 1053 was actually in breach of a prohibition promulgated in 1049 at the papal council of Rheims, since they were fifth cousins by a shared descent from Herbert II Count of Vermandois (d.943). As a penance they founded the abbeys of St. Stephen and the Holy Trinity at Caen. This prohibition insofar as it was observed, meant that kings had soon to look for their consorts in remote realms or outside the royal caste — a useful discouragement of inbreeding and the means of bringing within the circle of royal intermarriage Russian, Byzantine, Polish and Hungarian with French, Spanish, German and English.[97]

It is sometimes said that China has the oldest continuous culture in the world. In support of this it is contended that the ancestral forms of its present writing and language go back to the fourteenth century B.C. and that it never had a dark age, as Europe did, since 'even the deepest invasions and conquests by barbarians from the north never destroyed the Chinese culture and civilization as the Greek-Roman civilization was destroyed', since 'the invasions of the north promoted a more rapid Chinese expansion into the south, so that the loss of empire and rule in the north was always compensated for by more and more developments in the south'.[98]

95 *The Evolution of Man and Society*, 1969.
96 pp. 319-20.
97 pp. 413-7.
98 Owen Lattimore, 'China to-day. Some Social Aspects', *Journ. R. Soc. of Arts*, CXVI, 1968, p. 655.

One might counter this by pointing out that the Phoenician prototype of our own alphabetic script goes back to the fifteenth century before Christ, that archaic forms of the Greek language (in Minoan script) have been identified at the same or an earlier epoch, while Graeco-Roman civilization continued in Byzantium when barbarians invaded Western Europe and grew up again in the West before Byzantium fell.

It would be less easy, however, to counter Chinese claims to greater continuity if pedigrees deriving extant families from the time of Confucius (and indeed from Confucius himself) can be substantiated, and are not found to be rather adoptive than natural. Such pedigrees, I believe, exist but for all I know they may be myths. I therefore end by placing the ball in the court of the Sinologists and hoping that they may be able to return it.

POSTSCRIPT
THE JEWISH KINGS OR PRINCES OF NARBONNE

Professor David H. Kelley (sometime of Harvard, now of Calgary University) has increased my debt to him by drawing my attention to a recent work by Arthur Zuckerman, *A Jewish Princedom in Feudal France 768-900* (Columbia University Press, 1972). The author's scholarship, though not his conclusions, are vouched for by the foreword to his book by Salo W. Baron, Professor Emeritus of Columbia University, author of *A Social and Religious History of the Jews*, who writes that Zuckerman 'has definitely made a case for his alluring theory'.

There were many settlements of Jews, large and small, in both the Roman and the Persian Empires. The largest, probably, was in Babylonia, where 'Exilarchs' or 'Princes of the Captivity', claiming descent from the House of David, (Zuckerman, op.cit., pp. 90-1, quotes references to an eighth century exilarch in Baghdad who claimed to be of the seventieth generation in direct descent from King David) exercised both civil and religious authority both under the Parthian Kings and the Sassanians who followed them. The *Encyclopaedia Judaica* (Jerusalem, 1971, Vol. 6, pp. 1023-34) gives a broken pedigree of the exilarchs from c.A.D. 140 to Bustanai ben Haninai (c.618-670), (Zuckerman dates Bustanai c.610-660 and the beginning of his exilarchate c.637 (pp. 438, 104), living at the time of the Arab Conquest, c.650, and from him to Daniel ben Hisdai IV (c.1150-74). The exilarchate is said to have been brought to an end by Tamerlane in 1401.

According to one account the Caliph Omar (father in law of Muhammad) confirmed Bustanai as exilarch after the Conquest and gave him to wife Izdundad a daughter of Chosroes II the last Sassanian king but one, while Omar himself married her sister. But according to another account (that of the *Seder ha-Kabbalah* of Abraham ibn Daud a twelfth century writer) the Caliph concerned was Muhammad's son in law, the Caliph 'Ali (*ibid*, Vol. 4, p. 1557) and the father of Bustanai's Persian wife was the last Sassanian king, Yazdegerd III, son of Chosroes II. It seems to be agreed that there was subsequent conflict between the progeny of Bustanai's Persian wife and other Jewish lines, the latter seeking to enslave or at least oust the former. This conflict over the inheritance of the exilarchate is said to have culminated in 771, when the claimant Natronai ben Havivai, of Davidic origin but not descended from the Persian Princess, was compelled to leave Babylonia for the Maghreb, Spain or France (*Ibid.* VI, p. 1026 and XII, p. 887; Zuckerman, op.cit., pp. 77-80).

At Narbonne, near the Mediterranean frontier of France and Spain, there was from the later Roman times onward an important settlement of Jews. These were said to have given valued help to the Frankish king, Peppin (or Pippin) the Short, the father of Charlemagne, in his conquest of this region (then called Septimania) from the Muslims in 759 and to have been granted by him in reward the right to be governed by a Jewish king, and they certainly enjoyed a degree of autonomy a century or more later (Encyc. Jud. XII. p. 829).

Arthur Zuckerman (*supra cit.* p. 59) quotes from a twelfth century addition to the work of Abraham ibn Daud, the statement that Charlemagne, who exchanged embassies with the Caliph Harun-al-Rashid in 797 and 801, (as his father had with the Caliph al Mansur in 765-8, Zuckerman op.cit. pp. 74-5) asked the Caliph to send him a Jewish prince of the house of David and was sent by him one Makhir, who became ancestor of a dynasty of Exilarchs (Zuckerman, pp. 60, 80, 98, 109, 258). This Makhir Zuckerman, who connects him rather with Peppin's embassy than Charlemagne's, conjecturally identifies with Natronai ben Havivai, the exiled descendant of Bustanai, mentioned earlier.

Zuckerman goes on to propose a further ingenious identification (*inter alia*) of Makhir with Theuderic, father of St. William, Marquess of Septimania, 790-806, the father of Bernard, Marquess of Septimania, and Count of Autun (d.844), whose daughter is said to have married Vougrin (d.866), Count of the Palace under Emperor Charles the Bald, and Count of Angoulême. From him Isabel of Angoulême, wife of King John of England, was eleventh in descent, so that these theories, *if all accepted,* would give the later Kings of England and their countless progeny a descent from King David. The chronicle of Adémar de Chabannes, III 20, says that Vougrin married a sister of William of Toulouse, a statement accepted by L. Levillain in his article 'Adémar de Chabannes, genealogiste' *Bulletin de la Société des Antiquaires de L'Ouest,* 1934, p. 248: I owe this reference to Mr. C. F. H. Evans, F.S.A., who adds that Adémar was a descendant of Vougrin and that Levillain argues convincingly that this William of Toulouse could only be the son of Bernard of Septimania. He refers also to the later similar conclusion of J. Broussard in his 1957 Edition of *Historia Pontificum et Comitum Engolismemsium.* J. L. Werner in 'Ademar von Chabannes and die Historia Pontificum et comitum Engolismemsium', *Deutsches Archiv für Enforschung des Mittelalters,* 19 J (1963), 297-326, further discusses the relations of the text. Mr. Evans regards Mr. Zuckerman's identification of Theuderic the father of St. William with the Jewish prince Makhir as possible but not proved. Professor Kelley regards the identity of Makhir and Theuderic as virtually certain, but that of Makhir with Natronai as much more doubtful, though this need not invalidate Makhir's Davidic origin. Further evaluation and possible fascinating extensions of these possibilities must await analysis by authorities on the various aspects of these matters.

CHAPTER IV

THE RECRUITMENT OF THE ENGLISH
UPPER CLASSES

The quality of government depends on that of those in charge of it and as these have historically sprung from or been recruited to the upper classes, it is instructive to see who the members of these classes were and whence they came. The available evidence, though grossly incomplete, is yet so voluminous that an army of researchers working for years could not exhaust it. How then can one hope in a brief essay to make a useful contribution to so vast a subject? Perhaps one cannot. Yet, as a genealogist who in four decades has seen many pedigrees. I have slowly reached the view that they fall for this purpose into a few recognizable types and form a limited number of patterns. On that experience I found what follows.

The structure of English society before the Norman Conquest can be illustrated genealogically only to a very slight degree. A good deal is indeed known, especially from laws and charters, of the names, duties, tenure and standing of different conditions of men in different parts or the country. But the few known pedigrees tell us, if anything, less than can be gathered from other sources. There was a wide class of *gesiths,* later called *thegns,* whose eminence above the *ceorls* or free peasants is indicated by the differences in their *wergild* or blood price; that of the former in seventh century Wessex being six times that of the latter. This was the great social divide, though intermediate ranks existed. The *thegns* may thus be equated with the post-conquest baronial and knightly class and the later nobility and gentry. The word *gesith* means companion and points to those so named originating as the chosen companions of kings. *Thegn* means one who serves another and the standing of a thegn depended on whom he served, whether a king or some lesser lord. The chances of the latter were however considered much the greater by Sir Frank Stenton who saw 'the central course of Old English social development . . . as the process by which a peasantry, at first composed essentially of free men, acknowledging no lord below the king, gradually lost economic and personal independence'.[1] This happened, he believed, through organization under leaders for the sake of security.

The greatest servants of the king were his *ealdormen,* called from the time of King Canute by the Danish name of *eorl* or earl. Their office, the government of a shire, was conferred by the king and could in theory be ended by him at any moment. By degrees, however, it developed a tendency to become permanent and hereditary, so that in the generation before the Conquest the three great houses sprung from Godwin of Kent, Leofric of Mercia and Siward of Northumbria had attained an eminence beyond the king's power to undo. There were ordinary *thegns* also who by the same date seem to have built up estates, greater than their fellows', which must have taken more than a generation in the building.[2]

The Norman aristocracy, like the Norman nation, was a more recent creation. The future Duchy of Normandy, lying along the Channel coast of France between Brittany and Flanders, followed the bounds of a Roman Province which under the Franks became Neustria. The Vikings from Scandinavia, who had invaded England, ravaged this region too, until in 911 Rolf (called Rollo in France) coming from Norway, entering France by the Loire after raids in Ireland and campaigning north eastward, was defeated near Chartres by the Carolingian Emperor Charles III. He thereupon submitted to baptism and was granted lands on the lower Seine by the Emperor which his son and successor William Longsword (927-42) enlarged to the bounds of Normandy.

Though now nominally Christian the Norman Vikings took a long time to shed entirely their pagan ways and attachments. Duke Richard the Fearless (942-96) is referred to in a Rheims chronicle as *Piratarum dux* and in 1013 his son Richard II (996-1027) welcomed at Rouen a party of Viking invaders of Britanny.[3] Though the Dukes married daughters of neighbouring Frankish rulers and magnates, they carried on at the same time a pre-Christian custom of polygamy or concubinage, of which we may see a vestige in the six or more mistresses and upwards of twenty bastards of Henry I of England (1100-1135).[4]

By 1025, however, Scandinavian speech though still used in Bayeux was extinct in Rouen,[5] and by 1050 a fusion of Viking and Gallic elements had taken place which made the Normans into the unique force they then became; conquerors between 1050 and 1100 not only of England, but of Southern Italy and Sicily; passing into Spain,

1 F. M. Stenton, *Anglo-Saxon England,* Oxford, 1943, p. 463.
2 Ib. pp. 539, 480.
3 David C. Douglas, *The Norman Achievement,* 1969, p. 24.
4 *Complete Peerage,* Vol. XI App. D.
5 Douglas, op. cit., p. 25.

Scotland, Ireland and Wales; and critically involved with the rising
Papacy, at Byzantium and in the First Crusade, in which they
established a Norman principality at Antioch.[6] Powerful, ruthless,
singly minded and often repellent, they excelled in government and
domination through these very qualities and through ability to use the
skills, institutions and traditions of those they conquered.

Professor Douglas has concluded[7] that a largely new Norman
aristocracy took its rise in the early eleventh century, many of its
members being kin of the Duchess Gunnor (d.1031), first mistress, then
wife of Duke Richard I, some of whom certainly acquired former ducal
lands. It was to a small baronial group, thus linked by kinship and
marriage, that William, between 1070 and 1087, gave lordship over
nearly a half of conquered England, while they still kept their
possessions in Normandy. Though Robert of Torigny's pedigrees must
be distrusted,[8] they and other evidence suffice to link in this way
most of the Conqueror's earls and a number of his greater barons,
including the families of Clare, Beaumont, Montgomery, Giffard,
Montfort, Grandmesnil, Reviers, Vernon, Vere, FitzOsbern, Warenne
and Mortimer Peds. 45-6) (note p. 259). Professor Douglas points,
moreover, to close links between powerful Normans in Sicily, Normandy and England.[9]

Though their origins are largely unknown, there is evidence of a wide
admixture of blood. The tale told of the Duchess Gunnor was that
Duke Richard I fell in love with Senfrie, the beautiful wife of one of his
foresters; but Senfrie succeeded in substituting for herself her
unmarried sister Gunnor who thus became the Duke's mistress, the
mother of his heir and other children, and at length his wife. She
secured, it seems, important marriages for two of her sisters, while her
brother's grandson became Earl of Hereford and the forester's grandson
Earl of Shrewsbury.[10] Gunnor's son Duke Richard II (996-1027)
married the daughter of a Count of Brittany of Celtic descent. But their
son, Duke Robert (1027-35) left the Duchy to his bastard by a tanner's
daughter — William the Conqueror.

It was an age of violent upheaval when fortune favoured the strong
and those who served them, yet inherited right was the basis of all, so
that old and new were ever mingling. Whether in genetic or cultural
terms we must accept Professor Darlington's explanation of tenth
century Normandy (and its extraordinary consequences) 'as the place
where the southward movement of the barbarians and the northward

6 Douglas, op. cit., *passim.*

7 *William the Conqueror,* 1964, pp. 85-92.

8 William of Jumièges, *Gesta Normannorum Ducum,* ed. J. Marx, Soc. de l'hist.
de Normandie, 1914, pp. 320-9.

9 *The Norman Achievement,* pp. 114-7, 226-234.

10 G. H. White, 'The Sisters and Nieces of Gunnor, Duchess of Normandy', *The
Genealogist,* New Series, Vol. 37, 1921, pp. 57-65, 128-132.

movement of Romanized people were most actively interpenetrating' and we may well find validity in his further conclusion that 'it was the place where the Viking leaders, themselves a governing class, were hybridizing on a large scale with the newly established governing class of Capetian France', and that 'it was this hybridization which produced the race and the phenomenon we know as the Normans'.[11]

Though the origins of the mass of the knights who made Duke William's conquest of England possible can only be guessed, the natural assumption is that the compound was similar to that of the leaders, though we know that there were also a large Breton contingent and smaller groups from the countries of Boulogne, Picardy and Flanders. What is certain is that between 1066 and his death in 1087 these adventurers and their leaders, William's earls and barons, had displaced the English earls and greater landowners with few exceptions throughout the country, while the lesser thegns had been expropriated to a large but less certain extent.

For those greater old English families which did not altogether perish the choice, as Sir Frank Stenton has shown in detail,[12] lay between exile and decline into obscurity. Many moved to southern Scotland, where an aristocracy largely of English blood was already dominant. Others fled to Denmark, with which the recent Anglo-Danish monarchy of Canute had established close links. Among these were two sons and a daughter of King Harold, to whom Sweyn, King of Denmark was first cousin. The daughter, Gytha, was married to Valdemar of Holmgard, that is Vladimir of Novgorod in Russia, usually identified (though there is some discrepancy in the evidence) with Vladimir Monomachos (d. 1125).[13] Her descendants, if so, were numerous and through them the blood of Harold came back into the English royal house with the marriage of Edward III to Philippa of Hainault (Ped. 47, note p. 259).

This episode points to a route by which English exiles may have reached Constantinople, where many joined the Varangian guard of the Byzantine Emperors. A notable contingent seems to have taken service under Alexius Comnenus in 1081 and to have fought the Normans in South Italy.[14]

The pedigree (Ped. 51, note p. 260) of the English Earls of Northumberland illustrates both the Scottish link and the higher survival rate of English magnates in the North. Lucy, Countess of Chester, married successively to three Norman lords, was of English blood and perhaps allied to the house of Leofric of Mercia. The blood of that house was certainly represented in the Anglo-Norman nobility through a Welsh descent (Ped. 48, note p. 259). These, with the

11 C. D. Darlington, *The Evolution of Man and Society*, 1969, p. 431.

12 F. M. Stenton, 'English Families and the Norman Conquest' Tr. Roy. Hist. Soc., 4S., 26, 1944, 1-12, & *Anglo-Saxon England*, 1943, p. 610.

13 E. A. Freeman, *The Norman Conquest*, 2nd ed., 1876, IV. 752-5.

14 Ib. 845-8.

progenies of Colswein of Lincoln, Thurkill of Arden and Wigot of Wallingford, Harding son of Eadnoth and Colegrim of Fulbeck must stand for those landowners great and small who in one way or another came to terms with the Normans. That many more lesser thegns than we can identify probably did the same is suggested by the later attainment of importance by a number of families, whose origin was demonstrably English, though their ancestry cannot be taken back to the Conquest. The proof in these cases is simply that the first known ancestor bore an English personal name. English thegns' families, which kept the station of knights or in due course reached it, were bound thereby to become Normanized and so sooner or later gave their children Norman names.[15] In the class of freemen below the knights the same thing happened more slowly, this changeover often not coming before about 1300. Among presumably English families which had attained baronial rank by 1350 Sir Frank Stenton and others have noted those of Fitzwilliam of Hinderskelfe, Neville of Raby, Greystoke, Segrave, Multon, Berkeley, Cromwell, Audley and Ughtred.[16]

English blood came into the royal house through the marriage of Henry I to Maud of Scotland in 1100. There was no further infusion till in 1329 Edward III married Philippa of Hainault, a remote descendant of the houses both of Godwin and of Siward (Ped. 47). The resurgence of English families in the later Middle Ages is, however, well brought out by the number of English lines of ancestry which Edward IV (1461-1483) could claim through his grandmother Anne Mortimer and his mother Cicely Neville (Peds. 47 to 50).

The same point may be made in converse by looking at the successive disappearance of Norman male lines from among the earls. By 1400 St. Liz, Ferrers, Bigod, Clare, Warenne, Bohun and other great names had gone, but Vere, Beauchamp, Courtenay, Fitzalan, Mowbray, Stafford, Mortimer, Percy and Montagu remained. Of these by 1500 only Vere, Courtenay, Fitzalan, Stafford, and Percy were left, but an earldom had

15 EG. 50; *Notes & Queries*, 197, 1952, pp. 222-5, P. H. Reaney, 'Pedigrees of Villeins & Freemen'.

16 As this goes to press Sir Charles Clay's latest volume, *Early Yorkshire Families* (with illustrative documents edited by Diana E. Greenway. Yorkshire Arch. Soc., Record Series, Vol. CXXXV, 1973; published with help from the Marc Fitch Fund), makes (with much else) the greatest contribution to date to our knowledge of English post-conquest manorial survival. It deals minutely with approximately one hundred Yorkshire manorial families, traceable continuously, or nearly so, 'from an ancestor living before the death of Henry I, and some at least of whose lands passed by inheritance to the reign of Edward I or later.'

Sir Charles is able to show that, in addition to families descending from Gospatric the thegn, some seventeen can be shown to descend from Anglo-Saxon ancestors and that some show marriages between Anglo-Saxons and Normans, though most of these held undertenancies from Norman tenants in chief. Further illustrations of this and other aspects of our subject could have been drawn from this remarkable work, had it appeared earlier.

come to the Norman, though originally minor, family of Talbot. By 1600 Vere, Percy and Talbot alone remained, but there had been new Norman male line recruits to earldoms, such as Manners, Clinton, Clifford, Seymour and Devereux. By 1700 only Vere, Talbot, Clinton, Manners and Seymour remained of these, but there had again been new Norman recruits such as Sackville, Villiers and St. John. By this time, however, the Norman ancestry of all such families was so diluted with English that a new earl or duke of Norman male descent might well mean less and be a lesser rarity than one of English name whose inheritance from early Normans was continuous, as with the Dukes of Norfolk and Northumberland and Lords Leconfield, though these are respectively by male descent Howard, Smithson and Wyndham.

Through most of the centuries which here concern us the route of entry into the upper classes lay through the ownership of land though that ownership might itself, more and more, as time went on, arise from purchase with mercantile or other wealth. In the first century or two after the Conquest the chief mechanism of recruitment was subinfeudation. The King granted lands to the barons on terms of their producing for his service specified numbers of knights for specified lands. The barons in turn arranged this by granting manors to their knights on tenure of specified military service. Some knights, so enfeoffed, themselves enfeoffed others under them in fractional holdings, occasionally as small, even, as a hundredth of a knight's fee. This was among the factors which in time undermined the system, leading to the prohibition of subinfeudation by the statute *Quia Emptores* in 1295 and before that to the frequent substitution of payment (called *scutage*) for personal knight service and the replacement of the feudal levy by a paid army.

Before that stage was reached subinfeudation had brought many lesser men of varying status into the ranks of those holding by knight service and among them some who by degrees improved their position, adding acre to acre and manor to manor. We have a picture of the position on the estates of Ramsey Abbey, Huntingdonshire, about 1185, where a distinction is made between the knights, who held of the abbey on a military tenure not less than a hide and a half (a knight's fee being four hides), and the many franklins (frankelanni) 'Some of whom hold half a hide, some more, some less and ought and are accustomed to aid the knights to do service'.[17] Such franklins were expected to take up knighthood if they grew rich enough. The ladder of ascent by increase of wealth and lands may be seen from another angle as a ladder of ascent for lesser men who in one way or another served greater men, whether a king, baron or mere knight. At this as at other times the

17 *Cartularium monasterii de Rameseia*, ed. W. H. Hart, P. A. Lyons, Rolls Series 79, 1893, p. 49, quoted by G. C. Homans, *English Villagers of the Thirteenth Century*, Harvard U.P., 1942, p. 248.

process certainly went on at all levels, but the scantiness of early record makes it seldom clearly visible save at the highest.

In a brilliant essay on King Henry I Professor Southern points to factors which opened or kept upon the ladders of ascent for middling families in that king's time and ever after in England.[18] Chief among these he rates the preservation first by the Conqueror, then by Henry, of 'the tenurial complexities of Anglo-Saxon England'. A building up by their magnates of great compact fiefs, which the Norman kings could have encouraged but did not, might in the short term have made for effective government but would not have made all free tenants more or less equal in the royal courts and so would have prevented that growth of those courts, which gave royal officials their opportunities.

The consequent rise of Geoffrey de Clinton and other servants of Henry I from obscurity to great place is traced in its relation to this situation and shown as an early phase of the same process of family aggrandisement through service of the crown, which Tawney discerned in the sixteenth and Namier in the eighteenth centuries. If these historians and their followers have made modern English history seem surprisingly mediaeval, it is because this same pattern runs right through.

An early stage both of the process and the social patterns it produced can be seen in the records of the one class of men who rose from poverty to greatness by the pen rather than the sword — the great clerics and especially the bishops. Some of these were of knightly and even of baronial birth, but more, probably, were of prosperous franklin stock and a few, like the great Grosseteste, were of the humblest origin. Bishops' Registers (the earliest dating from 1209) give us our first detailed picture of the private arrangements of such men of modest birth and, since bishops shared the normal attachment to kindred, this may include light on their origins and social ambience.

Attitudes and ambitions naturally differed. Simon de Wauton or Walton, Bishop of Norwich 1258-65, born, probably, about 1180 of a franklin family at Walton in Wellesbourne, Warwickshire, was married before he took orders and had a son and two daughters. He rose by service in King John's household, became a judge under Henry III and at length a bishop. With the wealth thus gained he bought the manor of Walton d'Eyville, where he had been born, and granted it to his son. The son's daughter and heiress was thrice married, to a knight and two barons, her second husband being a descendant of King Henry I's second queen. (Ped. 57, note p. 261).

The family ambitions of Walter de Merton, Bishop of Rochester 1274-7 and twice Chancellor of England, took a different turn. He was born about 1200 at Basingstoke, Hampshire, son of William, called apparently 'the Cook', and of Cristina Fitz Ace or Fitz Oliver, one of a family of freeholders on the royal manor of Basingstoke with many

18 R. W. Southern, *Medieval Humanism and Other Studies* 1970, pp. 220-299.

connections there. There were Cooks in Walter's household and among his mother's tenants and it is probable that the Bishop's grandfather if not his father took the name from his occupation.[19] In 1264, when Walter's career as Henry III's Chancellor appeared to be ended by Montfort's rebellion, he turned to the establishment of a foundation to provide for his numerous nephews, nieces, cousins and ecclesiastical household. In 1262 he set about the foundation at Malden in Surrey of a college for clerical education and a charter of 1264 brought it formally into existence, some or all of his eight nephews being already there. Between 1266 and 1268 he acquired a site at Oxford to which he removed it, completing the foundation of Merton College by the issue of statutes in 1274. Thus was established the first self governing college at an English university, the model for all which have followed, notwithstanding that (as Mr. Highfield, the editor of the early rolls of the College, points out) the original objective of provision for the Founder's kin is at present out of fashion.[20]

His main object being to provide for his kin to become clerics, it is not surprising that Walter de Merton founded no knightly family. Indeed those who entered his College as Founder's Kin down to the late fifteenth century were of families otherwise of total obscurity. Nevertheless he had on two sides family links of some interest with the knightly class. In 1239 he had bought land at Ewell, Surrey, for the marriage portion of his sister Agnes when she married one Gilbert Ewell.[21] In 1265, following the crushing of Simon de Montfort's rebellion, Walter de Merton acquired land for his foundation from certain of Simon's supporters in circumstances which suggest that they may thus have been seeking favour with the winning side. One of the rebels from whom Walter acquired lands was one Robert Fitz Nigel, between whose son and namesake and Agnes, one of Walter's nieces, a marriage was arranged in 1266.[22] This Agnes seems to have been the daughter of Walter's sister Agnes and Gilbert Ewell, since on the death of their son William Ewell, canon of St. Paul's, in 1311 the marriage portion land at Ewell passed to Robert Fitz Nigel and remained in his family until 1369,[23] whence female descents might well be traceable through gentle families to the present day. Walter de Merton gave Maud, a sister of Robert Fitz Nigel, in marriage to Sir John de St. John,

19 *The Early Rolls of Merton College, Oxford,* ed. J. R. L. Highfield, 1964, p. 5n.

20 *The Early Rolls of Merton College,* ed. J. R. L. Highfield, Oxford Hist. Soc. N.S.XVIII, 1964, p. 77.

21 Ib. p. 40.

22 Ib. p. 28.

23 P. 40.

son of William de St. John, a member, probably, of the baronial family of St. John of Basing.[24]

Still more interesting was Walter de Merton's relationship to ... . family of Basing (Ped. 51, note pp. 260 1), which came to London in the late twelfth century, doubtless from Basing in Hampshire, and is remembered in Basinghall Street. Cristina Basing gave land to Walter in 1236 and his executors' accounts record an application by Maud de Basing for marriage portions which he had promised her two daughters, who were of his blood.[25] Her husband Robert Basing (dead by 1253) must have been near akin to Thomas Basing (Sheriff 1269/70), wool merchant, leading citizen of London and one of the few who took the side of Henry III against Simon de Montfort. He was Bishop Merton's principal financial agent and kept many of the Bishop's valuables in his house.

Through the marriage of Adam de Basing, sheriff of London in 1243, mayor in 1251 and owner of Aldermanbury, to Desiderata daughter of Ernulf fitzAlulf or Ruffus (Peds. 52-4, notes pp. 260-1), his family were linked to the group of intermarried aldermanic families who formed something like a patriciate or hereditary governing group in twelfth and thirteenth century London. The diversity of their origins is remarkable. The belief that two notable families were Italian, Bocointe (*Bucca uncta* = oily mouth) and Buckerel (Buccherelli) is now questioned.[26] However, Arnold fitz Thedmar, alderman of Billingsgate ward and compiler of the City *Liber de Antiquis* was the son of a German from Bremen. The families of Fitz Herlwin, Fitz Reinier and Blund were Norman, as also, presumably, were le Viel,[27] Fitz Alulf and Fitz Isabel.

Many citizens of Caen and Rouen came to settle in London because of its trading advantages, among them Gilbert Becket a merchant of Rouen and his wife Rose, from Caen, the parents of Archbishop Becket. Gilbert Becket became portreeve of London and his rich kinsman Osbert Huitdeniers was justiciar of London from 1139 to 1141.[28] But the great family of Fitz Ailwin, which gave London its first mayor in 1192, was of English origin, descending, probably, from Ailwin Horne, a thegn of Edward the Confessor. Professor Douglas,

24 PP. 87, 110. The pedigree of these St Johns in Baker's Northamptonshire, II 96 calls Sir John de St John (William's father) of Hambleton Co. Rutland, relying on a deed belonging in 1614 to Sir Valentine Knightly. But Coll. Arm. MS. Vincent 113 fo.40, using the same deeds, says merely of Hambledon: perhaps, therefore, Hambledon, Hants., where Sir Robert de St John of Basing held half a knight's fee in 1251.

25 PP. 87, 110.

26 *History*, Vol. 57 (1972). Susan Reynolds, 'The rulers of London in the twelfth century', pp. 339-40.

27 Susan Reynolds, *op. cit.*, points out that not all Blunds or le Viels need necessarily be akin and that some of Page's guesses have been mistakenly treated as established facts.

28 William Page, *London, its origin and early development*, 1923, pp. 80, 205.

moreover, has established the remarkable fact that a probable member of this family (and certainly an Englishman), Thierry of Barrow, son of Deorman, married (c. 1140) a Norman lady, Maud, who was akin to Earl Gilbert Strongbow) of the great Norman family of Clare, descended from the Dukes of Normandy.[29] The daughter and heiress of this marriage married William Blemund from whom Bloomsbury takes its name. English also was Ordgar, whose granddaughter, the wife of John Bocointe, endowed the church named from him St. Martin Orgar. So too was Algar Colessune, whose son Nicholas fitz Algar succeeded him as priest of St. Martin Chepe, while his daughter married Baldwin de Arras and became mother in law to Robert Fitz Herlwin. Edward of Cornhill was in 1125 among the fifteen English members of the *cnightengild* of London, a military organisation traceable back to the tenth century. His daughter and heir Agnes married Gervase, a Norman, who took the name of Cornhill (Ped. 53, and note p. 260).

William Page ends his account of these early London families with two interesting comments; he thinks that their intermarriages, though at first beneficial in blending the different races, ended by making them exclusive of new men, thus exciting a democratic party which at length took their place.[30] They were in fact displaced by Edward I in 1285.[31] His second comment is that their wealth attracted families from outside so that city heiresses married into baronial houses and carried their wealth out of London. Thus, the ultimate heiress of Henry Fitz Ailwin married Lord Bardolf (Ped. 52). The Cornhill heiress married Hugh de Neville, ancestor of the Lords Neville of Essex (Ped. 53, note p. 260). Her mother had been the heiress of a baronial family, the de Courcys of Stogursey, Somerset,[32] whose daughter by her second husband married the son of the Earl of Devon. Her uncle Ralph de Cornhill (d. 1199) married (c. 1191) the heiress of another baronial house, Alice, daughter of Robert de Hastings probably by the granddaughter of Walter fitz Other, a tenant in chief of the Conqueror, castellan of Windsor Castle, and ancestor of the Carews and Fitzgeralds.[33]

This Alice, after Ralph's death in 1199, married a cadet of a foreign ruling family closely related to the English royal house and settled in England. This was Godfrey de Lovaine, a half brother of the Duke of

29 Ped. 52, *infra*, note p. 260. Compare the relationship (R. W. Southern, *Medieval Humanism*, 1970, p. 226) between the wife of Reginald, Earl of Cornwall, (D.1175), illegitimate son of Henry I and a married sister, living in Launceston, of Peter of Cornwall, Prior of Holy Trinity, Aldgate, London, whose father Jordan, a Cornish country gentleman, was son of Ailsi, a master builder in the service of the canons of Launceston and grandson of Theodolf, an Anglo-Saxon landowner.

30 *London, its origin and early development*, 1923, p. 266.

31 Gwyn A. Williams, 'London and Edward I', *Tr. R. Hist. Soc.* 5S Vol. II, 1961, pp. 80-99.

32 I. J. Sanders, *English Baronies*, 1960, p. 143.

33 Ib. p. 130; E.G. (I) 77, (II) 84.

Brabant and Count of Louvain, (the husband of King Stephen's granddaughter) and a greatnephew of the second wife of King Henry I. Matthew de Lovaine (d. 1302), the grandson of Godfrey and Alice, married first a kinswoman of King Henry III and secondly a city heiress, Maud Poyntz. His son by the latter, Thomas de Lovaine (d. 1345), (it seems) completed the circle by marrying a daughter of Sir Robert de Basing, alderman of London 1292-6, one of the family related to Walter de Merton.[34] This Sir Robert was apparently the last of the city Basings. In 1294 he purchased the marriage of Margaret de Normanville, the orphaned heiress of a knightly family with lands at Empingham, Rutland, and in Nottinghamshire and Kent. He had meant to marry her to his elder son Reginald but as, when the time came in 1297, Reginald was a prisoner in Gascony, Sir Robert obtained consent to marry her to his younger son William. Sir William de Basing thus became the founder of a knightly family in Rutland. His male line continued there till 1445 and his Mackworth descendants in the female line remained at Empingham till 1723.[35] (ped. 55, note p. 261).

From this early, though small and scantily recorded sample certain points emerge. First of all we discern already in the thirteenth century, if not the twelfth, a socio-genealogical pattern for which England has since been notable; a pattern in which close links between the great and the humble can be traced through matrimonial cross-connections, which have arisen because of the absence of legal barriers between class and class; thus creating what Sir Lewis Namier has called 'the peculiar character of English society, civilian and plutocratic, though imbued with feudal habits and traditions'.[36] Walter de Merton, probably son or grandson of a cook, and with other humble kinsfolk, was also near akin to a London alderman whose son in law's stepmother was the King's kinswoman.

The arranged mercenary marriage was an important link in this kind of chain. Since a woman's (and indeed a male infant's) marriage was unlawful without her lord's consent, kings gave the marriage of their barons' heiresses to their protégés or sold them to the highest bidder. The wardship of orphans, being equally the lords's right, was similarly bought and sold. Thus Walter de Merton could marry his niece to Robert fitzNigel and the latter's sister to Sir John de St. John. Thus Robert de Basing, the alderman, could marry his son to the Normanville heiress. Thus, in general, men who had risen to wealth by whatever means could quickly knit their families into the class to which their wealth equated them. There were, however, exceptions to the rule of the arranged marriage. Rich widows, who at length were at their own

34 C.P. VIII.181 n(a).

35 V.C.H. *Rutland* II, 244; Blore, *Rutland,* 127. Sir John Basynges of Emping-ham (D.1445) owned an important Roll of Arms of c. 1395 now in the College of Arms (CEMRA, p. 71).

36 L. B. Namier, *England in the Age of the American Revolution,* 1930. p. 6.

disposal, sometimes pleased themselves by then marrying downwards. Such a case, perhaps, was that of Elizabeth of Juliers, widow of John, Earl of Kent, a grandson of King Edward I, who in 1360 broke a vow of chastity to marry a famous warrior, her countryman, Sir Eustace d'Aubrécicourt.[37] Her husband's uncle, Edward I's son, Thomas of Brotherton, Earl of Norfolk, about 1320, when some twenty years old, had made a marriage, which appears inexplicable on any basis of worldly calculation, to Alice, daughter of Sir Roger de Hales, coroner of Norfolk, a knight so obscure that the pedigree of his family has never been clearly traced.[38] From this marriage descend all the Mowbrays and the Howards, Earls and Dukes of Norfolk.

We also see already — in Becket, in Simon de Wauton, in Walter de Merton — the career open to the kinds of talent which kings and magnates could use, and not least administrative talent. In the same way Walter de Merton's official family or staff comprised kinsmen in relatively humble offices, as well as men of confidence, unrelated to him, on whom his organisation turned.

Two or three generations later William de Melton, son of a franklin of Melton in the parish of Welton in the East Riding of Yorkshire, entering the Church and becoming an usher of the King's Wardrobe in 1300, rose in 1317 to be Archbishop of York, dying in 1340. His Register mentions kinsmen in middle stations of life, not unlike Walter de Merton's, but again among them a family of successful London merchants, that of Swanland from the village of that name near Melton, whose London link was presumably the coastal trade from Hull. Simon de Swanland, who was an alderman of London from 1327 to 1334, acquired the manor of Harefield, Middlesex, in 1315. It remained in the Swanland family till about 1440, when Joan Swanland the heiress married John Newdigate and conveyed it to the Newdigates (also of Arbury in Warwickshire), who held much of it till very recently,[39] and are commemorated in the church there by one of the most remarkable family series of monuments in the country.

Archbishop Melton himself founded a family through his nephew Sir William de Melton, whom he brought up and endowed with the manor of Aston and other lands in Yorkshire.[40] In 1340, the year of his death, the Archbishop arranged a marriage for his nephew with Joan, daughter of Anthony de Lucy, who was summoned to Parliament as a baron. This before long linked the Meltons to the circles of greatness, for Joan's niece in 1381 became Countess of Northumber-

---

37 Complete Peerage, VII, 149.

38 For some of the scanty known data see F. Blomefield, *History of Norfolk*, ed. C. Parkin, 1808, Vol. VIII, pp. 18, 38. Harleian Society, Vol. 32 pp. 173, 187.

39 S. L. Thrupp, *The Merchant Class of Medieval London*, 1948, p. 368: V.C.H., *Middlesex*, Vol. III, pt. ii, p. 241.

40 Joseph Hunter, History of the *Deanery of Doncaster*, Vol. II, 1831, p. 162.

land and stepmother of Harry Hotspur, who was married to a great-granddaughter of King Edward III.[41] (Ped. 58).

It is difficult at this early date to establish similar close links between those of middling and of the humblest station, but I do not doubt their existence and have brought forward elsewhere some scraps of evidence.[42] It is sometimes said that the great social divide and barrier was between the free and the unfree. Certainly the Anglo-Norman lawyers tried in the two centuries following the Conquest to establish such a barrier, but they do not seem ever to have succeeded in making it impassable.[43]

The law which made their daughters, rather than their brothers, the heirs of men who left no sons meant that fiefs both great and small from time to time passed to new male lines through the marriages of such heiress daughters. The husbands might be junior members of long established families, but were by no means always so. The marriages were no doubt arranged by parents or guardians, but these often used such occasions to establish up and coming friends or protégés. It seems likely, indeed, that this was the biggest single source of the large infusion of wholly new names into the ranks of the knights and gentlemen which the heraldic evidence[44] of the later fourteenth and fifteenth centuries reveal.

Of course such rise by favour and marriage did not exclude rise by merit and self help. A guardian picking a husband for an heiress would look round for a man of promise. The families who rose by marriage were likely to be families of antecedent ability. No such case is more famous than that of the Howards, who made six marriages with heiresses, small and great, between Sir William Howard, who was made a Justice of the Common Pleas in 1297, and his descendant Sir John Howard who became Duke of Norfolk in 1483, whose mother was the eventual heiress of Thomas, Earl of Norfolk, a younger son of King Edward I.[45] The tradition was revived between 1555 and 1606, the Howard Dukes of Norfolk and Earls of Arundel marrying four great heiresses in that period.

However such gradual rise by inheritance over generations was naturally not a matter solely of marriage to heiresses. A point made by Professor Hoskins in relation to the Tudor and Stuart squires and gentry of Devon is of far more general application. Many of them were

41 L. H. Butler, 'Archbishop Melton, his Neighbours and his Kinsmen 1317-1340', *The Journal of Ecclesiastical History*, Vol.II 1951, pp. 54-67: C.P. VIII. 254.

42 EG., 2nd ed. 1970, pp. 69, 214-5.

43 Ib. pp. 138-140.

44 Pp. 42-3 *supra*.

45 Lawrence Stone, *The Crisis of the Aristocracy 1558-1641*, 1965, pp. 112-4 lists a number of previously obscure families who rose to greatness by marriage with heiresses; Touchet, Bourchier, Stanley, Parr, Devereux and Manners before 1500; Fane, Mildmay, Finch, Greville and others after; and, most notably, Cavendish.

simply the fortunate survivors out of a larger number of small freeholders' families of the thirteenth and fourteenth centuries. Some had died out. Others had produced many daughters and given away more land with them on marriage than their heirs had gained by marriage to others' heiresses. But the lucky few had produced enough males and not too many daughters and by successive marriages built up small into great estates.[46] It will be noted that this definition of luck identifies the family as the *male line* family. I do not defend this. I put it so because it is how people usually think of it.

The other principal means of money making[47] were the law, trade (not excluding land speculation) manufacture (mainly of cloth) office under the king or a great lord and the profits of war. When Paulin Peyvre a 'literate knight or soldier cleric' (*miles literatus sive clericus militans*) who became Steward of King Henry III's household, first came to court about 1230, he owned scarcely two carucates of land; but in a short time, Matthew Paris tells us he had fifty. The estate he finally built up, mainly in Bedfordshire and Buckinghamshire, made him a rival of the great nobles in wealth.[48]

The piecemeal building up of a landed estate on a smaller scale is seen in *The Estate Book of Henry de Bray of Harlestone, Co. Northants (c. 1289-1340)*.[49] Most of his immediate connections, of whom much detail emerges, seem to have been franklins, though his great-grandmother Quena de Armenters was of a knightly family, but lost her lands through marrying while under age without the leave of her overlord and guardian William Earl of Derby. Henry's grandfather recovered some part of these and he himself a little more. Henry's mother, he tells us, was the daughter of one Richard, who was called the Clerk, because he was literate, and who lived a hundred years.[50] This Richard, who was grandson of one Arnold le Lord, who held eight virgates in Harlestone, Althorp and Duston, Northamptonshire, had a daughter by his second marriage, whose son Robert of Holcot is called 'le Bonde'[51] meaning that he was a husbandman or possibly a villein. This Robert's son was in 1301 a citizen of London.[52] We know from the evidence of lawsuits that there were in the thirteenth century freemen near akin to villeins and it may have been so here.[53] We know also that flight to a town was among the ways by which villeins attained freedom. Simon Paris, a small landowner in Harlestone with

46 W. G. Hoskins and H. P. R. Finberg, *Devonshire Studies*, 1952, pp. 127-8.

47 See p. 119 *infra.*

48 *Complete Peerage*, X,513: N. Denholm-Young, *History and Heraldry 1254 to 1310*, 1965, pp. 32-4.

49 Ed. for the R. Hist. Soc. by Dorothy Willis, Camden 3rd. Ser. Vol. XXVII, 1916.

50 Ib. p. 79.

51 Ib. p. 74.

52 P. 72.

53 EG. (II) pp. 138-140.

whom Henry de Bray had transactions, was possibly the same man as Simon of Paris, alderman of London (1299-1319 and 1320-1) who by origin was a villein from Necton, Norfolk.[54] Henry de Bray married his daughter and heiress, Alice, to John Dyve of Brampton, a member of a minor knightly family,[55] whose second cousin had a half brother who in 1329 abducted and married (as his second wife and her second husband) a granddaughter of King Edward I (Ped. 59), the widow of Hugh le Despenser the younger, who had been captured with his master King Edward II and hanged in 1326. Thus we have here again a close family connection between great and humble people.

Few and lacking in detail though these examples are, they suffice, I submit, to show that the special pattern of social order and movement, which has characterised England in later times, was already established within two centuries or less of the Norman conquest. The distinctive feature of this pattern is its amalgamation of contrasted elements of stiffness and movement; a structure or skeleton of permanent hierarchical form supporting an organism of slowly changing and ever mingling and recombining substance.

The first element of this peculiar balance is the tenure of land. The great lords, with their baronies, are supported by knights with their manors, and these by tenants, free and unfree, with their several rents and services. But the invisible pyramid of land tenure is transected by other such pyramids of power, influence, worth, service and skill, all the time moving individuals slowly upstairs and down from level to level. A very few make great moves. More make smaller moves, most stay still. But the cumulative effect of the many small moves, combined with attachment to kin, is to establish at all levels unadvertised but influential links between classes and resulting sympathies and aspirations. Though at all times there have been great bulwarks and barriers at particular points in the class structure, these have come and gone and shifted, like sandbanks in a river mouth, without ever forming a complete and coherent system of barriers. The skilful and determined navigator, who wished enough to do so, has often, therefore, been able to circumvent them, so that in effect, if not intention, they have served more to ignite than to quench ambition.

The timing and placing of these barriers has been of great importance all the same. Separations and comings together have alternated, with momentous consequence. This has had both a racial and a class aspect. We have noted the early and frequent, though for a time interrupted, marriage links between Norman and English families. We may compare the many marriages between the English and the Scottish baronage

---

54 S. Thrupp, *The Merchant Class of Medieval London*, p. 359.

55 *Estate Book of Henry de Bray*, p. 95; possibly sprung from the family from Dives-sur-Mer, Normandy, one of whom was a knight of archbishop Lanfranc (L. C. Loyd, *The Origins of some Anglo-Norman Families*, 1951, p. 37. D. C. Douglas, *Domesday Monachorum of Christ Church Canterbury*, pp. 37-8).

which took place from the time of the settlement of Norman knights in Scotland under King David I (from 1124) down to the settlement of the frontiers in 1237, and again during Edward I's intervention in Scottish affairs. After Bannockburn (1314) such marriages were almost unknown till King James VI of Scotland became James I of England in 1603. There was a similar period of intermarriage between Welsh princely and English baronial families in the twelfth and thirteenth centuries. But here, though the Edwardian Conquest made a breach, it was not long before marriage links across the border were resumed. John Cherleton married Hawise Gadarn, the heiress of the princes of Upper Powys, in 1309. The three daughters of Owen Glendower married Englishmen; their kinsman, Owen Tudor married (c.1429) the widow of King Henry V; the two sons of this union married ladies of royal descent; William Herbert, who was made Earl of Pembroke, married (c.1455) the sister of Lord Ferrers; and then came the great Tudor influx of Welshmen into England.

Another love hate relationship, sometimes on, sometimes off, was that of aristocracy to mercantile wealth. Though intermarriage between them in early times was rare, we have noted such early instances as that of Thierry, son of Deorman of London, with a kinswoman of Earl Gilbert Strongbow (c.1140) and that of Henry of Cornhill to the Courcy heiress (c.1190). It might be argued that twelfth century London citizens were more knightly than their successors or early Norman barons more *parvenu* than theirs. But does this do more than express the facts in modern and perhaps misleading terms? We have noted thirteenth century examples in the Lovaine, Cornhill and Basing families. In 1366 Lord Burghersh married the widow of a Mayor of London, Sir Henry Picard, herself of the City family of Gisors. In 1383 John de Montagu, Earl of Salisbury, married Maud the twice widowed daughter of Adam Francis, Mayor of London. Her first husband had been sheriff of London and her second a Knight of the Garter.

About 1450 Anne, the eldest daughter and coheir of Thomas, Lord Hoo, Knight of the Garter married Sir Geoffrey Boleyn, Lord Mayor of London.[56] Their son married the heiress of the Irish Earl of Ormond; their grandson married a daughter of the Duke of Norfolk; and his daughter was the second Queen of Henry VIII. In 1465 Maurice Berkeley, younger brother of the then Lord Berkeley and later Lord Berkeley himself, married Isabel daughter of Philip Mead, three times Mayor of Bristol. His brother complained 'of the obscure parentage of the lady Isable, which he vainly called base: and of the unworthynes of his brothers match with so mean bloud, as he reproached it, making that a motive to his own vast expences, and of the disinheritance of this lord his brother, least any of her base bloud should inherite after him'.[57]

56 CP. VI, 564-5.

57 *The Lives of the Berkeleys by John Smyth of Nibley*, ed. Sir John Maclean, ii, 1893, p. 173.

About 1485 George Neville, Lord Bergavenny, married secondly as her fourth husband the widow of a Lord Mayor (Sir Robert Bassett) and of two citizens of London.

Professor Stone notes several sixteenth century marriages between peers' families and those of city merchants, but comments that these become very rare after 1520 and that the families recruited to the peerage from the city by way of the Crown service, such as North and Rich, dropped their city connections when once established. He adds, however, that after 1591 financial difficulties led some peers to look for city marriages once more.[58] Moreover, the new peers created by James I and Charles I, were, as he puts it, 'men who always had a sharp eye to the main matrimonial chance',[59] and with them city marriages were frequent.

An account like this of social classes and their development can well give a wrong impression of the nature and degree of contact and mobility between them. It has, therefore, seemed to me that a truer picture might be given by pedigrees illustrating lateral marriage connections between class and class at different dates. To what extent the connections shown may be typical or exceptional is a question to which no confident answer will be feasible until genealogical investigations have been made on a scale vastly greater than anything yet planned. My belief, however, is that such investigations would bring to light many such linkages at all dates where sufficient record exists.

For the twelfth, thirteenth and the early fourteenth century the examples, already discussed, of the London citizens, of the kin of Bishops Merton, Wauton and Melton and of Henry de Bray must at present suffice. For the mid-fourteenth century we may instance the great William of Wykeham (1324-1404), Bishop of Winchester (1367) and founder of Winchester College and New College, Oxford. He took his name from his birthplace, Wickham in Hampshire, but his father's name was John Longe, probably a husbandman and perhaps of unfree descent. About 1570 Humphrey Wykeham of Swalcliffe, Oxfordshire, made a claim to be Founder's Kin at Winchester and New College, which Sir Richard Fiennes, a descendant of the Founder's sister, opposed.[60] At these proceedings a life and genealogy of the Founder were produced by the Wardens of the Colleges, 'fayer written about twentie yeares after his death' in the Statute book of the College of Winchester, in which his father was 'covertly noted to discende from such as had receaved liberty from someboddie'.[61] Later in the

58 Laurence Stone, *The Crisis of the Aristocracy 1558-1641*, pp. 628-9.
59 P. 617.
60 G. D. Squibb, Q.C., Norfolk Herald Extraordinary, *Founders' Kin Privilege and Pedigree*, Oxford, 1972, pp. 37-8.
61 C. E. L[ong], 'Descent of the family of Wickham of Swalcliffe, Co. Oxon., and their kindred to the Founder of New College', *Herald & Genealogist*, V., p. 236.

proceedings the point was made again that 'according to the ould written note in the inside of the cover of the protocoll booke of Winchester Colledg (which is not knowne by whome or when it was written) John Longe, there supposed to be the father of the founder, is there also said to be of a servile or slavish condition, whereas the founder was a gentleman borne, witnes his armes'.[62]

These suggestions of servile origin may be a mere inference, and quite possibly a mistaken one, from a phrase in the life of Wykeham written in 1424 by Robert Heite or Heath, who tells us that Wykeham's father 'Johannes nomine, progenitorum libertate dotatus, honestum moribus et gesturis se omnibus exhibebat'.[63] Mr. John Harvey inclines to the view that Heite means that John Long's forefathers were free by origin, *not* manumission. Of course Wykeham's use of arms as a bishop is not really evidence that he was a gentleman *born*. Indeed it has been not implausibly suggested that the chevron in them alludes to his building achievements and his motto, *Manners makyth man,* to his self made eminence. The obscurity of several of those who benefited as Founder's Kin from his benefactions suggests (as with Merton) obscurity of origin on at least one side.[64] On the other hand his mother is credited with a knightly descent which there seems no reason to doubt.

Wykeham himself seems to have acknowledged a non-existent relationship to the Wykehams of Swalcliffe, Oxfordshire, whose name came from a Wickham in that county. His purchase in 1377 of Broughton Castle, three miles from Swalcliffe, and of the Swalcliffe Wykehams' assimilation of their arms to his may be connected with this. Complaisance of this kind is immemorial. Broughton passed on Wykeham's death to his sister's grandson Sir Thomas Perrot, alias Wykeham, whose granddaughter married Sir William Fiennes, son of Lord Saye and Sele, of ancient baronial descent, with whose progeny it still remains.

Our next example is a trio of able brothers of whom the eldest was Henry Chichele (c.1362-1443), Archbishop of Canterbury (1414), Founder of All Souls College, Oxford (1437) and a protégé of William of Wykeham (Ped. 60). Their father Thomas Chichele (d.1400) was a yeoman of Higham Ferrers, Northamptonshire, who became mayor of that place and was prosperous enough to be able to establish his family. At the Poll Tax of 1379 he had been assessed at 6d. But in the neighbouring parish of Ringstead three men of his name and probably

62 Ib. pp. 379-80.
63 G. H. Moberly, *Life of William of Wykeham,* 2nd ed. 1893, p. 323.
64 Coll. Arm. MSS.C.G.Y., 270, 271, Wickham Kindred. Moberly, op.cit., pp. 299-310. The occurrence of the surname Aas or Ace among them (ib.p.4.n.3) suggests the intriguing possibility of a link with Walter de Merton's FitzAce kindred at Basingstoke.

of his kindred, Thomas, Hugh and Richard Chicheley, were assessed as labourers at the minimum figure of 4d.[65]

Thomas Chichele's second son Robert (d.1440) was a grocer of London who acquired great wealth and became sheriff, alderman and twice mayor (1411-2 & 1421-2). In his will he made bequests to his poor relations at Higham Ferrers and at Souldrop, Bedfordshire. 'Item pauperibus de sanguine meo in parrochiis de Higham Ferrers et Suldrop necnon et aliis pauperibus in iisdem parrochiis de Higham et Suldrop' xx li.[66] The third son William (d.1426/7) was likewise a grocer of London and became sheriff and alderman. His daughter Florence married (as her third husband and his second wife) John Darell (d.1438), esquire, of Calehill, Kent, Steward to her uncle Archbishop Chichele and the son of a Yorkshire knight. John Darell's nephew, Sir Richard Darell, Under Treasurer of England, married the widowed Countess of Stafford, a Beaufort great-granddaughter of John of Gaunt (Ped. 60). The ups and downs of the Chichele descendants, or at least of the more prosperous among them, are well seen in the volumes of pedigrees, *Stemmata Chicheleana*, printed at Oxford in 1765 and 1775 for the benefit of candidates for fellowships at All Souls College, though Mr. G. D. Squibb's recent work has revealed some errors.[67]

To the two instances already noted[68] of humble connections with royalty through marriages of certain of the five daughters and eventual coheirs of Edmund Beaufort, Duke of Somerset,[69] we have now to add a third, but this was not because these ladies failed to make any noble marriages, two earls being numbered among their eight husbands. From the manorial records of Great Waltham, Essex, which run from 1248 to 1546 and are preserved among the Duchy of Lancaster Records in the Public Record Office, it has been possible to trace in unusual detail the pedigree of a family of Drake,[70] originally villein tenants of that manor. The stages of their gradual emancipation are unusually clear. In the late thirteenth and early fourteenth centuries more than one is recorded to have commuted labour services for money payments. In 1357 Robert Drake, a bondman of the lord, produced a charter by

65 Ped. 60, *and E.179/159/36. m.1., quoted by Sylvia Thrupp, The Merchant Class of Medieval London p. 330.*

66. *The Register of Henry Chichele*, ed. E. F. Jacob, 1938, Vol. II. p. 567.

67 G. D. Squibb, Q.C., *Founders' Kin, Privilege and Pedigree* (Oxford 1972), pp. 96-103. I suggest that the Robert Chichele, father of Philippa Chiche, ancestress of many claimants, though wrongly identified as the Founder's brother may have been one of the kinsmen whom we know him to have had (cf. Sylvia L. Thrupp, *The Merchant Class of Mediaeval London*, (1948), pp. 330-1).

68 Paston, pp. 10-11 *supra*; Chichele, *supra.*

69 Francis Sandford, *A Genealogical History of the Kings of England*, ed. S. Stebbing, 1706, pp. 333-4.

70 A. Wagner, *Drake in England*, Concord, New Hampshire Historical Society, revised edition, 1970,

which he had acquired land in an adjoining parish. His right to it was disputed but in the end admitted on payment of a rent.[71]

To a branch of this family (though his place in it is uncertain) doubtless belonged Thomas Drake, who in 1442 had a royal pardon for marrying without licence Elizabeth the widow of John Warner of Great Waltham, who had died in 1439.[72] Thomas Drake acquired property and became clerk of the peace for Essex. His son Thomas, who married the widow of his stepbrother John Warner, was Member of Parliament for Maldon in 1468 and, when his father died in that year, put up a monument to him in Maldon church.[73]

Elizabeth, wife successively of John Warner and Thomas Drake, was a Helion of Helion's Bumpstead, the descendant of an ancient knightly family.[74] Her brother John Helion (whose executor in 1450 was Thomas Drake) left two daughters, of whom Philippa married a famous warrior, Sir Thomas Montgomery of Falkbourne (d.1494), Knight of the Garter, whose second wife Lora (Berkeley) married thirdly Thomas Butler, Earl of Ormond and Wiltshire, whose elder brother had married Eleanor Beaufort, one of the five daughters of Edmund, Duke of Somerset, and a great-granddaughter of John of Gaunt (Ped. 61).

The Wars of the Roses, followed by the succession of the Tudor to the Angevin dynasty in 1485, did not make that complete change in the composition of the upper classes sometimes credited to them, but made a great change all the same. It is visible in the changed nature and origin of the men recruited to serve their sovereign at the highest level, some of them founders of great families. Where are the successors to Wykeham, Chichele or Warwick the Kingmaker? Where the predecessors to Dudley and Empson, Thomas Cromwell and Burleigh? The process had ancient roots and was neither quick nor sudden, but the warriors and churchmen were going down and the lawyers and merchants were coming up. With the Duke of Wellington, two centuries and more ahead, the warriors' day was not done; and lawyers had been coming up since Scrope and Howard and Bray two centuries back. The talents, also, though they differed, were not exclusive. Administrators may not differ greatly though chosen in one age from knights and churchmen

71 Ib. p. 66.

72 The Manor Court Rolls of Great Waltham, D/D Tu 243, record the attachment of Thomas Drakes and Isabell his wife of Great Waltham, junior, and Thomas Cornyssh, executor of the will of John Warner of Great Waltham, Junior, to answer Barnabas Faux in a plea of debt on 23 Dec. 1445.

73 College of Arms MS. C21 (Visitation of Essex 1634) fo.21. John Weaver, *Ancient Funerall Monuments*, 1631, p. 610, misprints Helion as Heydon. *History of Parliament, 1439-1509, Biographies*, p. 280.

74 I. J. Sanders, English Baronies, 1960, pp. 121-2: Morant, *History of Essex*, Vol. II., p. 531. Through her mother, Joan Botetourt, Alice Swinborne had an illegitimate descent from King Edward I and a legitimate descent from the Veres, Clares and Giffards.

and in another from among lawyers or merchants. Buccaneers too are found in all walks of life. Yet we think we see types which one age has exalted relegated to lower place by the next and conversely.

A new kind of segregation and conjunction sprang from the religious divisions of the sixteenth and following centuries. The 'religious apartheid' of the great Roman Catholic families begins, Professor Stone concludes, about 1570,[75] partly chosen, partly forced upon them. This much intermarried group includes the families of Tresham, Throckmorton, Stonor, Petre, Stourton, Howard (in its Roman Catholic branches), Arundell, Roper, Dormer, Browne, (Viscount Montagu), Vaux, Blount, Plowden, Tichborne and others. But their endogamy never approached in persistence or consistency that of the contemporary Roman Catholic royal families of Europe, who since the sixteenth century have almost formed a caste or selfcontained genetic group.

There were comparable marriage links, though for a far shorter time and much less exclusive, between some of the great Puritan families, and through them with some of the most active promoters of American colonization (Peds. 63-5, and note p. 262) Professor Carl Bridenbaugh gives some of the background of this movement in his *Vexed and Troubled Englishmen 1590-1642* (Oxford, 1968), where he brings together the changes, pressures and discontents of many kinds, which led in those years to the great migration to North America which he calls 'the first swarming of the English'. The discontented were not all of one kind or all subject to the same pressures. There were recusants as well as Puritans, adventurers as well as victims. It is clear, however, that the same forces which in 1642 ignited the Civil War had before that time largely given the impulse to migration. John Winthrop (1588-1649), a chief founder of New England, and so at long range of the United States of America, was in actuality a Cromwell guiltless of his country's blood. It is a characteristic paradox of genealogy that the late Duke of Norfolk was among his descendants.[76] From an early New England settler of another, mercantile, sort, William Vassall (d.1655), the son of a London alderman of Huguenot origin, descended the famous Whig hostess Lady Holland (d.1845).[77]

The same pattern of limited and shifting barriers and confluences may be discerned in the history of landownership. The fourteenth century had been a time when great estates became greater by heiress marriage and by purchase and when, despite occasional forfeitures and losses, no great family 'was permanently separated from the bulk of its estates except by failure of heirs'.[78] When that occurred the estates

75 Lawrence Stone, *The Crisis of the Aristocracy, 1558-1641,* p. 614.
76 V. L. Oliver, *History of the Island of Antigua,* 1894-9, Vol. II, p. 215.
77 EG., Ist ed., 251, 2nd ed. 295.
78 G. A. Holmes, *The Estates of the Higher Nobility in Fourteenth Century England,* 1957, p. 9.

either passed by arrangement to another family or escheated to the king, who regranted them to his friends or relations. On the other hand legal developments in this century made it easier than before for owners of land with many children to disperse the former among the latter.

There were geographical differences also. Professor Everitt concludes that the seventeenth century gentry of Kent were old established and deeply rooted by comparison with those of Suffolk.[79] Yet scarcely a name from those of the knights of Kent in the Dering Roll (c.1275) or the Parliamentary Roll (c.1312) and very few even from the County Roll (temp. Richard II) are still to be found in the Heralds' Visitations. Survivals of mediaeval knightly names among the gentry seem, however, to be more frequent in remoter counties such as Devon, Yorkshire and Cheshire.

Thomas Fuller wrote in *The History of the Worthies of England* (1662)[80] that gentry near London 'quickly strip and disrobe themselves of their estates and inheritance'; that in Berkshire estates 'are skittish, and often cast their owners'; that families of northern gentry are longer lasting, though 'northern gentry transplanted into the south, by marriage, purchase or otherwise, do languish and fade away within few generations; whereas southern men on the like occasions moving northward acquire a settlement in their estates with long continuance'. Some, he says, attribute this to distance from London, while he sees it as the effect of thrift and moderate expense.

The Wars of the Roses broke up or reduced some of the greatest estates and families, though their effect in this sense has been exaggerated. However lands escheated to the Crown by forfeitures and those much greater still acquired by Henry VIII's suppression of the monasteries were used by the Crown to endow new men by gift or sale, so that there was in the sixteenth century a large building up of new great estates. Among the greatest surviving from that time to our own are those of the Russells, Dukes of Bedford, the Cavendishes, Dukes of Devonshire, the Cavendish-Bentincks, Dukes of Portland, and the Thynnes, Marquesses of Bath.

One may fancy also that the sixteenth century growth of nationalism and of a certain separation of England from the continent was reflected in the prominence of certain rough hewn types, conspicuous among Holbein's drawings of the courtiers of Henry VIII and in other Tudor portraiture.[81] No doubt they existed earlier, though portraiture did not favour them, and they may equally have been of Norman derivation. We must not forget the great Tudor Welsh influx which by hybridization gave us two giants, Burleigh and Oliver Cromwell.

In this century the dispersal of monastic and other lands, the growth of population and industry and the rebuilding of houses, which now

79 Alan Everitt, 'The Community of Kent in 1640', *Genealogists' Magazine,* Vol. 14, 1963, pp. 229-258.

80 I. 162, 350; II. 554.

81 See also p. 116 n. 111 *infra.*

took place throughout the century, produced a new alignment and spread of social classes. A married clergy begins to grow into a professional class.[82] The division of labour grows more complex in the arts and crafts, trade, administration and property management. At the lower end of the scale poverty, vagrancy and crime increase. Religious division, as we have seen, both reflects and reacts on these social divisions.

In consequence between 1500 and 1600 the social ladder acquires more rungs, and our lateral chains connecting rich and poor, though no less normal and frequent tend to become longer. One contributory cause was perhaps the weakening of parents' control over their children's marriages,[83] which made arranged marriages between old blood and new wealth less general. Thomas Cromwell, the blacksmith's son, who became Henry VIII's chief agent for suppressing the monasteries and the papal power in England, was able to marry his son to a sister of Queen Jane Seymour (Ped. 62). This alliance, however, did not save him from execution at his master's hands two or three years later. But I know nothing comparable in later English history, if only because English royalty now, joining that of Europe, withdrew for about four centuries into an international royal caste.

Another contribution to the appearance, if not the fact, of this trend is the development of kinds of records which reveal to us more clearly the common people; most of all the parish registers, which Thomas Cromwell devised in 1536 after the suppression of the monasteries not, perhaps, without an eye to the need of a despotic government to enumerate and know its subjects. Thus we are brought naturally to a chain of connection based for the first time upon a man whose eminence, though literate, was not clerical, a man who sought and attained but the rank of gentleman, if he was not rather the archetype of Professor Everitt's pseudo-gentry, and yet is 'so sepulchred ... that kings for such a tomb would wish to die'.

Richard Shakespeare, William's grandfather, was a husbandman of Snitterfield, Warwickshire, and a tenant there of Robert Arden of Wilmcote in Aston Cantlow, whose daughter Mary his son John married. These Ardens of Wilmcote belonged, probably, to a remote cadet branch of the knightly Ardens of Park Hall, whose ancestor Thurkill of Arden was the son of Aelfwine, sheriff of Warwickshire in the time of King Edward the Confessor. John Shakespeare became a glover, burgess, alderman and at length bailiff of Stratford on Avon, though his fortunes later declined. In 1596, however, his son William,

---

82 Pp. 124-7 *infra.*

83 Laurence Stone, *The Crisis of the Aristocracy*, pp. 611-2, attributes this trend to the puritan ethic producing an idealized view of love and marriage. C. S. Lewis, *The Allegory of Love*, 1936, traces the descent of the romantic attitude to love and marriage, achieved by Spenser and Shakespeare, from the twelfth century Provençal cult of courtly love.

growing prosperous, applied, as we suppose, on his behalf for a patent of arms for him and in this he is styled gentleman.

The only extant known descendants of John and Mary Shakespeare derive from their daughter Joan, who married a Stratford hatter, William Hart. Her great-grandson was a glazier and plumber. In 1597 William Shakespeare bought from William Underhill, gentleman, a great house in Stratford called New Place, to which he ultimately retired. From this house no doubt his two daughters were married, Susanna in 1607 to Dr. John Hall, according to his epitaph a most skilled physician, and Judith in 1616, two months before her father's death, to Thomas Quiney of a family of Stratford burgesses and tradesmen.

Through the Quiney marriage Shakespeare is linked to his sovereign, Queen Elizabeth, by a lateral chain passing through perhaps nine, perhaps only five other families (Ped. 66 and note p. 262). The doubt turns on whether Katherine wife of Adrian Quiney (d.c.1533) and great-great-grandmother of Thomas, was by birth a Sheldon of Beoley, as Sir Edmund Chambers thought probable.[84] If so, it was her nephew (or possibly great-nephew) Ralph Sheldon, who married Anne, daughter of Sir Robert Throckmorton of Coughton by a sister of Henry, Lord Berkeley, whose son married Elizabeth Cary, a great-granddaughter of William Cary by Mary Boleyn, Queen Elizabeth's aunt.

This chain is a little longer than our earlier examples but the social steps up and down are shallower, the loftiest being the rise of the Shakespeare family itself and the marriage of Anne Boleyn to Henry VIII. If Katherine Quiney's Sheldon origin be not accepted, we come round a longer way through her second marriage to John Combe and the families of Blunt and Clare. That part of the chain between Throckmorton and Shakespeare illustrates the importance and closeness of local links between neighbours or adjoining classes in the ranks below the nobility. With the Throckmorton-Berkeley marriage we pass into the higher ranks whose focus was the Court rather than the neighbourhood. At this date the same pattern could be illustrated a thousand times.

The deep conflicts, religious, social, economic and political, which came to a climax in the Civil War, had divided England in one way and another at least since Henry VIII's divorce and suppression of the monasteries. Elizabeth's masterly tacks and compromises, James's turnabouts and evasions long held off the fatal collision to which Charles succumbed. Yet one might expect that the stresses, which had finally this fatal end, would in some way be reflected in the genealogical patterns of the century and more preceding. Though such reflections can be here and there discerned, they are far less conspicuous, far less pervasive than one might expect.

84 E. K. Chambers, *William Shakespeare*, Vol. II, 1930, p. 133.

One's impression — and it is no more — is of a pattern closely resembling the general English class and social pattern we have thought to discern; hard cores of not impermeable rock, that is of religious or social separateness, forming centres in a slowly shifting maze of shingle and sandbanks, that is of classes or areas with a bias one way or other but actually taking sides according to circumstances. Just as Queen Elizabeth herself had recognised as her cousin a Puritan preacher,[85] whose great uncle had been a cardinal (Ped. 63); just as Burleigh had recognised as kinsman and had helped as such the separatist Robert Browne whom the Congregationalists claim as their founder;[86] (Ped. 67):so Oliver Cromwell himself had a royalist uncle and namesake and was linked by a lateral chain of only three families to a Laud family which was probably that of the Archbishop while Oliver's son's marriage in 1665 linked the Cromwells by a lateral chain of only two intervening families to the Royal Stuarts.[87] Families were often split between King and Parliament. There were many who could never doubt which side was theirs, but many more who were pushed by events and some who took neither side. The Civil War allegiances of localities were largely governed by the local dominance of families and individuals, partly by long term economic and social patterns and partly by a

85 Arthur Hildersham's parents were devout Catholics who intended him for the priesthood, but sent him to Saffron Walden grammar school, where the master indoctrinated him with Puritanism. When his father took him from Christ's College, Cambridge, and tried to send him to Rome, he refused and was sent back to Cambridge by his cousin Henry, Earl of Huntingdon, who later, though he was then neither licensed nor in orders, appointed him lecturer at Ashby de la Zouch, where he preached on Puritan grievances. From this the High Commission suspended him in 1590, but in 1592 he was allowed to preach north of Trent and it is said that even this restriction was later removed through the intervention of the Queen, who called him 'Cousin Hildersham'. His son Samuel was among the Ministers ejected in 1662 (D.N.B.; Calamy).

86 Burleigh and Robert Browne were not blood relations though connected by the marriage of Burleigh's aunt to Browne's step-great-uncle.(Ped. 67)

87 Oliver's grandmother, the wife of Sir Henry Cromwell (D.1603), was the daughter of Sir Ralph Warren, Lord Mayor of London, by Joan (Lake), who married secondly Sir Thomas White (1492-1567), Lord Mayor of London and Founder of St. John's College, Oxford. George White (1569-1586) of Fyfield, Berks, nephew of Sir Thomas, married Mary, daughter of William Laud, joiner of London. Archbishop Laud, who entered Sir Thomas White's foundation, St. John's College, in 1589 and became its President in 1611, was son of William Laud, a clothier of Reading. A lateral chain with only two intervening families (Russell of Chippenham and O'Brien of Thomond) was established between the Protectoral House of Cromwell and the Royal Stuarts by the marriage in 1665 of Oliver Cromwell's son Henry to Elizabeth Russell, the stepson of whose sister (Sarah, Countess of Thomond) Henry, Lord O'Brien (*Complete Peerage* XII, i. 710) had in 1661 married Katherine (Stuart), Baroness Clifton, great-granddaughter of Esmé, Duke of Lennox, a first cousin of Lord Darnley, the father of King James I

geographical relation to the struggle as it developed. To expound this genealogically would be a valuable but a large and distinct exercise.

Though the sixteenth century had been a time when great new fortunes were built up, it was also a time of instability when some great families came to grief or got into difficulties. Professor Stone expounds the temptations to extravagance and the new risks which accompanied new opportunities.[88] Many old rich had had to sell to new families which were thrusting upward with the profits of office, or of the law, trade, farming, industry, speculation or maritime enterprise. The climax of change was reached, he concludes, between 1610 and 1620. Then the market dropped. Land values fell; rents and in due course taxes rose; and small men were harder hit than the great landlords.

When the Civil War and the Interregnum came, the sale of royalists' lands and similar policies, as Mr. Christopher Hill has shown, both pulled down many of the old gentry and played some part in building up a new race of 'improving' gentry.[89] In the later seventeenth and early eighteenth centuries a new building up of great estates took place, assisted by the legal device of the strict settlement, which made the dispersal of property harder. An oligarchy of a hundred or two great noblemen, rich, growing richer and determined that their successors should retain their wealth and eminence, amassed great estates, and built the great houses and furnished them with the great collections, by which they are best remembered. Politically as well as socially they were active, powerful and long successful, maintaining their exclusive pre-eminence from 1700 till after 1780.

Their origins, like those of English noblemen in general, were mixed. Some were descended in the male line from the mediaeval nobility and gentry, some from the new men of the sixteenth and seventeenth centuries. These two groups were by 1700 totally intermarried and the greatest were still augmenting their wealth by marriage to city heiresses. However, though there were exceptions, there came now a tendency for these great families to intermarry with one another. They were predominantly Whigs during the long Whig predominance and long after 1780, when Tory power was reborn, Whiggery remained the preserve of these great families.

A member of one of them, George W. E. Russell, wrote that 'Whiggery, rightly understood is not a political creed but a social caste. The Whig, like the poet, is born, not made. Macaulay was probably the only man who, being born outside the privileged enclosure, ever penetrated to its heart and assimilated its spirit . . . When Lord John Russell formed his first Administration [in 1846] his opponents alleged that it was mainly composed of his cousins, and one of his younger brothers was charged with the impossible task of rebutting the accusa-

88 *The Crisis of the Aristocracy, 1558-1641*, pp. 197-8.
89 *Puritanism and Revolution*, 1958, pp. 153-96.

tion in a public speech'. From John, Earl Gower (d.1754), he adds, were said to be descended 'all the Levesons, Gowers, Howards, Cavendishes, Grosvenors, Russells and Harcourts, who walk upon the face of the earth'.[90] Though to these names among his progeny there may, indeed, be added those of Churchill, Fitzroy, Fox, Greville, Cavendish and others, it has yet to be remembered that Earl Gower lived too late to be the ancestor, though he and his were kinsmen of many more intermarried Whig families (Peds. 71-2). The pedigree which exhibits a small arbitrary selection of these links would need to be five or ten times the size to approach exhaustiveness.

The predominance of these families is also seen in the fact that out of 5,034 members of the House of Commons between 1734 and 1832, 382 (that is one in every thirteen) belonged to thirty one families only.[91] Their political power and cohesion lasted well beyond the middle of the nineteenth century but then faded. When Bertrand Russell died in 1970 he was more than once referred to as the last of the Whigs. By this, I think, was meant that his was the last powerful, public voice within the circle of these families to express something like their old self confident aristocratic reformist ethos. The families continue and some of their influence and much of their wealth remain to them, but they no longer dominate and their members seem to be now assimilated to modes of thought deriving from other sources.

To see where the new rivals for power, wealth and leadership came from we must look far back and take account of a further element in social movement. We may call this the theory of new ground, for it is by looking for and occupying unoccupied ground that the hitherto unsuccessful, the disinherited, build up for themselves new strength, new strongholds, from which in time they issue to turn the tables on those who excluded them.

It was held that a villein who fled from his lord's manor to a town and lived there uncaptured for a year and a day was legally free. The charters of some early boroughs record their claim to admit such fugitives, though this was sometimes disputed. Other villeins might leave with their lord's consent and pay him for the privilege. For freemen movement into the towns was easier and frequent. The proportion of these immigrants into the towns who made their fortune there was small, and out of these that of the families which survived to return as landowners to the country was smaller, yet amounted to a

90 George W. E. Russell, *Collections and Recollections*, 1903, pp. 75-6.

91 Manners 21; Townshend 17; Buller, Finch & Fitzroy 15 each; Cavendish, Fane, Stuart (Bute), 15 each; Grenville, Spencer, 13 each; Bouverie, Ponsonby, Stuart (Galloway), Yorke, 12 each; Cavendish-Bentinck, Leveson-Gower, Paget, Pitt, Seymour, Smith (Carrington), Walpole, 11 each; Lowther, Onslow, Percy, Williams-Wynn, 10 each, See Gerrit P. Judd IV, *Members of Parliament 1734-1832*, Yale U.P., 1955.

steady trickle. Room was made for these and other rising men partly by colonization of new ground such as former waste or forest. Professor Everitt attributes the great setting up of new families and building of great houses in Northamptonshire in Elizabethan times to the opening given them there by extensive sales of Crown lands which had before been forest.[92]

The converse and no less significant situation was that of areas where the population pressed on the means of subsistence, because of increase in the one or decrease in the other. There are indications that because of invasion and immigration from the continent or because of the healthy climate, or of gavelkind tenure,[93] or other causes, the counties of Norfolk and Suffolk became between the eleventh and fourteenth centuries among the most populous in England. The greater number of the parishes and the ancient churches and houses, including many long since ruined churches, support this. Between the fourteenth and sixteenth centuries, the cloth manufacture, perhaps developed to cope with this, coupled with trade by sea, made them also among the richest counties. Witness the sumptuous churches built by the great clothiers. But in the seventeenth century technical and other changes removed the cloth trade to Yorkshire and elsewhere, and closed or reduced the seaports, leaving these two among the poorest of agricultural counties. This, combined with the religious dissent which here as elsewhere seems to have reflected the separate mindedness of the weaving community, must have been among the reasons why so high a proportion of the early settlers in New England came from those parts.

The Civil War, ruining some, made openings for others. The difficulties of the lesser country gentry did not end with the Restoration. For some of them debts accumulated till the sale of their lands was their only recourse and they departed to the towns or overseas or simply sank in the social scale. The heralds making visitations of counties at intervals of twenty or thirty years noted the disappearance of old names as well as the arrival of new ones. Gregory King, comparing the Derbyshire record of 1663 with the situation of 1687, noted that 'Nath: Bate of Little Chester, hath issue, but he sold all and died dead poor'; 'Robert Draper of Coland, decayd', 'Capt. Hope dyed a beggar,' 'Henry Houlden of Weston upon Trent, sold all or most, yet there is a Barr^r. a Rich parson and a Grasier remaining'. 'Bradshaw of Litton, a Derbysh Family, a Wollen Draper in P[aul's] Ch[urch]yard and several sons now remaining in London and at Litton'.[94] It is interesting, however, that these four were not established in 1663. Had the older trees in general the deeper roots and greater endurance?

92 Alan Everitt, 'Social Mobility in Early Modern England,' *Past and Present*, 1966, p. 66
93 P. 14, *supra*.
94 MS. in my possession, See pp. 45 *supra* and 112 *infra*.

Men in the law, trade, manufacture and (in Derbyshire especially) mining were stepping up to take the places of those who fell by the way. 'Mr. Jno. Burroughs was a sope boyler in Derby now dwells at Holland near Ashbourne, hath a great estate.' 'Mr Rob Heywood of Carsington a lead merchant a good Estate, he hath a son near Bucklersbury named Samll. Heywood a Norwich factor': 'Mr John Turner of Swanwicke near Alfreton several hundreds per ann. married Dr. Thoroton's daughter, his father a rich collyer.'

I suggested earlier (p. 104) that to discover the sources of the new families who came to wealth and power on the flood tide of industrial and other changes of the later eighteenth and the nineteenth centuries, we should look at those who in the centuries preceding, lacking outlets of the familiar kind for their energies and abilities, had sought to exercise these on new ground; upon previously unexploited land at home and overseas; in new developments of trade, craft and mechanism, and in due course in the refined forms of these called the professions; often, though by no means always, expressing the ethos of their new way of life in some new form of religion or political outlook.

The relative looseness of the social structure made it often possible for men of enterprise to move on to such new ground while still keeping links and sympathies with occupants of the old. Manufacturers still aspired to return to the land as gentry. Emigrants to America and Australia kept and renewed family links with their land of origin and continued through the generations to return to trace these. Immigrants from the continent slowly or quickly formed links by marriage, which enlisted them in the old pattern. Not only before and afterwards but at the height of the Whig oligarchy this happened easily.

Peter Godde (d.1716) of Westminster, a modestly successful Huguenot refugee, had, with a son Henry (1702-64), a daughter Frances (1694-1769), who became tirewoman to Queen Caroline, having previously (in 1715) married Richard Pigot (d.1729) of Peploe, Shropshire, and borne him three remarkable sons. George Pigot (1719-77), the eldest, entered the East India Company's service in Madras as a writer in 1737, rose to be clerk of the Court of Appeals there in 1742 and was made Governor and Commander in Chief of Madras in 1755. Resigning that office, in 1763, he was made a baronet in 1764 and Baron Pigot of Patshull in the Peerage of Ireland in 1766. He presented a cheetah from India to George III and about 1765 commissioned from George Stubbs a painting of it with two Indian attendants, which his family sold in 1970 for £220,000.[95] In 1775 he was again made Governor of Madras but died in 1777, while in a disagreement with his Council so serious that they had arrested him. The Pigot diamond, which had been his and weighed 188 grains, was disposed of by a lottery under Act of Parliament in 1800 for £23,998. Ali Pasha of Jannina bought it in

95 Sotheby's Picture Sale of 18 March 1970, lot 30.

1818, but ordered that at his death it should be crushed to powder, which, in 1822, it was.

The next brother, Robert (1720-96), who succeeded under a special remainder to Lord Pigot's baronetcy, was a soldier who fought at Lexington and Bunker's Hill and was made Lieutenant-General in 1782. The third brother, Hugh (1722-93), entered the Navy as an able seaman and rose to be Admiral of the Blue, a Lord of the Admiralty and Commander in Chief in the West Indies. In 1769 he married as his second wife Frances, daughter of the Very Reverend Sir Henry Wrottesley, seventh baronet and Dean of Worcester. Her mother was a daughter of the first Earl Gower (p. 104 *supra*) and a granddaughter of the first Duke of Kingston. Her sister was Duchess of Grafton (wife of the Prime Minister) and her aunt was Duchess of Bedford. Meantime (before 1729) Henry Godde, Mrs. Pigot's brother, had married the daughter of John Jackson, oilman, of Westminster. Thus in the heyday of the Whig oligarchy the nephew of an oilman's son in law who had risen by naval service could marry into its heart. Furthermore the Admiral's first cousin Mary Wilhelmina Godde married the King's hatter, George Wagner (1722-96),[96] son of a German immigrant, who on his mother's side had a cousin married to a bricklayer (Ped. 70). A still closer connection between high and low arose from the marriage to a Reading carpenter about 1728 of the widowed sister in law of the brother in law of the Duke of Wharton, herself a coheir in her issue of the Barony of Berners.

If my view of the case is right, close connections between high and low are liable to be turned up anywhere, at any date, in England when the records are full enough and sufficiently extensive work is carried out. Such work is done by genealogists who pursue all the links of their own families and by those others who set out to reconstitute the whole milieu of a great literary figure, as Sir Edmund Chambers did for Shakespeare. It is therefore no surprise to find the characteristic pattern emerging from the ten volumes of Alleyn Lyell Reade's *Johnsonian Gleanings*.

We have noticed the link between Johnson and his scorned, disdainful patron Chesterfield through the marriage of Johnson's cousin Parson Ford to Judith Crowley, whose step-greatniece married Chesterfield's brother. Besides this Johnson himself, son of a bookseller and grandson of two yeomen, had as first cousins — children of his father's brother — a labourer, a currier, an apprentice tinplate worker and a flaxdresser's wife. The labourer's sons were a stationer and a woolcomber and the woolcomber's son a framework knitter and publican (Ped. 73).

96 My own ancestor. The Admiral's wife's aunt, the Duchess of Bedford, was my wife's ancestress. EG. II, 260, 266.

By contrast Johnson's father's sister Catherine (c.1650-1725) was (it is almost certain) married as a young woman to an elderly physician of ancient family, Gerard Skrymsher (1618-1700) of Woodseaves in High Offley, Staffordshire — the equivalent in reverse, perhaps, of the marriages of rich widows to penniless young men. Their descendants were people of substance, their daughter Hester marrying in 1705 Thomas Boothby, (1686-1752) of Tooley Park in Peopleton, Leicestershire, 'a great sportsman, celebrated in the history of foxhunting'.[97]

Through Dr. Gerard Skrymsher's sister-in-law, the lateral chain from Johnson and his labouring cousins moves rapidly into loftier spheres. Her uncle, John Egerton, Earl of Bridgwater (c. 1579-1649), married a daughter of the Earl of Derby, whose mother was a greatniece of King Henry VIII. Her brother Francis Leigh, Earl of Chichester, married a step-niece of the royal favourite, George Villiers, Duke of Buckingham; while their daughter married Thomas Wriothesley, Earl of Southampton, the son of Shakespeare's patron. Through the Boothby, Clopton, Combe and Quiney families a longer lateral chain links Samuel Johnson to Shakespeare.

Within the circle of these rising families the prosperous dissenters to some extent formed a separate enclave, because for a century and a half their nonconformity cut them off from the universities and from public office. This concentrated their energies on banking, trade and industry, which combined with their frugal habits to enrich them. One must not, however, overrate their segregation. Not only was the time of their exclusion short by the time scale of social and genetic history, but there was, in true English fashion, a good deal of passing to and fro across the religious barrier. Some rich dissenters, their fortune made, returned to the Established Church. Some without doing so took brides from or gave their daughters in marriage to it.

The connection of dissent with industry continued and grew from the sixteenth century to the nineteenth, but neither this link nor the link between religious dissent and social exclusion must be pressed too hard. Their importance for our present purpose lies with that minority of dissenters whose abilities qualified them for a leadership which, because of their nonconformity, they could not take in political or public life. To these, manufacture in an unincorporated town such as Birmingham, free from civic and guild restrictions, at first offered optimal opportunity. But as they prospered so were they tempted to return to the fold of the Established Church and play their parts on a larger stage.

Professor Darlington points to the leading part played by the Unitarians and the Quakers, whose 'sceptical and rigorous intelligence

97 A. L. Reade, *Johnsonian Gleanings, Pt.X, Johnson's Early Life*, 1946, pp. 164-5.

underlay the greatest developments'. He argues that among them 'a new and genetically contrasted governing class grew up, with hardly more scientific enterprise than the Church of England's establishment but corresponding to it in wealth and preparing to challenge it in political power'. These groups, he says 'digging themselves in, became an alternative establishment based on their separately intermarried genetic communities', until at the end of the nineteenth century the beliefs which separated them began to crumble and amalgamation began.[98] This indeed, as he points out, had happened earlier in many single instances. Indeed it may be questioned whether the family separateness between the Established Church and protestant dissent ever came to be nearly as deep as that between Roman Catholic and Protestant or between Jew and Christian.

Ambrose Crowley (1633-1721) of Stourbridge, Worcestershire, was a dealer in iron and had become a Quaker by 1658 when his son and namesake was born. He disclaimed any right to gentility or arms at the Heralds' Visitation of Worcestershire in 1681/2. The only son of his first marriage, Sir Ambrose Crowley (1658-1713), came to London, where he became immensely rich, trading as an ironmonger, and reverted to the Established Church. He was knighted in 1707 when Sheriff of London. His monument at Mitcham, Surrey, tells us that his 'numerous family[sic] and great estate were the present rewards of an indefatigable industry' and application to business, an unblemished probity, and a sincere belief and practice of true Christianity, and particularly a boundless liberality towards the poor, many hundreds of whom he continually employed.

He is said to have been the original of Addison's satire in the Spectator for 12 February 1712: 'I am a person of no Extraction, having begun the World with a small Parcel of rusty Iron, and was for some years commonly known by the name of "Jack Anvil". I have naturally a very happy genius for getting Money'. Jack Anvil, having made a considerable fortune by trade, is knighted and and marries 'an indigent young Woman of Quality', who makes him change his name to Enville.

By his will Sir Ambrose left his four daughters £10,000 apiece in South Sea stock and bonds. One of them married a Lord Mayor of London, one a baronet, and the youngest the tenth Lord St. John of Bletso. Their brother John Crowley (1680-1727) became an alderman of London. One of his daughters married Sir William Stanhope (d.1772), brother of Samuel Johnson's patron Lord Chesterfield. Another (with a fortune of £200,000) married John, Earl of Ashburnham (1724-1812).

---

98 C. D. Darlington, *The Evolution of Man and Society*, 1969, pp. 513-4.

Meanwhile the old Quaker of Stourbridge, Ambrose Crowley (1635-1721) the father of Sir Ambrose, had a large family of sons and daughters by a second marriage. One of the daughters, Judith (1681-post 1732), married (c.1724) a clergyman, the Rev. Cornelius Ford (1694-1731), better known as Parson Ford, the first cousin of Dr. Samuel Johnson, and as 'the parson who sits next to the punch-bowl in Hogarth's *A Midnight Modern Conversation*'. But two at least of the daughters remained Quakers, marrying the two sons of Charles Lloyd (1637-98) of Dolobran, Montgomeryshire, who became a Quaker in 1662. He, having suffered much persecution, settled eventually in Birmingham, while his brother Thomas, (1640-94), likewise a Quaker, settled in Pennsylvania. Sampson Lloyd (1664-1724), son of Charles and of his wife Mary Crowley had a daughter Olivia (1707-75), of whom Dr. Johnson was enamoured when she was eighteen years old. From her brothers, Charles Lloyd (1696-1741) and Sampson Lloyd (1699-1779) of Birmingham descend the Lloyds of that place, founders of Lloyd's Bank and notable for their humanitarian, religious and mercantile activities. Charles Lloyd married Sarah Carless, whose grandfather Richard Carless is thought to have been a legatee and kinsman of Col. William Carless or Carlos (d.1689), who hid Charles II in the oak tree at Boscobel. The Carless family were connected also with Johnson's friend Edmund Hector.[99]

The Lloyds of Birmingham remained Quakers until Sampson Samuel Lloyd (1820-99) was baptised at St. Peter's Birmingham in 1853. He became Member of Parliament for Plymouth in 1874 and bought back the family property of Dolobran and the old Friends' Meeting House there in 1877. His grandson, George Ambrose Lloyd (1879-1941), director of Lloyd's Bank, Governor of Bombay and High Commissioner for Egypt, was created Baron Lloyd in 1925 and married a first cousin of the Earl of Harewood, the son in law of King George V (Ped. 68).

A younger son of Sampson Lloyd (1699-1779) was Charles Lloyd (1748-1828), who appears in the *Dictionary of National Biography* as a Quaker, banker and philanthropist. His son Charles Lloyd (1775-1839) was a minor poet and a friend of Samuel Coleridge and Charles Lamb, while his daughter Priscilla (d.1815) married the Rev. Christopher Wordsworth (1774-1847), Master of Trinity College, Cambridge, brother of William Wordsworth the poet (1770-1850) and father, by her, of the two bishops Charles Wordsworth (1806-1892) and Christopher Wordsworth (1807-1885). The Lloyds and the other Quaker banking families of Hanbury, Gurney, Barclay and Buxton were

99 Alleyn Lyell Reade, *The Reades of Blackwood Hill . . . with a full account of Dr. Johnson's Ancestry . . .1906, pp. 151-2, 158-178: The Dictionary of Welsh Biography down to 1940*, 1959, pp. 570-1; Coll. Arm. Reg. Norfolk XVIII, p. 132.

intermarried, but the other marriages of these families were not confined either to Quaker or to banking families.

A second important dissenting group of late eighteenth century formation was that of the Birmingham Unitarians, including the linked families of Kenrick, Beale, Martineau, Chamberlain and Nettlefold. But these families also had links by blood and marriage outside their own community (Ped. 33). They were drawn to Birmingham by business and religion, from different places, as Protestants from different countries were drawn to sixteenth and seventeenth century Geneva. Archibald Kenrick (1760-1835) was a scion of petty nonconformist gentry in Denbighshire. He came to Birmingham about 1780 and there became an Unitarian. In 1791 he set up an iron foundry at West Bromwich with which his family is still connected. Though sending sons to Rugby and Oxford since 1887, they remain Unitarians and have never figured in Burke's *Landed Gentry* nor obtained a grant of arms.[100]

Three of Archibald Kenrick's granddaughters married into the Chamberlain family, which sprang from a maltster of Lacock, Wiltshire, whose son Joseph (1752-1837) (the first of four generations of boot and shoe manufacturers in the City of London) married Martha Strutt. Her uncle Jedediah Strutt (1726-97) had in 1756 invented a machine for making ribbed stockings and in 1771, with Richard Arkwright, built the first water powered spinning mill at Cromford in Derbyshire. The Strutts remained in the Church of England. Jedediah's grandson was created Lord Belper in 1856 and his great-granddaughter is Lavinia, Duchess of Norfolk.

The Chamberlains became Unitarians and Martha (1794-1866), daughter of Joseph and Martha (Strutt), married in 1819 John Sutton Nettlefold (1792-1866), of a family of London leathersellers and coal-meters, originally from Surrey. J. S. Nettlefold, likewise an Unitarian, founded the Birmingham screw manufacturing firm which grew into Guest, Keen and Nettlefold. In 1854 Joseph Chamberlain put his eighteen year old son and namesake into this firm, as the representative of his own interest in it, and it was this Joseph Chamberlain (1836-1914), the third, who became Lord Mayor of Birmingham, President of the Board of Trade, Secretary of State for the Colonies and a major political force. Two of his three wives were Kenricks. His son, Sir Austen Chamberlain, was sent to Rugby in 1878 and was granted arms in 1926 (for his grandfather's descendants), having been made a Knight of the Garter in 1925. Frederick, son of John Sutton Nettlefold had been granted arms (for his father's descendants) as far back as 1866. Both the Chamberlain and the Nettlefold families appeared in

100 *The Dictionary of Welsh Biography down to 1940,* 1959, pp. 533-4; J. E. Griffith, *Pedigrees of Anglesey & Caernarvon Families,* p. 277; *Chronicles of a Nonconformist Family. The Kenricks of Wynne Hall, Exeter and Birmingham,* ed. Mrs. W. Byng Kerrick, 1932; R. A. Church, *Kenricks in Hardware. A Family Business — 1791-1966,* 1969.

Burke's *Landed Gentry* in 1965. A grandson of J. S. Nettlefold was sent to Rugby in 1888.[101]

Gaston Martineau, a Huguenot refugee surgeon, settled about 1690 in Norwich, where his son, grandson and great-grandson were likewise surgeons and latterly Unitarians. The last of these had no son and his brothers went different ways. Three sons became brewers in London, one a partner in Whitbread's brewery, and three lines of their descendants have figured in Burke's *Landed Gentry*. The youngest son, Thomas Martineau (1764-1826), a Unitarian and a manufacturer of camlet and bombazine in Norwich, was the father of two figures of some eminence, Harriet Martineau (1802-76), the writer, and James Martineau (1805-1900), the Unitarian divine.[102] Another son, Robert (1798-1870), moved to Birmingham, of which his son, grandson and great-grandson have been Lord Mayor, the first of these marrying into the Kenrick family.[103]

A connected and no less powerful element in the displacement of landowning as the basis of entry to the upper classes was the growth of a non-landowning element within the class of the gentry. We have seen that from the thirteenth century or earlier men could rise by favour, administrative skill, trade, speculation and otherwise from lower stations in life into the upper ranks. Then and long after, however, it was a part of this acceptance that they should acquire lands and manors and become not just equal to the country gentry but actually country gentry. In the later seventeenth century, however, a class become much in evidence to which, as we have noted,[104] Professor Everitt has given the name of pseudo-gentry, 'that class of leisured and predominantly urban families who, by their manner of life, were commonly regarded as gentry, though they were not supported by a landed estate.'

Gregory King, then Rouge Dragon, noted from letters of Francis Sandford, Lancaster Herald, among 'Persons for Grants' — that is, eligible for grants of arms — in Derbyshire in 1686-7. 'Bagnold (Jn[o].) Town Clerk of Derby an Attorney looks high' and Mr. Horne of Butterly, another Cole Merch[t]. near Alfreton in Derbysh. though he was a poor Colliers boy yet now proud and ambitious and exalts his home as high as any of his Neighbours, his son hath lately married a Citizens da[r]. with a prettie good portion, a letter by Derby bag will find him'.[105] 'Mr. Chambers of Derby a rich attorney, Sir Jn[o]. Shore

101 Austen Chamberlain, *Notes on the Families of Chamberlain and Harben*, 1915: J. L. Garvin, *The Life of Joseph Chamberlain*, Vol.I, 1932; Burke's *Landed Gentry* 18th ed. pt.i, 1965.

102 Walter Rye, *Norfolk Families*, 1913, pp. 537-8; D.N.B., Harl. Soc., Vol.39, p. 1107; Burke's *Landed Gentry*. 2nd, 3rd, 4th, 8th & later edns., Coll. Arm. Reg Norfolk XLI, p. 9.

103 *D.N.B.*

104 P. 46 *supra*.

105 P. 105, *supra*: A. R. Wagner, *Heralds of England*, p. 313 and MS. in my possession there cited.

married his dau^r and Mrs. Joseph Parker of Derby another dau^r;' 'Joseph Parker of Derby is said to be worth 8 or 10,000 *l.* his father was a Baker'. The next chapter deals with another group within this class.[106] As the eighteenth century wore on, the non-landed gentry — or pseudo-gentry — acquired an ever larger stake in the country and more firmly rooted status, while the nineteenth century saw the development from earlier roots of an institution for completing their qualifications and credentials, and indeed for producing them — the Public Schools.

The principle was not new. Sons of aspiring parents in earlier days sometimes acquired manners and accomplishments as well as learning by being put to clerkly service in noble households. But the growth of population and wealth, with a general increase of the pace of life, made a market for quicker mechanisms of social adaptation. G. D. H. Cole, discussing the nineteenth century progress of the middle classes, notes how newly rich dissenters were assimilated to gentility through the public schools,[107] as we have seen Birmingham manufacturers sending their sons to Rugby.

The coming, with the nineteenth century, of a vast growth of population and the spread to a large part of this of new wealth, produced, by mere numerical multiplication, a longer gradation and greater spacing out of classes, though fortified, I do not doubt, by the determination of each class to cling to its position and standards, old or new, in the midst of flux. Unexpected lateral chains linking class to class continue, however, as before, though these factors make them longer. Upward moves from class to class become more frequent than ever.

At this point it becomes possible to exhibit the nature of the movement with something clearer and more complete than a lateral chain. Some years ago my friend Mr. Marc Fitch allowed me to use the material he had assembled on the history and genealogy of his family to illustrate an earlier work.[108] He now permits me to draw on the same source for my present purpose. The Fitch pedigree here shown (Peds. 74-5) begins with Richard Fitch, a yeoman of Steeple Bumpstead, Essex, who died in 1494. He was related, though it is not known exactly how — and it may have been fairly distantly — to a somewhat richer yeoman family of the name in neighbouring Wicken and Widdington, which made the upward passage into the gentry by a marriage about 1490 to the heiress of a small property in Lindsell near by. The senior line sprung from this marriage appears with arms in the seventeenth century Heralds' Visitation books. Their younger branches

106 P. 123 *infra.*
107 Studies in Class Structure, 1955, pp. 43-4.
108 EG (1960), pp. 192-6.

entered the professional class and an extant line descends from an early New England settler.[109]

The progeny of Richard of Steeple Bumpstead were more numerous and mostly poorer. They subsist at the present day in many known branches and no doubt in many more which are not known. None of them appears in the Heralds' Visitations, but one junior line achieved a baronetcy in 1688, and the baronet's younger brother became a country gentleman whose male progeny continued till the early nineteenth century. It is now, through a female line, represented in the higher peerage. Two yeoman branches sent sons to University before 1700. They became clergymen but one left no issue and that of the other, whose son was an attorney, is not now known.

From a cadet line of dissenting small farmers at Great Dunmow, spring branches in a variety of stations in life. Some went down, some went up, some went overseas; but it is perhaps characteristic of an Essex family that the common fate was to go to London — though escaped by a Felstead farmer, who after trying a draper's shop in Bures, migrated in 1851 to New Zealand. Samuel Fitch, farmer of Chigwell in 1813, was a labourer two years later and in 1851 his son was a coachman of Nottingham Place, Stepney. Samuel's nephew George (c.1799-1872) was a farmer of Romford. His son was a milkman in Hackney, his brother a pork butcher, first in Whitcomb Street, Westminster, then in Crawford Street, Marylebone. Charles (b.1794), a first cousin of Samuel, was a porter in St. Bride's parish in the City of London in 1851.

The descendants of another of Samuel's cousins had more worldly success. James Fitch (1762-1818), whose brothers were a farmer in Writtle and an innkeeper in Whitechapel, opened a cheesemonger's shop at 83 Leadenhall Street, two doors from St. Catherine Creechurch, in 1784. His nephew George (1780-1842), the Writtle farmer's son, succeeded to this, but in 1827-8 the business nearly succumbed to the depression which followed the Napoleonic war. However a dissolution of partnership and move to 66 Bishopsgate Within, were followed by an improvement, from which the firm (now Fitch Lovell Ltd., with assets exceeding £20m.) has never looked back. George's son Frederick (1814-1909) moved in the late 1840s to Hadleigh House in the semi-rural, newly developed Highbury New Park. From 1894 this branch of the family appears in Burke's *Landed Gentry*.

It is not the social variety which seems to me so unusual in the Fitch family pattern as our full knowledge of it. Genealogists ordinarily concentrate their efforts on tracing direct ancestries and the closer and more notable collaterals. To trace the more obscure collaterals is not only thought unrewarding but can be very difficult. To anyone but a

109 Ib. pp. 192-3.

true genealogist of exceptional persistence the labour of pursuing these obscure Fitch branches from parish to parish in Essex and into London would have seemed disproportionate. With a commoner surname the task might in any case have proved impossible.

Though I know no other instance so fully worked out, I am clear that the social pattern this pedigree reveals is repeatedly paralleled by smaller sections of pedigree otherwise known and may be taken as typical of a major element of the English social structure; of that broad band, namely, of middling families of whom some branches have moved up, while more have moved down and others have stayed where they began. To demonstrate this pattern in an agnatic stem a prolific family with a rare surname is needed. To trace *all* descendants of a given couple many generations back, by female lines as well as male, is a task which has been attempted, but not, to my knowledge, achieved save where social elevation has confined the progeny within a limited circle.

The prevalence of the pattern can be tested in another way by tracing complete (or as near as possible complete) ancestries of individuals. I have written something of this elsewhere.[110] Little work has been done in this field in relation to its size and I can give no more than an impression. For what it is worth my impression is that, if one could trace the sixty four ancestors in the fifth generation back of any gentleman or non-royal nobleman of the nineteenth or twentieth century, one would find among them in every case one or more and in some cases many members of the middle or lower classes. In support of this I would mention the simple fact that in all the cases where I have seen it attempted there are either positive instances or else gaps in the record which at least show that the missing ancestors were not members of well known families. My conclusion is that the slow and limited but steady infusion of new blood from below into the upper classes is an immemorial and uninterrupted English phenomenon.

If we take it that these patterns are typical, what tentative conclusions can we draw as to their effect upon or relationship to social and political history? I speak only of tentative conclusions because the facts at present known appear too slight to justify firm conclusions. On that footing the most obvious suggestion is that the absence, on the one hand, of lasting barriers between groups and classes, with the frequency of hidden links and bridges between them on the other, have produced a situation in which great changes have from time to time been possible with a minimum of violent upheaval. For a nation with a temperamental or climatic need for periodical violent revolution and political drama this would be a drawback, but it seems on the whole to suit the English, with their rain and mists — and their tolerance.

110 EG. (ii. 1972). pp. 231-3.

A question one would like answered is whether this social pattern tends to bring particular types of men to the top.[111] To discuss this we must roughly classify the types to be considered. Let us call them the military, the adventurous, the administrative, the judicial, the money-getting and ambitious, the demagogic, the theocratic, the subtle, the decorative and the creative. The Norman warriors, who established the pattern, were military adventurers, but adventurers of the hard headed kind, pursuing defined objectives rather than adventure for adventure's sake. They had, further, a strong sense of cohesion and a marked capacity for using abilities different from their own. Hence administrative and mercantile gifts were from the first means of rising, but especially if their possessors had also that deferential temperament which disposed them to accept and support the system they found. That the two gifts were not unconnected is suggested by the emergence of some notable administrators from merchant families.

Demagogic talent — so destructive elsewhere — this system has kept in its modest place. Wat Tyler, John Wilkes, Horatio Bottomley and their like have stirred things up without achieving responsibilities for which they were unfitted. We have not had to suffer the rule of a Cleon, a Savonarola, a Danton or a Hitler.

In the cultivation and application of creative talent in the arts there have been marked alternations. In England kings with the gift of taste have too often been ineffective kings. Henry III, Richard II, Henry VI and Charles I are examples. But the special impulses given to the arts by those kings did not die with them. The best artists have often, though not always, come from families bred and trained in the arts over some time. The existence of such families only, I think, arises from sustained fashions of taste and expenditure.

There are many other instances of a particular cause or movement gaining strength through the acquirement of power by a ruling group or ruler who had it at heart. The rise and fall of puritan aesthetic attitudes can be seen in these terms. So can the rise of tolerance, of humanitarianism, indeed of almost any fashion one may think of in morals, knowledge, the arts, the crafts, and in attitudes to government and the social order. Define the movement, list its prime movers, then look for their origins and relationships.

Can we look deeper into our pattern and its consequences by trying to see in it the kind of family types and structures which Frédéric le Play (1806-1882) thought he discerned in the population as a whole? His scale runs from the patriarchal family at one extreme, in which the

111 May we hope that the anthropologists may be able in time to sort out for us more closely these types, both psychological and physical. As Margaret Mead reflected in 1931 (*Blackberry Winter. My Earlier Years*, 1972, p. 216), 'What if human beings, innately different at birth, could be shown to fit in to systematically defined temperamental types', with male and female versions, and if a society . . . could place its emphasis on one type of temperament . . . ?

whole progeny of the patriarch lives together, to the 'unstable' family of parents and their children only at the other, with his special concept of the *famille souche* or 'stem family' in between. In this middle type, the very existence of which some of his successors questioned,[112] he saw the virtues of the Aristotelian mean; some of the security given by the patriarchal family, without its deadening gerontocracy; some of the unstable family's freedom but with more effective enterprise arising from greater security and an anchor in tradition. Civil liberty and paternal authority, he thought, went together and would collapse together.[113]

Without accepting all this one may see it as a promising approach to the question of the relationship between genealogical patterns and social attitudes. If the society of large, tightly organized kinship units is seen as one extreme and the rootless, atomic, urban-industrial society as the other, it is arguable that the best hope lies in a mean or balance between the two. In political terms this will mean a balance between the hereditary principle of government on one hand and the representative or elective principle on the other. Such a balance, it has been argued, was at times achieved by 'the late lamented British constitution' in which King, Lords and Commons were supposed to check and balance one another. But it follows from this view that the balance will be upset if one of the partners develops weakness. Much history has been written in terms of the strength and weakness of kings and dynasties, but the nature and causes of similar alternations in upper, middle and lower classes have been less explored, at all events on that side which genealogy might illuminate.

Stability has alternated with change at different times for different classes. In the fourteenth century and again in the first two thirds of the eighteenth the position of the great landowners was especially stable and secure. Yet at those very times other classes were involved in upheaval and the stability of the upper class was a factor in the turmoil of the others. In the same way the nineteenth century power and thrust of the middle classes played its part with other factors in that decline of the aristocracy, so well analysed by Mr. W. L. Guttsman,[114] which has taken place in the past century. Though this consequence was feared from the 1832 Reform Bill and still more at the time of that of 1867, the process still took some time to gather momentum, but at length became pronounced, and not least in the weakening of the link between membership of the upper class and the ownership of land. Yet despite this and many more hostile forces the recuperative power of the traditional elements of English society cannot yet be written off. Some readers may share the writer's belief that the hereditary principle being

112 Michael Z. Brooke, *Le Play: engineer and social scientist,* 1970, p. 107.
113 Ib. p. 109.
114 *The British Political Elite,* 1963.

deeply rooted in our biological nature is best held back from more savage manifestations if accorded that respectability and recognition which the English traditional order gave it. If so, they may feel dismay that a balance so long and fruitfully preserved should now be disparaged by its beneficiaries.

That is a matter of opinion. What is certain is that the social and political theories, on which the contrary view rests, rely on grossly imperfect knowledge, certainly on the genealogical side and probably on others. The genealogical omission is due to simple neglect of a huge and important field — a neglect itself probably due to the bias and social attitudes of former genealogists and recent historians. Nor, in my humble opinion, can this omission be made good or circumvented by any process either of mathematical sampling or of simplistic moralization. A virtue of the genealogical approach is that it impels us to see society rather as an organism than as a machine and to make better allowance for its complexity and unexpectedness. It drives us to see men not as mathematical units but as individuals in a human context. We are fortunate to have in England a wealth of records from which genealogies may be traced and clothed in living detail. Let us dignify and understand ourselves by using them to the full.

POSTSCRIPT

The appearance in 1973, since this chapter went to press, of *The Nobility of Later Mediaeval England, The Ford Lectures for 1953 and Related Studies* by the late K. B. McFarlane calls for a note of its bearing on our subject.

McFarlane lists the roads to success in the fourteenth and fifteenth centuries as the Church, the law, service, trade (including industry and finance), the spoils of war and marriage. It was easy for a prelate to promote his kinsmen in the church, harder for him to help lay relations, because it must be done out of his income. But the richest churchmen were those, like Robert Burnell and William of Wykeham, who were more than churchmen and whose wealth was the reward of service to the king (pp. 11-12).

The wealth of the most successful lawyers came to them also largely through their service to the king as judges, e.g. the founders of the families of Scrope of Bolton and Masham, Bourchier, Norwich, Cobham and Howard, and later those of Gascoigne, Paston, Fortescue, Yelverton, Littleton, Catesby and Fairfax (pp. 12-13, 164-6).

At a lower level hereditary service to the nobility, as their private civil servants or household officers, made the fortunes of the Hugfords and the Throckmortons, who served successive Earls of Warwick, the Whitgreaves, who served the Staffords and the Hungerfords and Leventhorpes who served the Dukes of Lancaster (p. 140).

Among merchants of the fourteenth and fifteenth centuries the De la Poles were unique in rising to be Earls or even Barons. Most of the many citizens from the twelfth century to the fifteenth, who prospered and invested in land, settled for the status of gentleman. Had they waited longer, they might have flown higher, but only if they or their issue had not perished first, as so many more seem to have done in towns than in the healthier life in the country (pp. 13-15, 167). On the risks of total extinction of the male line even in the most favourable circumstances and the consequent special advantages accruing to the rare survivors McFarlane's analysis in instructive (pp. 78-80, 142-9).

The means whereby English captains and soldiers in the French wars acquired wealth by ransoms paid for their prisoners, as well as by pay and spoils, are fully analysed and appear a more important source of new wealth than has hitherto been realized (pp. 19-40). One recalls, however, Nicholas Upton's reference of c.1440 to the many poor men who had become noble through their service in the French wars, many of whom had taken arms to be borne by themselves and their heirs.[1]

1 E.G. II; p. 118.

An important change in the possibility of rising in the world by marriage to an heiress (p. 90, *supra*) is shown to have occurred between the earlier and later Middle Ages (pp. 151-2). In 1189 Henry II and Richard I could make the fortune of William the Marshal by giving him Strongbow's daughter and heir in marriage. But by 1300 resistance to the disparagement of heiresses and to the royal right of betrothing infant children had weakened not only the king's position in this matter but that of overlords in general, so that heiresses became rather the subject of bargaining and instead of being used to endow new men were more often married to heirs of fortunes equal to their own. Even kings' younger sons and grandsons were not often or easily so well provided for as were Thomas of Woodstock, the son, and Henry of Bolingbroke, the grandson of Edward III, when they were able to marry the two daughters and coheirs of Humphrey de Bohun, Earl of Hereford and Essex, who had died without a male issue, aged thirty one, in 1373. It was this growing tendency to bring great estates together in marriage which produced in the fifteenth century such vast aggregations of estates, lordships and titles as those of the Nevilles and Staffords, and indeed of the houses of Lancaster and York.

All the same the marriages of obscure men to ladies not at the time in line for great inheritance, but who later became so by failure of senior heirs, could still, in the fifteenth century, promote the offspring of such unions to great estate from relative obscurity. Thus after the death of Anne Mowbray, Duchess of Norfolk, in 1481 her great inheritance passed to the Howard and Berkeley descendants of her great-great-aunts. The chances of such unforeseen promotion were enhanced by the high rate of extinction of male lines, which McFarlane analyses in some detail (pp. 78-80, 142-9). Similar, as we have seen (p. 91 *supra*) was the good fortune of the few families whose male lines happened to survive.

Examples are given of another important exception, which we have already mentioned (p. 89 *supra*) to the rule of arranged marriage, the liberty, namely, of widows, to marry whom they would, which often led to mésalliances. Thus in 1297 Joan of Acre, daughter of Edward I, married secondly, to her father's great displeasure, Ralph de Monthermer, one of the household of her first husband the Earl of Gloucester. Katherine (Neville), Duchess of Norfolk, about 1465, when over sixty, married as her fourth husband Sir John Wydville, aged twenty. Both the Wydvilles and the Tudors, in fact, owed their rise to royal mésalliances (pp. 11, 153).

Important changes in succession law and practice which took place, between 1300 and 1500, must considerably have affected the means and nature of recruitment. Though in 1300, as McFarlane puts it (p. 62), the rights of an eldest son were secure against cadets, and were so again by 1500, there was a phase in between when many possessors had the will and found the legal means to endow younger sons and sometimes even bastards and strangers in blood with portions of their inheritance. The use of entails and the vesting of lands in feoffees for such purposes is expounded (pp. 69-74, 78-82, 276-9), as also the later developments which by 1500 had once again reduced these possibilities. In the interval, however they had produced in late mediaeval England a group of younger sons and even bastards of magnates who became magnates in their own right (p.71), such as John Fitzalan, Lord Maltravers (1408-1435), William Beauchamp, Lord Bergavenny (d.141), Hugh Stafford, Lord Bourchier (d.1431), John, Lord Devereux (d.1393), Thomas Percy, Earl of Worcester (1343-1403) and John Beaufort, Earl of Somerset and Marquess of Dorset (c.1371-1410).

Between heirs female and collateral heirs male the battle went sometimes one way, sometimes the other. When Guy, the eldest son of Thomas Beauchamp, Earl of Warwick, died in his father's lifetime, his daughter Katherine was made a nun and her uncle Thomas succeeded in 1369 to what would have been her inheritance. However, her grandfather Earl Thomas would in any case have diverted much of this from her by entail and conveyance to feoffees (pp. 72-3). On the other hand Sir John Wingfield of Wingfield, Suffolk, settled estates on his daughter (who married Michael de la Pole, (d.1389), later Earl of Suffolk) to the prejudice of his brothers and their descendants.

A growing inclination towards tail male and against inheritance by heirs female is seen by McFarlane as the background to the creation of peerages with remainder to heirs male. What some have seen as a special objection by the Crown to dignities held in fee, he regards rather as a general prejudice 'which kings naturally shared' (p. 273). As new grades of peerage were successively introduced — dukedoms (1337), marquessates (1385), baronies by patent (1387) and viscounties (1440) — it was natural that they should be given remainders accordant with the general trend.

He further associates this introduction of new ranks in the peerage with a general hardening of barriers against too easy mobility and a growth of stratification (pp. 122-5). He cites in evidence the codes of precedence which begin to appear at this time and might have mentioned the sumptuary laws too. However, our own earlier comments[2] suggest some need for caution here. Be this as it may, we owe a great debt to McFarlane's combination of historical learning with that deep interest in 'heraldry, genealogy, and the study of manorial descents', for which he nevertheless felt it necessary, as recently as 1953, to apologize (p. 2), as 'even now slightly disreputable occupations'. The truth is that without the genealogy his analysis of social mechanisms and developments not previously understood would have been impossible.

2 pp. 88, 92, *supra.*

To digest these and the further distillations of McFarlane's work which his editors promise will take time. The question above all questions to which one hopes attention may be directed is that of the detailed effect on governing persons and their government of the special conditions of their selection and survival now revealed. Can an optimum be discerned between too much and too little security of tenure and continuity, between degrees and methods of mobility, between French and English or between thirteenth and fifteenth century norms of noble living? One hopes for some advantage here in the relative freedom of the context from current political obsessions.

CHAPTER V

THE RISE OF THE PROFESSIONAL CLASS: AN ETON MICROCOSM

Social classes other than the highest are so large that exhaustive genealogical study of their origin and growth has not so far proved feasible. We can only, therefore, proceed by sampling and the problem is to extract a true sample. Our first attempts may well be full of fallacies, yet must be made if better is to follow. In the last three centuries a class can be discerned with growing clarity of families addicted to the learned professions. This does not mean that all their members entered those professions. In Victoria's reign, indeed, the alternatives socially open to those members might hardly stretch beyond the armed services, but in earlier times a nabob, a city merchant, and even a tradesman might be brothers to a bishop, dean, or judge. Still, the aspiration of this class was to be gentlemen as well as scholars and by the nineteenth century many families had attained to this.

Where did they come from? How were they moulded? How and how far did they become knit into a coherent group? It seems to me that some answers to these questions may emerge from looking at families attached over generations to some one learned institution and thereby linked, intermarried and assimilated to a common style and ethos. For such a scrutiny a University might be most apt were it not so large and were its continuity not impaired by the celibacy of its members; or an Inn of Court might do, were it less metropolitan. But it seemed at length that a much smaller group, which I know better, might serve the turn, namely that of the Fellows and Masters of Eton College.

Mr. Christopher Hollis in his recent excellent history of the school has dealt somewhat harshly with these.[1] Members of the Fellows' families in the eighteenth century tended, as he points out, to intermarry, and this he attributes to their living in a 'curious isolation'

1 *Eton. A History,* 1960, p. 140.

produced 'by their indeterminate social position in a world in which
social positions were as a rule strictly determinate. For they liked to
think of themselves as gentlemen, whereas other people did not quite
accord them that rank. Therefore it was more convenient for them to
restrict themselves to one another's society'.

This is an interesting diagnosis but, in my view, a mistaken, or at
least, an imperfect one. The mistake in it derives partly, I would argue,
from an insufficiently full examination of the particular facts, but
much more from wrong assumptions about the general social background. These assumptions are of course, in no way peculiar to Mr.
Hollis. He, indeed, has, I take it, adopted them just because they are
general, and need the genealogical approach for their refutation.

The fact is that the eighteenth century Eton fellows' families present
an example of a process widespread in their day, namely the coming
together into a new learned or professional class of families of diverse
origins and their consequent association and intermarriage with one
another. From the point of view of older established classes they might
seem to be neither flesh nor fowl — but that is necessarily the position
of a new class till it has established itself.

While some legal and official families are found earlier, in the service
of the crown, great lords and religious houses, the effective root of the
class we are considering is, I think, to be looked for in the permission to
the clergy to marry, granted in 1548, lost under Mary and restored by
Elizabeth in 1559. Long after it had ceased to apply to the clergy as
such, — till about 1870 indeed — the rule of celibacy was still imposed
on the fellows of Oxford and Cambridge colleges and it might have
been expected still similarly to apply to such a foundation as Eton. In
fact, however, Edward VI appointed Thomas Smith, a married man, as
Provost in 1547 and it seems that after 1548 some of the Fellows also
married, while William Barker the Headmaster had a Royal Licence in
1551 to retain his post though married. The married Fellows were
expelled under Mary but marriage was permitted again under Elizabeth
and indeed encouraged by the dispensation she gave the Fellows of
Eton on 11 June 1566 each to hold one living of the value of 40 marks,
while still retaining their Fellowships, though this was forbidden by the
Statutes of Henry VI.[2]

From this moment and not merely from the eighteenth century, Eton
family links and groupings began, though, as we shall see, the first,
sixteenth century, intermarried group of Eton families, appears to die
away in the latter part of the seventeenth century and has not so far
been linked with the new grouping of the same kind which then
originated. A part of the Founder's plan having been to furnish the

2 H. C. Maxwell-Lyte, *A History of Eton College*, 1875 pp. 129, 137, 182.
Robert Avis, Fellow 1552-4, was married, but it is not known when. John Johnson,
Fellow 1553, was deprived in 1554 as a married priest.

Church with educated priests, acceptance on the Foundation led on naturally for a large proportion of the scholars to scholarships and then Fellowships at the sister foundation of King's, Cambridge, and thence to Eton or King's livings or to masterships or fellowships at Eton. Furthermore, between 1474 and 1820 forty one Provosts, Vice-Provosts, Fellows, Head Masters, Lower Masters and Assistant Masters were appointed to Canonries at Windsor.[3] Election therefore, to an Eton scholarship at the age of ten or twelve was often, in a modest way, a life provision. This, doubtless, was the Founder's plan. His children were, if possible, to be provided for through life. The Fellows in the period which concerns us were almost all Etonians, but not all though most of the assistant masters were.[4] It is indeed only latterly that the record of these last becomes complete. Before 1698 the names of ten are known, between that date and 1753 we know fifty two, and between 1753 and 1790 twenty eight, the much smaller number in the latter period reflecting longer tenure. Of the ten, three became Fellows of the fifty two, eight and of the twenty eight, thirteen.

Dr. Richard Okes, Provost of King's, wrote in 1869 at the time of the reforms, that the small number of places to be filled and the small number of those electing to the Eton Fellowships had 'led to a snugness in the body and the "family party" principle has been acted upon with very little exception, ever since I have known the place. If there was no *relative* to be served, there was some near friend and pliant person a friend of a friend . . . the Assistant Masters were invariably appointed from King's and in process of time became Fellows. The best Kingsmen, such as Sir John Patteson and others, though few, preferred striving in more active scenes and the choice of good men for Assistants was not great, and as a mediocre man was thought good enough for the place generally, mediocre men were appointed through interest of some friends, or from previous family connexion . . . Old pupils, of former tutors and existing tutors found favour'.[5]

It would be of great interest if we could make a complete analysis of the occupations and ranks from which the masters and Fellows were drawn, but our present information is too imperfect for this, so that we can only form an impression from those origins which we happen to know. Nineteenth century reformers were inclined to argue that such benefactions as King Henry's were meant for paupers but were diverted by later ages to the assistance of a higher class. Sir Wasey Sterry, the editor of the earliest Eton Register will have none of this and points out that the Founder's Statutes themselves in effect define the qualifying

3 S. L. Ollard, *Fasti Wyndesorienses: The Deans and Canons of Windsor,* 1950, p. 163.

4 *Etoniana*, No. 85, 1941, pp. 550-552, R. A. Austen-Leigh, 'The Early Assistant Masters' says that only three Assistants were taken in early times from any College but King's.

5 *Etoniana.* Vol. I. No. 15, 1913, pp. 234-5.

degree of poverty as possession (by the scholar, not his parents) of not
more than five marks a year, which at 10d. a week, as provided by the
Statutes, would provide for a scholar's board for a year and a half, and
was equal to one fifth of the headmaster's then salary.[6] He points
out that the earliest election list, that of 1444, includes children of the
gentry, a Cruwys of Devon, a Catesby of Northamptonshire and a
Yarborough of Lincolnshire. The social strata drawn on down to the
eighteenth century seem in fact to range from sons of the lesser gentry,
through those of officials, clergy and yeomen, to those of local
tradesmen and College servants. All these are represented in the families
which we shall consider more closely. We are not, of course, here
concerned with those sons of the nobility and gentry, who attended the
school but were not on the foundation, since they were not the source
from which the Masters and Fellows were drawn. These lived at their
own expense both in the College precincts and in the town. It should be
noted that the Founder himself had planned for these Oppidans.

The pedigrees which follow are in no way complete pedigrees of the
families in question, being designed to give merely such information as
illustrates the subject here discussed. Accordingly children who were
not at Eton or King's and wives with no Eton or King's connection are
usually omitted.

Pedigrees 76 to 79 show the intermarriages of twelve families who
furnished Eton and King's with fellows between the reigns of Henry
VIII and Charles II, with a postscript in the Montague family running
over into the eighteenth century. The social origins of these families so
far as known range from the minor gentry and yeomen (Day, Montague, Rowe, Woodhall, Bateman) to Windsor and Eton tradesmen
(Goad, Dee), and in this respect they do not differ greatly from those
which follow them, though the contribution of the gentry to the latter
seems rather smaller. Where they do perhaps differ more markedly from
this second crop is in their greater academic distinction. Three bishops,
two Regius Professors and a Vice-Chancellor suggest a level of intellectual attainment which the Eton families did not touch again until the
nineteenth century. In this connection we may note the link with the
family of William Barlow (d. 1568), Bishop of Chichester, whose five
daughters all married bishops.

In this period, no less than later, one notes the advantage enjoyed by
those who chanced to live on the doorstep of a great foundation. Eton
and Windsor tradesmen and College servants and tenants clearly had
certain chances, if they cared to use them, of getting their sons elected
as scholars on King Henry's foundation. The same pattern could, I
think, be worked out in relation to Oxford and Cambridge Colleges, as
earlier in relation to *monastic* foundations. It is a part of the great
general importance in former times of the ties of neighbourhood,

6 Sir Wasey Sterry, *The Eton College Register 1441-1698*, 1943, p. xiv.

service and tenancy. Crown servants came from Crown manors, College servants from College manors and so forth.

It is curious that despite such links as these, making for continuity, there seems on present evidence to be a definite breach between our first and our second group of intermarried families. This may be mere accident, yet one cannot but think in this connection of Mr. Gladstone's dictum that 'the palmy days of the College ended with the Revolution of 1688. After that almost everything was sacrificed to nepotism and favouring. The College became exclusive and insignificant'.[7] The reference here is to the successful assertion by the College after 1688 of the right to appoint its own members which the Crown had previously breached. Such reassertion by corporations of their rights as against the Crown was characteristic of the period and contributed here as elsewhere to nepotism and particularism. Nevertheless our second group of families, though initially, perhaps, less distinguished, in time, as we shall see, produced scions of some eminence.

In both these groups, at all events, we see at work three of the factors which build up new classes; first the attraction from diverse sources to a specific way of life of individuals suited to it by ability and temperament; secondly their marriage into the families of others of the same kind; and thirdly the recruitment of their children to their way of life. In the new grouping which began after the Revolution the second of these factors grew into something almost distinct in kind — a largely self-contained community on a basis at once social and geographical. It would seem that by the end of the seventeenth century the Eton community had grown large enough to provide its own marriage market and accordingly we now encounter a linkage of Eton Fellows' and masters' families on a much greater scale than before, continuing strongly from that time onwards down to the abolition of the resident fellows in 1877, and leaving vestiges even at the present day. There were of course still many fellows and masters who did not marry into this connection. There were also some continuing Eton families which did not do so. Yet these last are in more than one case found to be fairly closely linked with the main group through marriages with families of the same sort outside Eton, thus confirming that this Eton nexus was a section and microcosm of a growing class in the country at large.

To link the distinguished Lyttelton group with the rest of Pedigree 84, we have in fact, as will be seen, gone away from Eton (through Pedigree 83) and returned there. In the same way the Thackeray group of Pedigrees 91-3 is joined to Pedigrees 88-90 only through the external

7 Observations by W. E. Gladstone on Maxwell Lyte's 'History of Eton College', 1875, quoted in *Etoniana*, No. 115. (1954), pp. 231-2. In the course of these Gladstone admits rather grudgingly the excellence of Disraeli's picture of Eton.

junctions of the Plumptre and the Stephen families. It might well be,
however, that more extensive searches than I have made would link
many more Eton families to the main body.

Lord Annan has written[0] memorably of an 'intellectual aristocracy' formed by the intermarriages in the nineteenth and twentieth
centuries of middle class families of a particular type. He dwells
especially on the gifted philanthropic families of the Clapham sect,
Gisborne, Babington, Macaulay, Elliott, Venn, Stephen, Thornton and
Wilberforce, and on a group of Quaker families Gurney, Fry, Gaskell,
Hoare, Hodgkin, Fox, and Barclay, some of these intermarried already
before 1800, and tending to secede to the Church of England. He shows
how they and others were drawn to Cambridge and thus intermarrying
formed a linked group of outstanding ability. In Pedigree 90 I have shown
a link between the Eton families and this Clapham group through the
Sumner-Bird marriage. I have elsewhere argued[9] that it would be
possible by following such intermarriages further to take the connection into every county and every learned institution in England and in
so doing to give the group character a rather different bias.

I would now make the distinct but related point that Lord Annan's
intellectual aristocracy was the fine flower of a less eminent, but older,
wider and still valuable class, but for whose prior existence that fine
flower could not have blossomed. The class in question is that wider
scholastic class which we have been discussing, the learned clergy and
laymen, and among them the Eton masters and fellows; for the most
part men not of genius but of sound learning; men whose standards,
spreading outward and downward, in manners as well as scholarship,
were the basis of such education as their nation has. It may, however,
here be noted that Eton has had its share of Lord Annan's fine flowers
of intellect. Thackeray, Warre-Cornish, Benson, Conybeare, Howson,
Lyttelton, Lubbock, Hill and Elliott are families on his list, from which
Eton masters have been drawn, and yet others have significant connections there.[10]

Our present quest, however, is not a pursuit of genes or genius but of
the genesis of a class.

The social range of origin is, much as before, from sons of the lesser
gentry, through those of clergy, merchants and yeomen, to the children

8 *Studies in Social History. A Tribute to G. M. Trevelyan*, ed. J. H. Plumb,
1955, VIII, pp. 241-287, N. G. Annan, 'The Intellectual Aristocracy'.

9 *English Genealogy*, I p. 173. II p. 199. For a further interesting series of
intermarriages between such families see the pedigrees at the end of Belinda
Norman-Butler, *Victorian Aspirations. The Life and Labour of Charles and Mary
Booth*, 1972, linking the families of Macaulay, Trevelyan, Potter, Meinertzhagen,
Cripps, Hobhouse, Fletcher, Llewelyn-Davies, Du Maurier, Booth, Ritchie,
Thackeray and Butler.

10 Among other names in Lord Annan's catalogue which also appear in Etonian
contexts are those of Stephen, Hobhouse, Huxley, Darwin, Keynes, Haldane,
Willink, Furse and Wedgwood.

of Eton and Windsor tradesmen and College servants. I have seen it asserted that members of the four professions, the Church, the Armed Services, the Bar and Physic before 1800 were almost without exception either younger sons of the landed gentry or sons of other professional men. It will, however, be clearly seen that this is not true of our present sample and in my experience it is equally untrue in general. I should guess that the proportionate intake from other classes than those two into this class before 1800 was as great as after that date. Edward Hawtrey (Pedigree 80) who entered College about 1617, was the second son of a Buckinghamshire gentleman of ancient Norman lineage but modest estate.[11] The Plumptres (Pedigrees 88, 89, 90) were wealthy burgesses of Nottingham, established there since the Middle Ages and intermarried with the county gentry. Huntingdon Plumptre (1601-60), a famous physician, was the first of his line to engage in learned pursuits. His grandson Henry (1681-1746) was President of the Royal College of Physicians and the academic bent and Cambridge links were well established before the Eton connection began.

The Naylor, Reynolds, Chamberlayne, Newborough and Durnford families all seem to have moved from the yeoman into the clerical class in the seventeenth century before they became connected with Eton. Thomas Thackeray (1693-1760), son of the parish clerk of Hampsthwaite, Yorkshire, became a scholar of Eton in 1706, probably through the help of his uncle Elias, who had himself in 1682 come to Christ's College, Cambridge, as a sizar — an undergraduate, that is, who worked his way through College by menial service to his richer fellows. All the Thackerays save the descendants of Thomas remained in the yeoman and tradesman class in Yorkshire; while Thomas ended as Head Master of Harrow and left a tribe of academic and professional descendants — among them the novelist. Thackerays have been Eton scholars in six generations.

Windsor and Eton tradesmen as before contribute their quota. Joseph Pote (d. 1787, Pedigree 82) acquired the Eton bookshop by marriage, at one time kept a boys' house, had two sons in College and sent one to Eton as an Oppidan. John Foster, son of a Windsor bricklayer, entered College in 1743 and in 1765 became Head Master of Eton, though not the most popular or successful holder of that office.

College servants and their families made good use of their opportunities. It is likely that the son of Edward Wise (d. 1684, Pedigree 82), the College butler, became a boarding master, and *his* son entered College in 1729. One son of Robert Woodward (Pedigree 92), College butler, entered the school as an Oppidan in 1678 and became Chapel clerk, while the other succeeded his father as butler, but left daughters of whom one married Dr. Thackeray, the Head Master of Harrow, and the other first a City linendraper and secondly the Honourable and

11 F. M. Hawtrey, *The History of the Hawtrey Family*, 1903, Coll. Arm. Reg. Norfolk XXVIII, p. 83.

Reverend Nicholas Boscawen, Prebendary of Westminster, eighteenth child of the first Viscount Falmouth. This looks like an instance of the kind of equivalence, which according to the Swiss Jean Rouquet, writing in 1755, every Englishman tests in the pair of scales he keeps always by him, 'wherein he exactly weighs the birth, the rank, and especially the fortune of those he is in company with, in order to regulate his behaviour and discourse accordingly'.[12] Boscawen had birth, his wife, we may suspect, had fortune. He as a nobleman's eighteenth child had sunk into the clerical station. His wife's family through ability and good fortune had risen into it.

The possible subleties of these situations come out well in a passage of the diary of Margaretta Brown, the sister-in-law of Dr. Keate. Referring on the 20th of March 1823 to the attachment formed by the Rev. George John Dupuis (1795-1884), then an Assistant Master (Pedigree 83), for Julia, the daughter of the Rev. William Roberts, the Vice-Provost, she notes that 'the father and mother seemed to approve of the attachment till William came — who has chosen to set his face against it as he thinks an Eton master not a good enough match for Miss Julia. Marry come up! and he was a private tutor'.[13]

George III's bishops, it has been said, were almost without exception either relations of noblemen, former chaplains to noblemen or tutors to their sons. A study of Austen-Leigh's Eton Registers brings out the frequency with which schoolboy friendship between a nobleman's son and a boy of humble origin led in due course to the latter's preferment in Church or State, by way of tutorship or otherwise. Horace Walpole's 'Quadruple Alliance' was a classic case of such friendship. Richard Carter (1751-1843), the ancestor of a notable Eton family (Pedigree 86) was of a yeoman family of Purton in Wiltshire, where they were neighbours and perhaps tenants of Lord Suffolk, whose secretary Richard Carter became. Another distinguished Eton family, the Lux-moores, were the boroughmongers of Okehampton, Devonshire, an activity more easily associated with Charles Scott Luxmoore (1792-1854), Dean of St. Asaph, 'a gigantic pluralist',[14] than with that venerated, ascetic figure, Henry Elford Luxmoore (1842-1926; Assistant Master 1864-1908). Another variant of the pattern was the recommendation of a young scholar as tutor to a nobleman's son by a Provost or Head Master who had been a schoolfellow of the nobleman or one of his family. It was thus that Henry Michell Wagner (K.S. 1808) became tutor to the Duke of Wellington's sons in 1817 on the recommendation of Provost Goodall.[15]

12 Rouquet, *The Present State of the Arts in England*, 1755, p. 17.
13 *Etoniana*, 1940, p. 471.
14 *History of Parliament, House of Commons 1754-1790*, p. 72.
15 *Sussex Archaeological Collections*, XCVII, 1960, p. 46, A. R. Wagner, 'The Wagners of Brighton and their connections'

It was a world in which enterprise might pay, as the edifying tale of Canon John Bostock of Windsor (Pedigree 89) illustrates. His obituary notice,[16] narrates that he 'obtained this preferment without a patron, and without the least prospect in the early part of his life of attaining to it'. Of plebeian origin in Cheshire he had made his way to Brasenose College, Oxford, and had probably a good singing voice, for three years after taking his degree he became a Conduct at Eton and two years later, in 1735, a Minor Canon of Windsor. This preferment he still held in 1757, when 'at the crisis of a contested election for the Borough of Windsor between Mr. Rowley and the late Mr. Fox, afterwards Lord Holland, it happened that Dr. Balthazar Regis (Pedigree 91), a Canon, died. Dr. Bostock, then Vicar of New Windsor, went to Mr. Fox, flattered him with the great assistance he could lend him, but knowing the nicety on which the election hung, told him such assistance depended on his procuring him the vacant stall. Mr. Fox, having drawn on the Treasury to the extreme, and knowing that a single vote was of the utmost consequence sent express to the Minister to inform him that unless Mr. Bostock was appointed Canon he should lose his seat for Windsor. The messenger brought back the tidings of the reverend gentleman's preferment. Mr. Fox did get his election, but save his own single vote little advantage further was made of Mr. Bostock's promise. He enjoyed it near thirty years, and may be said through life to have been the most lucky man that ever entered into it'.

A correspondent pays tribute to him as 'sincere in friendships, benevolent to his parishioners, hospitable to his acquaintance, particularly to those of the clerical profession, indulgent to his servants, a kind and attentive parent, tender and affectionate husband, an easy landlord, candid and upright in all his dealings, this worthy patriarchal clergyman, . . . sincerely regretted by his friends and justly lamented by everyone who had the least dependence on him'. His son married the only daughter of a baronet, took his father in law's name and, on his death, was made a baronet himself.

In 1841, following the appointments of Hodgson as Provost and Hawtrey as Head Master, the old system of nomination to scholarships at Eton, with a purely nominal examination, was replaced by examinations which in effect limited entry to boys who had had an expensive preparatory education. This raised the intellectual standard sharply. It also meant that Eton tradesmen's sons and clever country boys, who in earlier days might sometimes have got in by favour or perception of their promise, had now no chance.

In a rather similar way the nineteenth century movement, which multiplied the Public Schools and made them factories for the mass production of gentlemen, made Eton more than before the preserve of the upper classes, because it was now the highest rung of a longer

16 *The Gentleman's Magazine*, Vol. 56, 1786, Pt. i, pp. 182-3.

ladder. The 1841 reform of entry to College was followed by the appointment in 1871 of a new governing body under the Public Schools Act of 1868 and its issue in 1877 of new statutes which did away with the old Fellows and much else. In the face of these enactments and the greater changes of the age the hold on Eton of the old Fellows' families quickly faded, though the links of some of them with the College have continued and members of these have been among its brightest ornaments.

Perhaps the most original and influential teacher of all the nineteenth century Eton masters was one who had entered College under the old regime, William Johnson, afterwards Cory, (Pedigree 87), a kinsman of Sir Joshua Reynolds, best known to the world at large by his translation of a Greek epigram 'They told me, Heraclitus, they told me you were dead . . .'. His great-greatnephew John Carter quotes a pupil of the days after he had left Eton who recalled his 'miraculous power of teaching twenty things at once which seemed to have nothing to do with the subject on hand. So that you were in the midst of the French Revolution or the law about English Juries, when you thought you were learning the First Aorist or mastering some dates in Greek History'.[17]

The reforming away of the 'family system' makes it the more remarkable that the late nineteenth century saw the rise of a new scholastic Eton dynasty, that of the Lytteltons, a family of ancient Worcestershire gentry (baronets from 1618, peers from 1756), members of which had been Oppidans in each generation since 1725. The eight sons of the fourth Lord Lyttelton who was appointed in 1871 one of the first Fellows under the Public Schools Act, renowned both as Scholars and as cricketers, overlapped at Eton from 1854 to 1875. The eldest son like his father was a Fellow, from 1891 to 1918. Edward, the seventh, who captained both the Eton and Cambridge elevens, returned to Eton as an assistant master in 1882, took orders, became Head Master of Haileybury in 1890 and came back to Eton again as Head Master in 1905. The presence at Eton between 1882 and the present day of two Fellows, two Head Masters, and seven Assistant Masters of this family and its connections, is due to other causes than the earlier family sequences. Its social composition and its wider than Etonian character illustrate Eton's position and drawing power in a sphere now enlarged far beyond the bounds within which the old Eton families grew. From another angle it may be seen as a part of the tendency of the professional class in the past century to draw a proportion of its membership, as it had not done before, from peerage families.

Though I believe that this small Eton sample exhibits many features of the growth of the professional class as a whole, I am also clear that

17 William (Johnson) Cory, *On the education of the reasoning faculties*, Halcyon booklets, II, 1964, p. 5.

there will be differences and that the larger class and other parts of it will exhibit elements not shown here. It would be of great interest and it should be possible to make genealogical and social analyses of other types of public school and grammar school, and indeed of these schools generally, and to deal with Oxford and Cambridge Colleges in the same way, though such close and embracing family ties as those found at Eton and King's would not necessarily recur. Nor does it seem beyond the bounds of possibility to extend such research to the Inns of Court, the Army and Navy and other professional groups and institutions. Before this could be done, however, a genealogical foundation not yet existent would have to be laid.

CHAPTER VI

THE TWO NATIONS: MYTH OR HISTORY

To dissect an epigram may be to break a fly upon the wheel, yet some epigrams have stings so potent that only dissection can make them harmless. Trevelyan long since pointed out that Disraeli's division of England into the two nations of the rich and the poor[1] was, like all epigrams, only half true, since the Industrial Revolution, while increasing the disparity of wealth between the richest and the poorest, also increased the range of the classes intermediate between them.[2] Yet the two nations have not merely remained a commonplace of politicians' history but were still referred to as historical fact in 1954 by so careful a writer as Professor Court[3] and in 1963 by Mr. John Goldthorpe and Mr. David Lockwood,[4] who stress the emergence *since Disraeli's day* of intermediate strata to bridge the gap between the two nations. They refer in this connection to G.D.H. Cole's *Studies in Class Structure* (1955) and to *The Changing Social Structure of England and Wales 1871-1951* (1958) by David C. Marsh. Mr. Marsh, however, says nothing about the two nations, while Cole points out that even in the early industrial phase, when it looked 'as if there were a tendency, likely to gain further force, towards the fusion of the working class into the mass of "abstract, undifferentiated labour power" of which Marx wrote', there was a simultaneous contrary development of new skills and new social groups.

In his recent important work, *The Making of the English Working Class*, (1963), Mr. E. P. Thompson propounds a view, which could be looked on as a more sophisticated form of the Two Nations myth. The central thesis of his large and fascinating picture is that the years

1 *Sybil, or the Two Nations* appeared in 1845.
2 G. M. Trevelyan, *English Social History*, 1942, p. 546.
3 W. H. B. Court, *A Concise Economic History of Britain from 1750 to recent times*, 1954, p. 298.
4 John H. Goldthorpe & David Lockwood, 'Affluence and the British Class Structure', *The Sociological Review*, N.S. Vol.II, 1963, p. 133.

between 1790 and 1830 saw the formation of 'the working class' in a sense in which this did not previously exist and the vast range of information which he brings together is organized about this theme.

There had, of course, been working classes time out of mind, farm workers, weavers, tailors, builders, porters, servants and the rest, who might be generally, if vaguely, described as the labouring people or the lower ranks or orders, though where the line should be drawn between them and the ranks above them was an arguable question, admitting only of an arbitrary answer. Mr. Thompson's point is that the traumatic experience of the Industrial Revolution between 1790 and 1830 brought into existence a new and unified Working Class with a common outlook and ethos, built up of older elements, but nevertheless new and distinctive.

As if to disarm a potential adversary, Mr. Thompson quotes a seemingly opposed opinion from a pamphlet written in 1834 by Francis Place, the champion of trade clubs and of parliamentary reform. Place complains — 'If the character and conduct of the working-people are to be taken from reviews, magazines, pamphlets, newspapers, reports of the two Houses of Parliament and the Factory Commissioners, we shall find them all jumbled together as the "lower orders", the most skilled and the most prudent workmen, with the most ignorant and imprudent labourers and paupers, though the difference is great indeed, and indeed in many cases will scarce admit to comparison'.[5]

'Place', says Mr. Thompson, 'is, of course, right: the Sunderland sailor, the Irish navvy, the Jewish costermonger, the inmate of an East Anglian village workhouse, the compositor on *The Times* — all might be seen by their "betters" as belonging to the "lower classes" while they themselves might scarcely understand each others' dialect. Nevertheless', Mr. Thompson continues, 'when every caution has been made, the outstanding fact of the period between 1790 and 1830 is the formation of "the working class".' A literal-minded reader might conclude that Mr. Thompson, however politely, is flatly contradicting the view of Place, an informed contemporary. Those, however, with experience of discussing such topics will be more cautious and may suspect that the difference may be largely, if not entirely, one of terminology.

Let us first, then see how Mr. Thompson supports his contention. He points first to the growth of a class consciousness, which he defines as the consciousness of a common interest among the different groups of working people as against the interests of other classes, and secondly to the growth of specifically 'working class institutions — trade unions, friendly societies, educational and religious movements, political organisations, periodicals — working class intellectual traditions, work-

5 *Op.cit.* p. 194, quoting M. D. George, *London Life in the XVIIIth Century*, 1930, p. 210 quoting British Museum, MS. Add. 27834, fo. 45.

ing class community patterns, and a working class structure of feeling'. His detailed account of these matters draws on a wide range of sources and is in itself of absorbing interest. One is left, however, with the feeling that, while some of the phenomena described are shared by working class groups with groups outside the working classes, others conversely relate only to limited groups within the working classes, so that the essential working class quality we are looking for remains elusive.

Inevitably in the centre of Mr. Thompson's picture is the truly new industrial working class. The impression of novelty, horror and amazement made upon contemporaries of widely differing cast of mind by the human products of the factory system is well brought out in Mr. Thompson's citations of observers of all political complexions from Tory to Jacobin.[6] We are told of a new race of men, exploited by the new work discipline as mere machines, brought together, segregated and brutalized in crowded hives. These descriptions, however, are specifically of the manufacturing districts of South Lancashire, the West Riding and the adjoining part of Derbyshire and by no means apply to the country as a whole. Even within these regions there were gradations for as Mr. Thompson points out, the economic cleavages were by no means so sharp in the West Riding as they were in South Lancashire, the scene of Disraeli's *Two Nations,* 'where the gulf between the great manufacturers and workers was deepest', and where accordingly 'the working-class reform movement was most "independent", keeping its distance from even the active middle-class reformers of Manchester', while 'in Birmingham where social gradations shelved less steeply and where the artisan still aspired to becoming a small master, there was a vigorous indigenous Radicalism supported by many employers and to some degree under middle-class leadership.'[7]

London was another case again. As by far the greatest centre of wealth and luxury it was a magnet for workers from the whole kingdom and comprised within itself not only the extremes of wealth and poverty but all gradations and varieties within the working classes of prosperity, employment and circumstance, together with great social mobility. This pattern was established long before 1790 and continues still. The political impact of the French Revolution and the War was felt in its fullest force in the metropolis but its economic impact was so dispersed and varied between different trades and circumstances that it seems impossible, so far as London goes, to assign to this single epoch any one radical change in the social pattern. Political changes of course there were.

The social contrasts of London were widely distributed. In many parts squalid overcrowded rookeries of old, tumbledown houses, abutted on well built and well occupied properties. The greatest contrast,

6 pp. 190-3, 342-9.
7 P. 611.

however, was between the East and the West: the latter consisting largely of fashionable and prosperous streets and squares; the former of the crowded quarters of seamen and shipbuilders and of Spitalfields silk weavers, whose trade had long been subject to extreme vicissitudes and depressions. Among artisans in many trades there were elaborate hierarchies of skill of which the highest were looked up to as 'a species of aristocracy' by the rest 'with feelings half of respect, half of jealousy'.[8] This aristocracy of labour was, moreover by no means confined to London and was found in new industries as well as old. Some of its members thought themselves the equals of small masters, shopkeepers and professional men.[9] The immense variety of types, grades and attitudes in the working populace of London was no less when surveyed by Henry Mayhew in the middle, or by Charles Booth at the end of the nineteenth century.

With the farmworkers the picture differs again. Their miseries during the French war through the pressure of rising prices and taxation, and later through the tightening and harsh administration of the game laws and the Poor Law are not to be questioned. Migration overseas and into the towns and factories was evidence of this pressure, as well as that of growing numbers, and the return of prosperity to the land in the 1850's was but shortlived, for in the 1870's came a new depression which lasted till our own day.

But even if we concede all this and grant also (which is much more disputable) that the pressures of the wartime period squeezed out of the farm labourer's life some quality of happiness which never returned, this is still far from amounting to the emergence of a new rural working class in anything like the sense in which the class of the factory workers was a new one. The mechanization of agriculture and the revolution in communications, which have come much nearer to effecting this, did not arrive till our own century, in the early years of which Cecil Sharp was still able to collect from the living lips of farm labourers hundreds of folk songs embodying a traditional peasant culture.

The boot is indeed rather on the other leg, for as Mr. Thompson himself points out 'rural memories were fed into the urban working-class through innumerable personal experiences'.[10] Nor were these memories of oppression only, if, as he suggests, the yearning for land was an integral part of them. There is perhaps a parallel with other elements distinguished by Mr. Thompson as formative in the culture of the working class. His account of the contribution of Dissent and particularly of Methodism and his analysis of its relation to the new

8 A reference to the position of the body makers among the coachbuilding trades, quoted by Thompson, op.cit. p. 236, from W. B. Adams, *English Pleasure Carriages*, 1837.

9 Thompson, pp. 237-9.

10 *Op.cit.* p. 229, citing Richard Hoggart, *The Uses of Literacy*, 1957, pp. 23-5.

work discipline[11] are peculiarly striking. But the Chiliastic and revivalist religious trends of the period had an ambit much wider than the working classes, though certain forms were better adapted than others to that particular milieu.

The same thing may be said of the community spirit or collective element exemplified in working class culture by the Friendly Societies and similar bodies.[12] Such societies were not new but go back, if not to the mediaeval guilds, to the box clubs and benefit societies of the seventeenth and eighteenth centuries,[13] while their nineteenth century kin includes bodies ranging from London clubs, learned societies and professional institutions to regimental and old school associations. They had, indeed, a special function to perform where poverty enhanced the value of mutual help, but when it is suggested[14] that the values they embodied are those which differentiate 'the 19th-century *working class* from the 18th-century *mob*', one cannot but feel that this increased seriousness and discipline are characteristic rather of the Victorian age as a whole than of the working classes in particular.

We feel ourselves on firmer ground when Mr. Thompson in his last chapter brings the argument round to a political point. Grey's purpose in the 1832 Reform Bill was 'to associate the middle with the higher orders of society in the love and support of the institutions and government of the country'.[15] A crucial part of the mechanism devised for this purpose was the extension of the franchise to the £10 householder. Mr. Thompson quotes a letter from Edward Baines to Lord John Russell reporting the result of a survey of its application to Leeds made in 1831. The conclusion was 'that the £10 qualification did not admit to the exercise of the elective franchise a single person who might not safely and wisely be enfranchised . . . in the parts occupied chiefly by the working classes, not one householder in fifty would have a vote. In the streets principally occupied by shops, almost every householder had a vote.'[16]

We are here in the familiar realm of political calculation. The principle is that of the fulcrum, lifting the beam at the centre of gravity, the point at which it will balance. Mr. Thompson is certainly right in his view that such political lines make their own contribution to class division. He quotes James 'Bronterre' O'Brien: 'We foresaw that its effect would be to detach from the working classes a large portion of the middle ranks, who were *then* more inclined to act with the people

---

11 Ch. XI.
12 *Op.cit.*, Ch. XII.
13 M. D. George, *London Life in the XVIIIth Century*, 1930, pp. 302, 398-9.
14 Thompson, *op.cit.* p. 424.
15. p. 817, quoting A. Briggs *The Age of Improvement*, p. 56.
16 Thompson, *op.cit.*, p. 816, quoting Baines, *Life of Edward Baines*, pp. 157-9.

than with the aristocracy that excluded them'.[17] All the same political detachment is not the same thing as social detachment and is unlikely in such a case to amount to this.

We have in fact to consider what we mean by a social class. Mr. Thompson offers no definition, but I believe his view would be my own, that a social class is a body of people within a nation, who feel themselves to be one in virtue of shared feelings, attitudes, experiences and ways of behaviour. Because basic attitudes and feelings are normally acquired in early childhood, they are passed on from parents to children, and it is arguably this, and not in the main genetic or economic factors, that makes social classes largely hereditary entities. For a genealogist the surest test of a social class is that its members intermarry mainly with one another — a test, however, whose application may be exceedingly hard to ascertain.

New classes, on this view, are formed by the subdivision, coalescence or reassortment of old ones. Political, economic, technological or other change reshuffles the pack, dividing those who were before together and perhaps bringing together some who were before apart. The process may take place gradually, as it did for the professional class between the sixteenth century and the nineteenth, building up the class character and enlisting the class recruits so slowly and discreetly that the process can be watched and analysed. Or it may be cataclysmic, as it was, perhaps, for the factory workers in the years round 1800.

When the process is cataclysmic it may be easier to see its outlines but harder to discern its details. We should like to know far more than we do, and probably far more than we ever shall, of who the factory workers were and what happened to them. With immense research over many years Mr. Thompson has gathered evidence, from official and private papers, from local and obscure journals and from a great range of literature. He has disentangled influences, illuminated states of mind and shed many rays of light on much that before was altogether dark. And yet how much is still unknown.

Of two important elements Mr. Thompson gives us a clear picture. The rest remain an unanalysed residue, nor are we given figures which convey a clear notion of the proportion these two classes bear to each other and to the rest. The first class is that of the old handloom weavers who, without moving or wishing to change, saw their old employment by degrees transformed over their heads into something new and cruel, so that many were degraded, more or less abruptly from artisan to unskilled labouring status. Among these the croppers had been the élite of the woollen industry and the woolcombers of the worsted. Even these, however, were by no means a wholly static population. We are

17. P. 821.

told that in the 1820s many combers came to Bradford from Kendal, North Yorkshire, Leicester, Devonshire and even Ireland.[18]

The other element Mr. Thompson distinguishes is that of the Irish immigrants, to whom by the 1830s whole classes of heavy, ill paid work had passed, 'since the English either refused the menial, unpleasant tasks or could not keep up with the pace'.[19] We know that besides the Irish there were in those years great numbers of other immigrants into the northern clothing districts, but we do not know in any detail who or how many they were or whence they came.

How many came from farms and villages within a hundred miles, how many from farther afield, from towns and from London? How many were from families long on the verge of destitution, how many had fallen far in the world through folly or the blows of fate? How many were skilled workers ground down in their own trades by technological change? By knowing more of this we might surely guess more of the stock of thoughts and feelings which informed the new class as it emerged.

By the middle of the nineteenth century there is much to help us answer such questions. The census returns of 1851, and to a lesser extent those of 1841, with the general civil register of births, deaths and marriages begun in 1837, could in principle tell us much of who the factory workers were from about 1830 or a little earlier. The analysis would be laborious but it could up to a point be made. For the earlier years the position is different. The wealth of English archives far back into the Middle Ages is indeed so great that in this country, unlike most, the pedigrees of poor families as well as richer ones can often be traced for many generations. Certain conditions are, however, required to make this possible in a given case and to most of these conditions the special situation of the first factory workers is peculiarly hostile.

I have elsewhere distinguished four determinants of success in tracing pedigrees – status, record, name and continuity.[20] Of these the factory workers in the nature of things lack two – status and continuity – for they were men abruptly moved from old to new surroundings at the base of the social pyramid. The possibilities therefore rest on the other two factors, record and name, and it is to be feared that without some special piece of local luck the record position is likely to be unfavourable. Poor law and burial records perhaps offer the best chances. We are likely then to be peculiarly dependent on the incidence of rare and localized surnames. One might hope, for example, to get some impression of the proportion of Yorkshire and Lancashire surnames, many of which are distinctive and of local origin, but the comprehensive survey of English surnames now begun at Leicester

18 Thompson, *op.cit.* p. 283, quoting W. Scruton, *Bradford fifty years ago.* 1897, p. 95.

19 P. 434.

20 *English Genealogy.* (I) pp. 362-370, (II) 411-9.

University by the Marc Fitch Fund is a prerequisite. The labour involved might be formidable. One may sometimes have the kind of luck which enabled A. L. Reade to trace the descent of pottery workers in Burslem from Samuel Johnson's negro servant. But I recall on the other hand the enormous, though at length successful, efforts made to trace the origin of a labourer, who appeared in Manchester in 1764. His origin was found at last in a Leicestershire village, but only after many years of costly research, in spite of the helpful rarity of his surname.[21] There may, however, be possibilities for large scale research, distinct from those applicable to individual searches such as this.

If, *pace* Mr. Thompson, we conclude that the only new working class of his period was that of the northern factory workers, we are left with the question in what measure and at what pace in the years after 1830 their special ways of thinking and feeling became spread through the working classes at large. We have first to define these working classes. Mayhew in the 1860s and Booth and Rowntree in the 1890s have marshalled for us important sections of the available evidence, without however coming near to exhausting it, for, with all their wonderful detail, these surveys were limited to certain times, places and types of evidence. Nevertheless one is left with the impression that as late as the 1890s large sections of the working population still remained obstinately pre-industrial in their ethos.

For the purpose of his analysis Charles Booth divided the population of London into eight classes minutely defined by the nature of their occupations, the amount of their earnings and their employment, if any, of others. He makes it clear that such classification must be somewhat arbitrary, that there are no sharp dividing lines and that within each class there are many grades of social rank. Finally he points out that it is difficult to draw the line between the lower middle class and the so called working men and that in practice in East London they consort together in a free and friendly way.[22]

This agrees with the impression from other sources that the normal profile of English society has long been a continuous gradual slope, unbroken by sharp distinctions between contiguous classes. *The Two Nations* of South Lancashire in the 1830s formed a striking but a local and probably temporary exception. The analysis of such a society into classes all too easily becomes arbitrary and personal because each shades off into the next and the information we should like is never all available. If a formulation is required, however, I would submit that what Mr. Thompson has described with such learning and insight is not the making of the working class but the addition to the working classes of a new working class, which in time affected all and more or less absorbed many.

21 EG. (II) 414.

22 Charles Booth, *Life and Labour of the People in London, First Series: Poverty.* Vol. I, 1902, pp. 33, 61, 99.

142

POSTSCRIPT

Since the above was written a new turn has been given by Professor Perkin[1] to the doctrine of Professor Thompson that the nineteenth century working class was a new creation of the Industrial Revolution. In Professor Perkin's view England had developed, since the decay of the feudal society in the fourteenth century, a hierarchical, but paternal, open and mobile society, which was classless and unique, or nearly so. This was the soil in which the Industrial Revolution grew, and in which alone it could grow. The Revolution, however, when it grew to maturity, destroyed the structure of this Old Society, replacing it by a new structure, of which the elements were economic classes, opposed in interest, ethos and sentiment to one another. Between 1815 and 1820, according to this view, the class society took over as the effective social and political structure from the old society of ranks and orders, so that at that time, not only the working class, but the middle class also was born.

This interpretation Professor Perkin supports with evidence and inferences no less striking and informative than Professor Thompson's. To a genealogist, nevertheless, the neat pattern which emerges may seem to represent reality no more closely than the effort of the Anglo-Norman lawyers to classify all men as freemen or villeins and less closely than the sumptuary legislation of the fourteenth century whose authors tried in a more convincingly untidy way to regulate men's apparel according to their rank and wealth. It may seem to him that the changes of nomenclature, from rank to class, from 'lower orders' to 'working classes' and so forth, pointed out by Professor Briggs,[2] were rather, as Professor Briggs himself seems to suggest, portents of change in political thought and climate than indices of radical changes in social structure.

Great social changes were of course on the way. But when in England, since the Norman Conquest at least, had they not been? The historian of a special period is apt to see other periods as woods but his own merely as trees. Hence specialization in a long term topic may have its use as a corrective of specialization in short term topics or in periods. In the Old Society of England, whose fine gradations and ties of patronage and dependency Professor Perkin so well describes, the sense of class distinction as a determinant (though not the only one) of whom one married, fought, lived or did business with, was surely not absent. Conversely lines of patronage, dependency, local allegiance and family relationship have continued in the nineteenth and twentieth

1 *Harold Perkin, The Origins of Modern Society 1780-1880*, 1969.
2 Asa Briggs, 'The Language of "Class" in early 19th Century England', in A. Briggs and J. Saville, eds. *Essays in Labour History*, 1960. E.G.

centuries to cut across class lines with the same fascinating force and complexity as before.

The question has been approached from another angle by Dr. Kitson Clark[3] who has argued that for much of the nineteenth century 'there were . . . in Britain two nations struggling in the bosom of one land — an old nation based upon the old nobility, upon the squires and upon the Established Church, and a new nation based upon commerce and industry, and in religion largely dissenting'. Lord Blake comments[4] that 'this conflict was far more important than that between the two nations of *Sybil* and in many ways more bitter', but interprets it in political rather than social terms.

To a genealogist a peculiarity of the English pattern seems still to lie in its continuing refusal to crystallize in any one political or class pattern for long enough to enable politics to divide the nation consistently on class lines. Equally our political divisions do not stay long enough on any one line of social division to turn political into social groups or reduce the accustomed fluidity of the latter. If a social class is to become a hereditary or genealogical class, it can scarcely do so without a segregation of three or more generations, and to be lasting, needs much more still. This is something English History has not yet produced.

---

3 G. Kitson Clark, *An expanding society*, 1967, p. 11.
4 Robert Blake, *The Conservative Party from Peel to Churchill*, 1970, p. 93.

CHAPTER VII

GENEALOGY AND THE COMMON MAN

No true genealogist needs to be told that his study is a fundamental one. This truth, however, has not yet fully penetrated the world at large. There are still those who think of us as fools with long memories, devotees of the cult of Sir Walter Elliot of Kellynch Hall who 'for his own amusement, never took up any book but the Baronetage'. The view that pedigrees are the prerogative of the great and noble has of course prevailed in many times and places and the history of its currency in England forms an important chapter of our social history. Some development, however, of the contrary view, that genealogy may be a pastime of the people at large and an essential element in their history, can safely be inferred in the year when the Society of Genealogists celebrates its fiftieth birthday.

Pastime, however, is one thing and scientific history another. Genealogists from ancient times have been stigmatized as wishful thinkers and it would be rash to claim that this original sin was dead. Here it is that the giants of feudal and manorial genealogy, Dugdale and Horace Round, Geoffrey White and Sir Charles Clay, have such great lessons to teach us. We have recently witnessed the greatest genealogical event of our generation, the completion of the new *Complete Peerage.* I would recommend any student of our subject, who wishes to understand how evidence should be used, to apply himself to some of the mediaeval articles in the later volumes of that work, turn up the evidence cited in the footnotes and master the method which has governed its assembly and use. He will find that he has gained a fresh vision on the one hand of the strictness needed in assessing evidence, on the other of the vast possibilities which the range and value of English Records open to those who have learned to understand them.

Having stressed the supreme importance of the scientific approach, I should now like to emphasize the real, if lesser, value of genealogy as pastime. Genealogy for pleasure is the soil in which scientific genealogy grows and without which it would not grow. To mix the metaphors, the

pleasure of this kind of chase is the mainspring which makes genealogists tick and without which they would soon cease to tick. There are
several elements in this pleasure. Of these I would stress two. The first
is an aesthetic pleasure in the patterns formed by pedigrees as they
ramify through history and through one another. A precondition of this
pleasure is a facility in grasping these patterns, a gift, possibly not very
common. The second element I wish to distinguish in the genealogist's
pleasure is more important. This is the profound satisfaction we derive
from establishing and maintining links with our own roots. I suspect
that this satisfaction has deep biological and instinctive origins. Clearly,
however, some states of society foster it, while others tend to kill it.
Where the family or tribe are paramount and when legal rights depend
on kinship or descent, it is everyone's interest to know his pedigree. In
industrial societies, however, the unit is the individual and economic
links largely supersede the ties of kinship.

This brings us back to the critics, referred to earlier, who think of us
as fools with long memories. Their minds not being adapted to grasp
the pedigree form, they are repelled by its complexities and in present
day life they see no practical use for ancestors. Over and above this,
however, they often, it seems to me, feel a more or less conscious
dislike of genealogy because they associate it with snobbish attitudes or
fear it as likely to lead to painful revelations. It is important for us to
understand this point of view, mistaken though we may think it, for it
constitutes a real obstacle to the progress of our studies. The repug-
nance felt by some people for pedigree springs, I believe from a
generalized reaction against the status-hunger, the passionate interest in
social niceties, so easily turning to snobbery, long prevalent in England
and much discussed at the present time. These things have themselves
deep roots in our social history and are doubly of interest to the
genealogist because his studies can throw light on their nature. He can,
for example, help to correct certain widespread current misconceptions
as to the origins of the phenomenon. Some writers on the subject today
seem to think it all began with the industrial revolution and the
nineteenth century growth of the public schools. For my own part, if I
had to put my money on a single root cause, I would sooner plump for
the Norman Conquest.

England is by no means the only country in which the growth of
scientific genealogy has been closely linked with the proof of succession
to lands and titles. The pedigrees of their possessors have great historical
and technical interest and, with the record evidence on which they rest,
go back in general to a much earlier date than those of others. Everyone
knows this but there is another side to the picture little known outside
the ranks of the genealogists, who therefore, would do well to impress
it on the world at large. This is that in England we have a wonderful
abundance of Records whereby the pedigrees of the poorest families
can often be traced back for three of four centuries and sometimes

much further still, while the technique of such research has been pursued and steadily improved for more than two centuries.

There is of course an obvious sense in which the Annals of the Poor are in Thomas Gray's words, short and simple

In the Country Churchyard:

> *Their name, their years, spelt by th' unletter'd Muse,*
> *The place of fame and elegy supply*

In other words one cannot expect much biographical detail. What there is comes mainly from collisions with the law, even if it be only the Poor Law. But this is a condition which, the genealogist must sadly recognize, applies to nine tenths of the results of his work, whatever rank it may deal with. Did not Professor Tout remark regretfully that despite the historians' best efforts many feudal lords remained for him 'as like each other as a row of peas'? The ancestor who emerges from the records as an individual is sadly rare in most times places and stations.

The genealogist, however, is not solely or mainly a biographer and in a sense of the words, which is of great importance both to him and to the social historian, The Annals of the Poor may be neither short nor simple, but complex and extended. The Annals I mean are those, not of individuals, not mainly even of individual families, but of the groups of families and the kindreds which in sum have made up the people of England. The frontier region between genealogy and social history is a dangerous and difficult terrain, but I do not doubt that, if the resources for its full exploration could be marshalled, results of the greatest importance to genealogists and historians alike would be forthcoming.

Recent attempts have shown what remarkable results such explorations can produce even when limited to what is within the compass of individual effort. Mr. Noel Annan (now Lord Annan) in his essay on 'The Intellectual Aristocracy'[1] analysed the family interconnections of a group of nineteenth century families, whose members showed outstanding ability of a particular kind. Quaker and Evangelical philanthropy and the Clapham sect lead on to Cambridge in the last century and Bloomsbury in this; Thorntons, Wilberforces, Venns and Macaulays to Darwins, Wedgwoods, Butlers, Stephens and Stracheys. From a correlation, of which genealogy is the backbone, Lord Annan has built up a vivid piece of social history.

Research of the same kind but in a widely removed field is included in Miss Sylvia Thrupp's book on *The London Merchant Class in the Middle Ages 1300-1500.* A section of this work is devoted to a detailed analysis of the family histories of the Aldermanic class in these two centuries, from which elsewhere in the book many interesting conclusions are drawn.

---

1 *Studies in Social History*, ed. J. H. Plumb, 1955, pp. 241-87,

The men and families dealt with in these two important works could fairly be called uncommon. No such thing could be said of the village families whose fortunes are traced through five or more centuries by Dr. W. G. Hoskins in his book *The Midland Peasant, The Economic and Social History of a Leicestershire Village.* It is true that the survival in the archives of Wyggeston Hospital of a remarkable series of charters recording peasant land transactions between the twelfth and the early sixteenth century gives us information of an exceptional kind for Wigston Magna, the village in question. On the other hand Wigston almost entirely lacks early manorial records, such as exist for many other places, while other important sources used in the book are in no way special to Wigston. Indeed Dr. Hoskins himself in an earlier study of 'Leicestershire Yeoman Families and their Pedigrees',[2] has indicated possibilities of tracing more or less connected lines of families in this rank from the fifteenth century or even earlier.

Now before in imagination we take wing from this point and picture ourselves tracing back the pedigrees of nineteenth century labourers to 1350 or earlier, we had better pause and reflect upon the difficulties we must expect to meet with even in the most favourable case. I have elsewhere expressed the view that four factors above all govern success or failure in tracing pedigrees. These are status, name, continuity and record. If a family is of eminent status; has a rare surname and distinctive Christian names; maintains continuity with its past, by living in, or owning land in, the same place, pursuing the same occupation or otherwise; and finally if the relevant records happen to be well preserved; then indeed we may hope for success. But in proportion as one or more of these requisites is lacking, we must brace ourselves to encounter difficulties.

In the cases we are now considering the first of these factors — status — will *ex hypothesi* be lacking. We shall therefore depend all the more on a favourable disposition of the other three.

A statement I made earlier must now be qualified. I said that the technique of tracing humble pedigrees had existed and had been improved for more than two centuries. This is true, but it is also true that this improvement has not yet been brought to anything like its maximum potential. The main reason for this is very simple; namely that, the problems being not only difficult in kind but very large in scale, the funds and energies required have not so far been available. It is not so much that the available funds have been spent mainly on distinguished ancestries. There is some truth in that, but less than might be thought, if only because the rich have often had poor ancestors and have been interested in them. The real trouble is that to tackle this material effectively and economically one needs to tackle it wholesale and its sheer bulk makes this an enormous task. Furthermore most of

2 Tr. Leic. Arch. Soc. xxiii, 1947, pp. 30-62.

the money spent has been spent by individuals in pursuit of their own families, not on general research into groups of such families.

This is not of course a criticism of those who have carried out such particular researches or of those who have furnished the funds for them. They have proved most valuable in themselves and, until more comprehensive work is done, give us the only guidance we have, however limited this may be, on important historical and technical questions. I would single out for mention here the enormous work on the history of his own name and family carried by our past Chairman of Council,[3] Mr. Marc Fitch, the results of which I was allowed to summarize in *English Genealogy*. This, as I wrote, has made it 'possible to envisage the social wanderings of a whole agnatic kindred in a way possible for few if any other English families'.[4] There is no substitute for such work as this. One's only regret is that there can never be enough of it. One fears, indeed, that in relation to what is needed there will never be very much.

Is there then some other possible approach, more comprehensive in character, less costly in relation to results obtained, which would not only build up for us a general picture, but would give the genealogist valuable help and guidance in tracing individual lines? Not only do I believe that there is such an approach, but it is my privilege to be allowed to announce that a beginning on the lines I have in mind may shortly[5] be made. The plan in question is for a comprehensive historical Survey of English surnames. This project, though of great interest and potential value to genealogists, is not in itself a genealogical project. I want, however, to suggest that it might in time be used as the foundation of a history of English families in general. In 1958 the study of surname etymology took a great leap forward with the publication of Dr. P. H. Reaney's book *A Dictionary of British Surnames,* yet Dr. Reaney himself stressed that this was only a beginning and that a full scale etymological dictionary, even of English surnames only, would be too vast a work to interest a commercial publisher.

Happily commercial publication is not in this case our only resource. In 1956 Mr. Marc Fitch established the Marc Fitch Fund for the forwarding of learned projects of certain kinds. As a trustee of this Fund it might not become me to praise the work it has already done, though I would in passing emphasize that Mr. Fitch's discrimination has fully equalled his generosity. It is however, without any doubt of its importance that I refer today to a recent decision of the trustees, on the personal initiative of Mr. Fitch, to undertake a large scale work on English surnames. The plans are still at an early stage and much remains to be settled. I am, however, allowed to say that on the linguistic side

3 Of the Society of Genealogists.
4 *infra* Pp. 113-5 and Peds. 74-5.
5 1961.

we shall have the help and advice of Dr. P. H. Reaney and on the side of social and local history that of Dr. W. G. Hoskins. It is in the hope of securing advice and help from some of those who hear or read these words that I mention the matter now.

Dr. Reaney's plans for new work on the etymological side are extensive, far reaching and of great interest. Some of us may, however, feel that Dr. Reaney's published work has already carried the etymological side of surname history so far ahead of the rest that for the genealogist and the social historian the most pressing need at this moment is for a full and reliable study of surname distribution. On this side the very foundations have still to be laid. The only attempt at a general survey of the subject known to me is H. B. Guppy's *Homes of Family Names in Great Britain* (1890) which is based on analysis of the surnames of farmers in County Directories. For a simplified small scale approach to a vast and technical subject this was probably as good as any, but its main achievement is to start far more questions than it answers and to bring out both the interest and the difficulty of the subject.

How can a beginning be made with a more serious approach? It has seemed to Mr. Fitch, Dr. Hoskins and myself that the first step must be a complete extraction and analysis of selected taxation or similar returns covering as fully as may be the whole country on a uniform basis at certain key periods. The earliest returns which meet this specification for the whole country (though there are good earlier ones for part of it) are the Subsidy Returns of the years 1327-1332. It will, we think, be necessary to select from among these returns because those of some years are deficient for some localities and some for others. The levy was on the movable property of individuals and a large proportion of the whole population ought therefore, to be covered,[6] though we know that there are in places large deficiencies.

Next we have in mind to take the Poll Tax returns of 1377 to 1381. These taxes were levied on all over the ages of fourteen and fifteen respectively except the destitute, and so in principle represent the great bulk of the population. Their detail and completeness vary considerably, however, and their interpretation is in places difficult.[7]

Thirdly we plan to take the vast and magnificent series of the Subsidy Returns of 1524 and 1525. For rural parishes this, apart from gaps in the record, should give a nearly complete picture of heads of households, but in the towns something like a third of the poorest may have escaped assessment.

6 J. F. Willard, *Parliamentary Taxes on Personal Property 1290-1334*, 1934; S. K. Mitchell, *Taxation in Medieval England*, 1951.

7 See M. W. Beresford, 'The Poll Taxes of 1377, 1379 and 1381', in *The Amateur Historian*, Vol. III, No. 7 and Sir Charles Oman, *The Peasants' Revolt of 1381*, 1906.

Fourthly we should take the Protestation Returns of 1642, preserved in the House of Lords,[8] which contain the names of all males over eighteen who subscribed the Oath of Protestation, and of those few who refused to subscribe.

At some future time, if our plans prosper, one cannot but hope that it might be feasible to deal similarly with one or more of the later and still vaster returns, such as the Hearth Tax Returns of 1662-74 or even (dare one mention it?) the Census Returns of 1851 or 1861.

The general plan would be to make photographic reproductions in duplicate retaining one set for central reference and distributing the sections of another to helpers, whom we shall hope to find, one for each county or group of counties. These helpers we should ask in the first place to transcribe the returns for their areas and send their transcripts, with all queries, for central checking, where necessary with the original Returns in the Public Record Office or House of Lords.

The next step would be to analyse the checked transcripts for the distribution of surnames throughout the country — in all probability region by region in the first instance. So stated this may sound a simple, if laborious, operation, but it would in fact be one of great difficulty and complexity. Here, indeed, it is that we come to grips with the central difficulty of the subject, that of changing forms of names. What starts as one name may diverge into different forms, not only in different families, but in different branches of one family. Conversely names originally different may become assimilated into one form. It is therefore often impossible to know the original form (and, therefore, the etymology) of a family name till one has traced it back to its earliest form by tracing the history of the family. It is exactly as with place names, where the names of two places which are now identical may have two distinct origins.

At this point the surname etymologists may begin to demur. If we are to wait, they may say, for the completion of our work, till the pedigree of every family has been carried back to the fourteenth century or earlier, we shall never see the work done. Such fears, I believe, are groundless. Though the different approaches — the etymological, the distributional, the genealogical — will in many ways help one another, they are also largely independent and need not wait on one another. Furthermore it is to my mind an essential feature of such an enterprise as this that its use it not limited to a specific publication or publications. If the raw material brought together for these purposes can be kept together and made accessible to students, work on it could continue long after the primary publication and could form the basis of revisions and further projects.

I therefore make no apology for outlining, as a basis for discussion and thought, possibilities which go far beyond what is now or ever may

8 Hist. MSS. Comm. 5th Report 1967, pp. 120-134.

be practicable. Suppose, then, that our chosen returns of the different periods have been analysed by names and localities for a county or group of counties. We shall find, I think, that certain names will turn out to be distinctive enough and consistent enough in form for us to work out with comparatively little further effort an outline history of their origins and of the movements over the centuries of the families who bore them. By working through these distinctive names we may hope thus to establish general historical patterns which will help us when we come to those which for one reason or another are harder to disentangle. With some of these the trouble will be a similarity of form acquired by names distinct in origin. Here the help of the etymologist is indispensable. With others the difficulty will be that of separating the several branches of numerous families, while commonest and hardest of all will be that of distinguishing entirely separate families, which nevertheless bear the same name, ranging all the way from the rare surname taken by two families to the miseries of Smith and Brown.

Somewhere in the long spectrum between De Vere and Smith we may have to give up the attempt to sort out actual families, but the comprehensive approach should take us a long way. Our chosen subsidy returns will peg out the framework and, where possible and justified, special research will bridge the gaps between them.

It must be admitted at once that such research, on one surname and for one locality alone, could be enormous. In the very few cases, where it has, to my knowledge, been carried out, the labour and time taken have been very great. There is, however, an important mitigating factor. To deal in this way with all the families in a region together would be a far smaller task than to deal with each of them singly. This is because in three separate ways the comprehensive approach should simplify many problems which present great difficulties when a single family alone is dealt with.

The first of these has been familiar for many years to the Society of Genealogists as the principle of cooperative research. A genealogist, about to search a particular group of records for a single name, has often advertised his willingness to search at the same time for others, which may be of interest to people willing to share the cost of his time and expenses. If enough of these come forward each may get his work done for a tithe of the cost of doing it individually. This is the first helpful principle which would be brought into play.

The second is no less familiar to the professional genealogist. Up to a certain point the actual arrangement of records helps him in his ordinary individual approach. Nothing could be more straightforward than to list from the Calendars the wills of persons of the name which concerns him and then to abstract those wills. Sometimes, when all goes well, no other kind of approach is needed. But sometimes this straightforward method fails to yield the answer and we are driven to more difficult gambits. One such gambit is to plough through some great mass of unindexed records relating to a locality or type of transaction applicable to our problem in the hope of finding the needle in the bottle of hay. There can, of course, be no certainty that the method will work but it is nevertheless the basis of some of our neatest conjuring tricks. Its relevance here is simply this. For the solution of our problems certain records hold a key position because they bridge gaps or serve as signposts. If these can be discovered and then transcribed and indexed, as the Apprenticeship records, for example, were indexed by the Society of Genealogists, they will give us help at those difficult points where family continuity is broken.

A third principle, distinct from the last though closely linked with it, is brought into play by the same approach. We may call it the principle of identification by elimination. Problems of identity, as we know, are among the worst we have to contend with. We are looking for the origin of a John Smith. We find one whose origin is known and who, so far as our data go, could be the same man. The name being so common, however, we think we need more proof and do not know where to find it. In this situation the large scale analysis of a group of records will often afford help of a kind not to be looked for from research limited to the specific problem. By working out the history of a whole group of families one will often eliminate what at first sight looked like possible solutions. The case for what is left is thus strengthened. Furthermore this kind of total analysis is likely to bring out patterns not previously apparent, which can themselves then be used as arguments or clues. I have in mind especially patterns of occupational change and of population movement.

Now I may be told that the project I have outlined could occupy a small army of scholars for two generations. I therefore hasten to forestall my critics by saying that I understand this. My answer is that the value of the project does not depend on its completion, for each of its sections would have value in itself, both individually and as a sample of the whole, and this would arise largely from the correlation implied in their conformity to the larger plan.

There is one aspect, already touched upon, to which I wish to return before I close. The large project I have outlined is not larger in scale than others which are going steadily forward to completion. It is, I suggest, comparable in magnitude to the programmes of the English Place Name Society, the Victoria County History, the History of Parliament, to mention only a few. If it is not undertaken or completed the reason will be simply that it has not behind it so strong a force of public or private interest as these great projects. If there existed in England anything like the Clan Societies of Scotland or the Family Associations of the United States, the desire thus organized of a certain number of large kindreds would give my plan the impetus it needs to set it moving. Or the needed breeze might blow from another quarter, from acceptance by historians and sociologists of the light their studies might derive from a general history of English families. But 'the wind bloweth where it listeth, and thou hearest the sound thereof, but canst not tell whence it cometh, and whither it goeth'. It is no part of my purpose to try to whistle up the wind from one quarter or another. My aim today is less ambitious though still perhaps optimistic. It is, first, to appeal to those whose special knowledge, especially of local history and local record, would qualify them to do so, to give us help in our primary plan of mapping surname distribution and history. Secondly it is to make a wider, longer term appeal to those with cognate knowledge and interests who may help to guide our efforts into the most useful channels.

I have no idea whether the replies to this will be few or many. If they are not many I shall hope to answer them all soon. If my answers are delayed, it may be because there are more of them than I expect. On the whole I am disposed to think that the views I have put forward will make their way slowly but steadily and will spread, as our knowledge grows from the beginning now planned, which Mr. Fitch and his Fund have made possible.

POSTSCRIPT

Though, as set out above, the trustees of the Marc Fitch Fund had decided in 1960 to endow research into the history of English surnames, it was not until 1965 that they were able to find the right home for the work. It was then, however, established within the Department of English Local History at Leicester University, at that time headed by Professor W. G. Hoskins, and Mr. R. A. McKinley was appointed Marc Fitch Reader in the History of English Surnames.

It was decided to begin with East Anglia, as a sufficiently large, self-contained and distinctive region and by 1969 Mr. McKinley was able to print an account[1] of four years' intensive indexing and analysis of Military Survey and Lay Subsidy Rolls of 1522-3 for Norfolk and to draw a number of interesting, provisional conclusions. Among these was that there had been in the later Middle Ages a great deal of movement over fairly short distances, producing a distribution of individual surnames in geographically concentrated groups, together with considerable movement over greater distances and into the county from other regions.

In 1973 this was followed by the publication of a larger work on *The Development of West Riding Surnames from the Thirteenth to the Twentieth Centuries* by Dr. G. Redmonds. The scope of this was made feasible by the existence for the West Riding of printed editions of numerous record sources of different dates, such as are at present available for few other counties. It was also helped by the large number of relatively rare and highly distinctive surnames there, derived at early dates from isolated upland farmsteads, most of which can with probability be inferred to have given a surname to only one family apiece. These facts have enabled Dr. Redmonds to build up, step by step, a convincing picture of families spreading slowly, in the course of centuries, from hill to dale, from west to east, latterly to the conurbations, and at all dates also to the south. His evidence further suggests that, while mortality extinguished families in towns, healthy upland families were outbreeding others.

Meanwhile Professor Alan Everitt, successor at Leicester to Professor W. G. Hoskins, has drawn attention to the sharp contrasts between different patterns of rural society, not merely between counties but within them.[2] The 1873 *Return of Owners of Land* shows in

1 Department of Local History. Occasional papers, Second Series. ed. Alan Everitt. No. 2. *Norfolk Surnames in the Sixteenth Century*, by R. A. McKinley. Leicester Univ. Press, 1969.

2 Alan Everitt, 'The Community of Kent in 1640', *Genealogist's Magazine*, Vol.14, 1963, pp. 229-258; *The Community of Kent and the Great Rebellion 1640-60*, Leicester U.P., 1966; 'Social Mobility in Early Modern England,' *Past and Present*, 1966; 'The grass-roots of history', *Times Literary Supplement*, 28 July 1972, p. 889.

Leicestershire forty eight per cent made up of parishes dominated by small freeholders and only just over half controlled by handed magnates; but in Northamptonshire two thirds by magnates and only a third by small owners; while in Kent the weald belonged largely to the yeomen, but seventy per cent of the downland to the squires. Professor Everitt further stresses how such differences are reflected in different surname distribution patterns, where these have been worked out, The East Kent farming family of Denne, from some six branches in the seventeenth century had increased to some forty in the 1870s, nine headed by farmers, twenty one by tradesmen and ten by minor gentlemen. Dissent he finds, contrary to preconception, to be as strong (or stronger) in the countryside as in the towns. But in three areas examined he found three quarters of the countryside dissenting groups in freeholders' parishes, while in eighty per cent of the squires' parishes there was no organized nonconformity.

At this stage of analysis wide margins of uncertainty are noted which genealogy should in due course narrow. Genealogy, whether studied directly or through the medium of surname distribution, is evidently only one source among others of light on such questions. Yet the further such studies go, the more does its contribution seem indispensable.

Sabine Baring-Gould remarked as 'one of the most perplexing facts to the student of genealogy', that 'whereever a great family was seated, there are found also a shoal of individuals, distinctly of an inferior social class, bearing the same patronymic'.[3] He declined to admit the view, often, he says, expressed, that these were poor relations, possibly illegitimate, of the great families, save perhaps in rare cases. He thought them rather 'descendants of menial servants', who took their surnames from their masters, as in a parish register entry which he quotes:

1596. 3 July. Buried, William, servant to Arthur Carew, Esq., commonly called William Carew.

He cites also Pepys' entry on 14 Feb. 1660/1 'My boy Wareman [his servant lad] hath all this day been called young Pepys, as Sir W. Pen's boy [servant] is young Pen.'

To ascertain the proportion which such cases, (or those of foundlings named from popular heroes of their day), bore to the local clans truly of one stem, which *pace* Baring-Gould equally exist and are in my own view numerous,[4] is a challenge to the genealogist and the surname historian.

3 *Old Country Life*, 1890, pp. 17, 296-8.
4 EG. II, pp. 214-6.

THE PEDIGREES

PEDIGREE 1   THE SWAN BADGE (I)

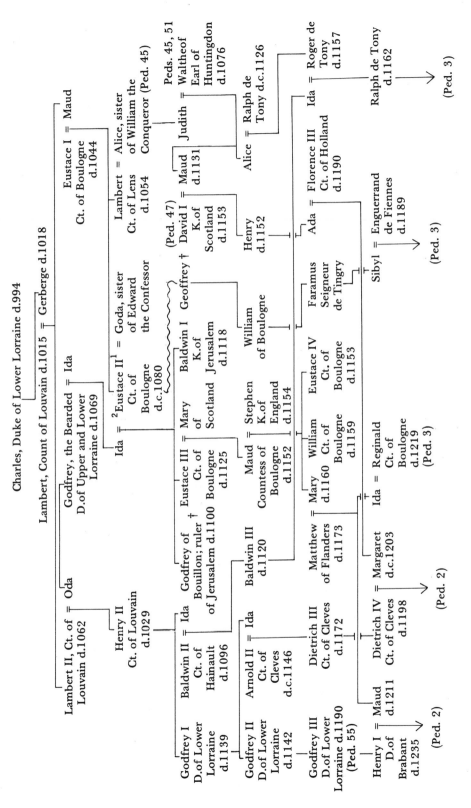

† Note p.253

PEDIGREE 2   THE SWAN BADGE (II)

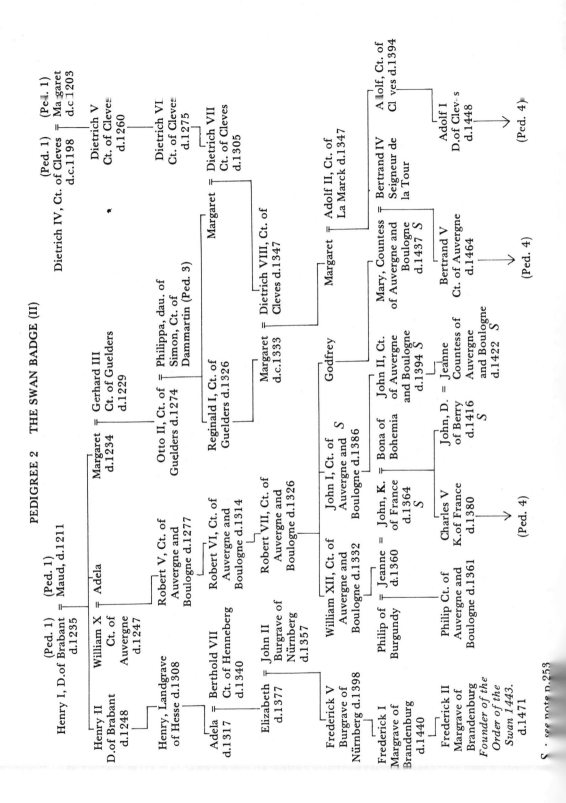

S : see note p.253

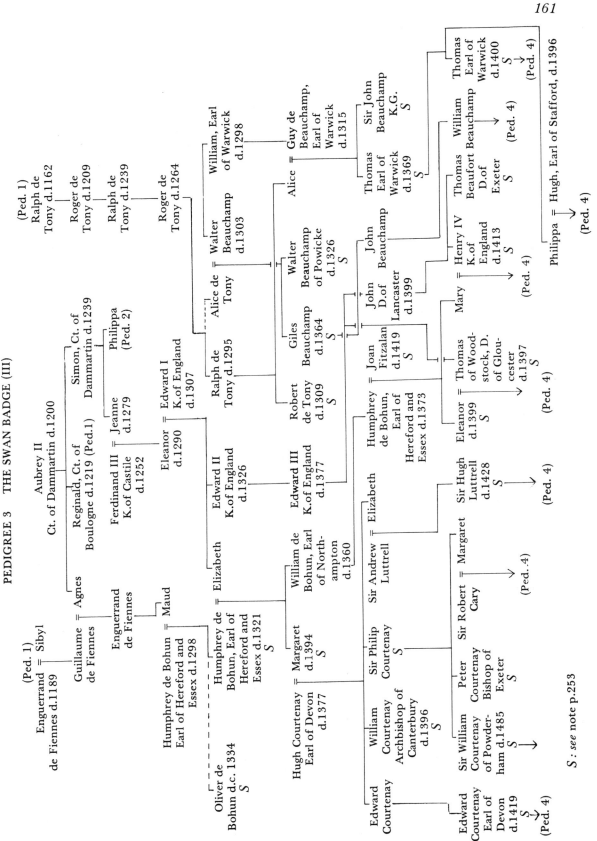

PEDIGREE 3   THE SWAN BADGE (III)

S : see note p.253

PEDIGREE 4   THE SWAN BADGE (IV)

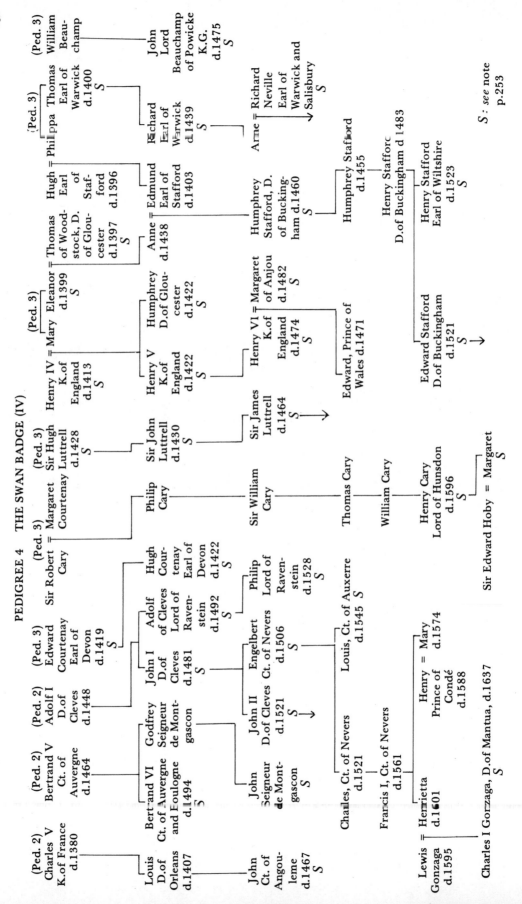

S : see note p.253

PEDIGREE 5   LYDIA, MEDIA, PERSIA, ACHAEMENIDS

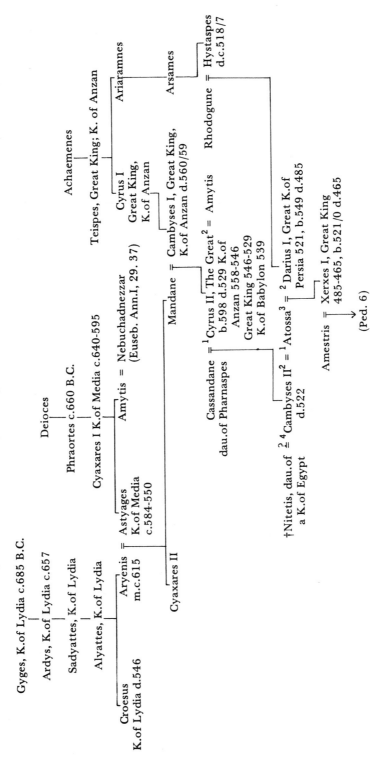

† Note p.254

PEDIGREE 6   PERSIA, ACHAEMENIDS

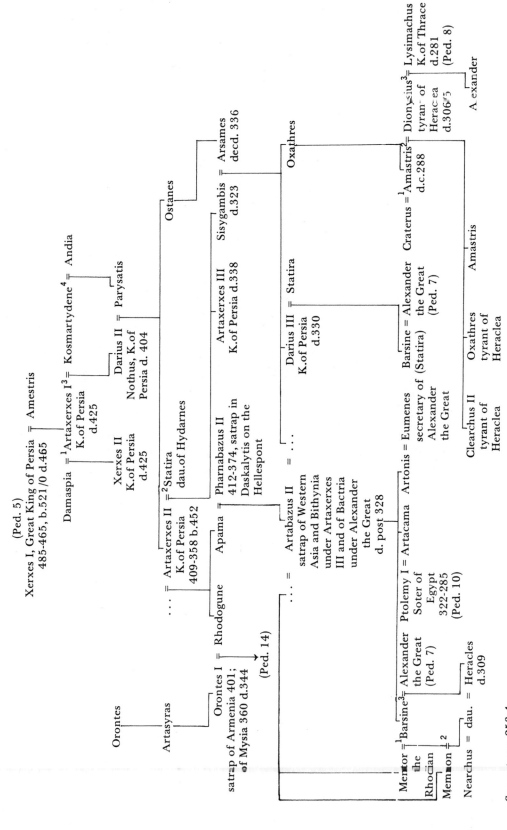

See note pp.253-4

PEDIGREE 7   MACEDONIA (I)

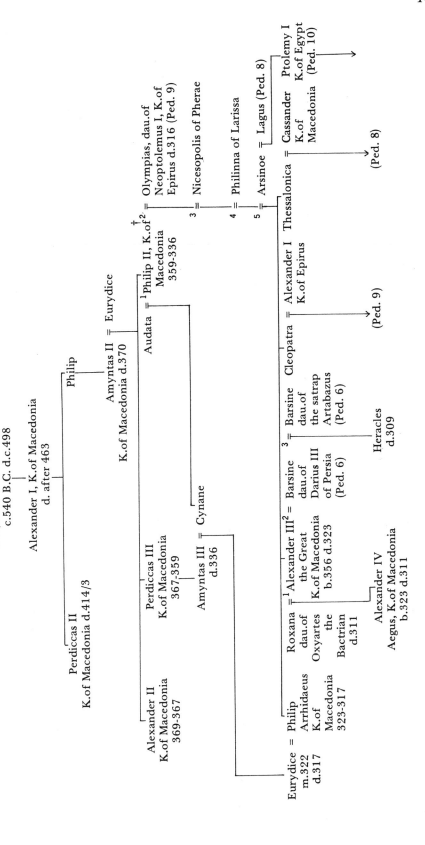

† Note p.254

PEDIGREE 8   MACEDONIA (II)

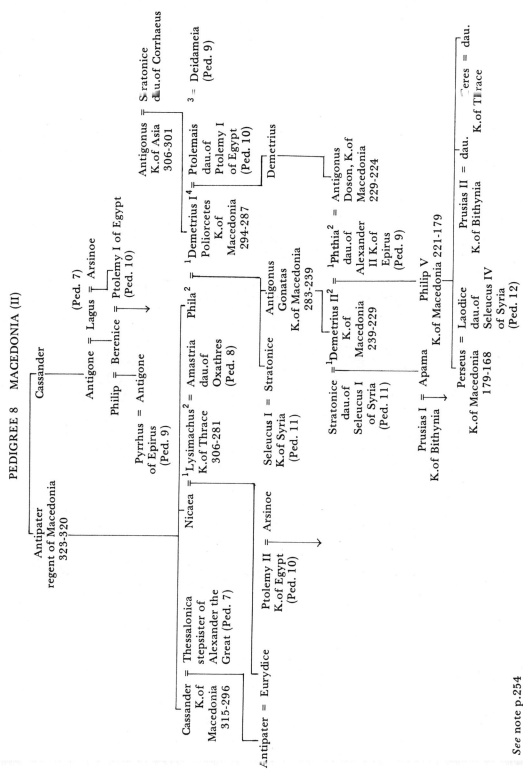

See note p.254

PEDIGREE 9 EPIRUS

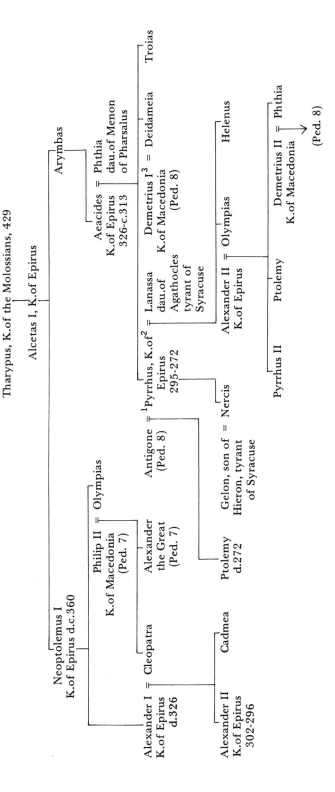

See note p.254

PEDIGREE 10   PTOLEMIES OF EGYPT

Artacama = [1]Eurydice ⊤ [2]Ptolemy I, K.of Egypt[3] ⊤ Berenice
dau.of Artabazus   dau.of   322-285 son of Lagus   dau.of Lagus by
satrap of Bactria   Antipater   and Arsinoe, concubine   Antigone, niece
(Ped. 6)   of Philip II K.of   of Antipater
                                       Macedonia (Ped. 7)

Arsinoe ⊤ Ptolemy II
dau.of   Philadelphus
Lysimachus K.of Egypt
            285-246

Ptolemy III ⊤ Berenice   Berenice = Antiochus II
Euergetes   dau.of Magos K.of   Theos K.of Syria
K.246-221   Cyrene by Apama   (Ped. 11)
              dau.of Antiochus I
              K.of Syria (Ped. 11)

Ptolemy IV ⊤ Arsinoe
Philopator
K.221-203

Ptolemy V ⊤ Cleopatra
Epiphanes   dau.of Antiochus III
K.203-181/0 of Syria (Ped. 12)

Ptolemy VI Philometor ⊤ Cleopatra
K.181/0-145

Alexander = [1]Cleopatra[2] ⊤ Demetrius II [3] = Antiochus VII   Cleopatra ⊤ Ptolemy VII
Balas usurper d.121   K.of Syria   K.of Syria   Euergetes
of Syria   (Ped. 12)   145-139/8   139/8-129   (Physcon)
150-146   K.of Egypt
                                                                                 145-116

Antiochus IX[2] = [2]Cleopatra[1] ⊤ [1]Ptolemy VIII[2] = [1]Cleopatra[2] = [2] Antiochus VIII[1] ⊤ Cleopatra
K.of Syria   Soter   (Selene)   K.of Syria   (Tryphaena)
(Ped. 00)   (Lathyrus)   (Ped.12)
                                     K.116-108/7
                                     and 88-80

... ⊤ Ptolemy IX = [1]Berenice   Ptolemy XI ⊤ Cleopatra
      Alexander I   Philadelphus   Neos Dionysos
      K.108/7-88   (Auletes) K.80-51

Ptolemy X = [2]
Alexander II
K.80

Archelaus = Berenice   Ptolemy XII   Ptolemy XIII   C. Julius = Cleopatra ⊤ Mark
high priest   K.51-48   K.47-44   Caesar   Q.of Egypt   Antony
of Comana   (Ped. 18)   (Ped.19)
(Ped. 16)

See note p.254

PEDIGREE 11   SELEUCIDS OF SYRIA (I), BACTRIA

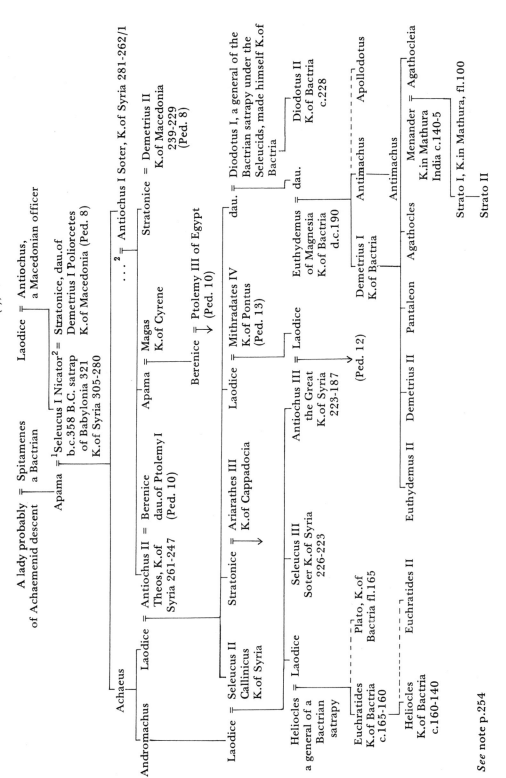

See note p.254

PEDIGREE 12   SELEUCIDS OF SYRIA (II)

Antiochus III, the Great = Laodice, dau.of Mithradates IV
K.of Syria 223-187 (Ped. 11)   of Pontus (Ped. 13)

Ptolemy V = Cleopatra   Antiochus = Laodice   Seleucus IV   Antiochus IV   Ariarathes IV = Antiochus
K.of Egypt   Philopator   Epiphanes, K.of   K.of Cappadocia
                                        K.of Syria   Syria 175-163
(Ped. 10)   187-175

Demetrius I   Perseus, K.of = Laodice   Antiochus V   Mithradates V = Laodice
Soter K.of   Macedonia   Eupator K.of   K.of Pontus
Syria 162-150   179-168   Syria 163-2   (Ped. 13)

Antiochus VII Euergetes   =³ Cleopatra
(Sidetes) K.of Syria   dau.of Ptolemy VI
139/8-129   of Egypt (Ped. 10)

Cleopatra ²=¹ Demetrius II Nicator ² = Rhodogune
dau.of Ptolemy VI   K.of Syria 145-139/8   dau.of Mithradates I
of Egypt (Ped. 10)   of Parthia (Ped. 17)

Laodice = Phraates II   Antiochus IX ²=² Cleopatra   ³=³ Cleopatra
K.of Parthia   Philopator   dau.of   (Selene) dau.of
(Ped. 17)   (Cyzicenus)   Ptolemy VII   Ptolemy VII of
¹ Antiochus IX   of Egypt   Egypt (Ped. 10)
Philopator   (Ped. 10)
(Cyzicenus)

Antiochus X
Eusebes
Philopator, K.of
Syria 115-95

Antiochus XIII
Asiaticus, K.of
Syria, dethroned
by Pompey 65 B.C.

Seleucus I   Cleopatra ²=¹ Antiochus VIII   Antiochus XII   Laodice = Mithradates I
K.of Syria   (Tryphaena)   Philometor   Dionysus, K.of   Thea   K.of Com-
125   dau.of Ptolemy   (Grypus) K.of   Syria   Philadelphus   magene
VII of Egypt   Syria 125-121
(Ped. 10)   ²=² Cleopatra   (Ped. 15)
(Selene) dau.
of Ptolemy VII
of Egypt
(Ped. 10)

Seleucus VI   Antiochus XI   Demetrius III
Epiphanes   Epiphanes   Philopator
Nicator, K.of   K.of Syria   Soter, K.of
Syria   Syria

Philip I
K.of Syria

Philip II
K.of Syria

See note p.254

PEDIGREE 13   PONTUS

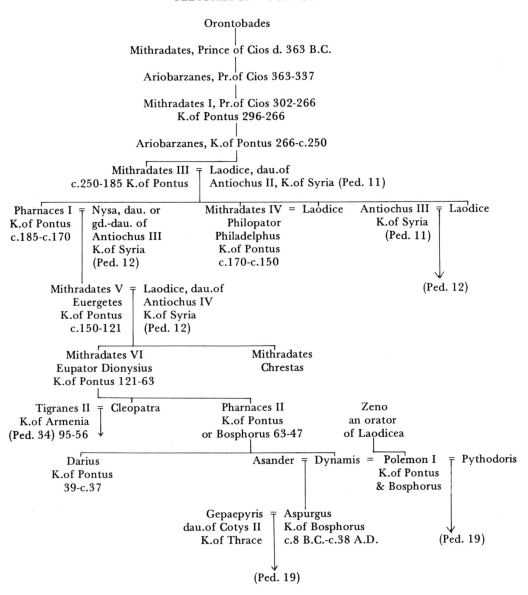

Orontobades

Mithradates, Prince of Cios d. 363 B.C.

Ariobarzanes, Pr.of Cios 363-337

Mithradates I, Pr.of Cios 302-266
K.of Pontus 296-266

Ariobarzanes, K.of Pontus 266-c.250

Mithradates III = Laodice, dau.of
c.250-185 K.of Pontus   Antiochus II, K.of Syria (Ped. 11)

Pharnaces I = Nysa, dau. or
K.of Pontus   gd.-dau. of
c.185-c.170   Antiochus III
                K.of Syria
                (Ped. 12)

Mithradates IV = Laodice
Philopator
Philadelphus
K.of Pontus
c.170-c.150

Antiochus III = Laodice
K.of Syria
(Ped. 11)

(Ped. 12)

Mithradates V = Laodice, dau.of
Euergetes   Antiochus IV
K.of Pontus   K.of Syria
c.150-121   (Ped. 12)

Mithradates VI   Mithradates
Eupator Dionysius   Chrestas
K.of Pontus 121-63

Tigranes II = Cleopatra
K.of Armenia
(Ped. 34) 95-56

Pharnaces II
K.of Pontus
or Bosphorus 63-47

Zeno
an orator
of Laodicea

Darius
K.of Pontus
39-c.37

Asander = Dynamis = Polemon I = Pythodoris
                    K.of Pontus
                    & Bosphorus

Gepaepyris = Aspurgus
dau.of Cotys II K.of Bosphorus
K.of Thrace   c.8 B.C.-c.38 A.D.

(Ped. 19)

(Ped. 19)

See note p.254

PEDIGREE 14   ORONTIDS OF ARMENIA AND COMMAGENE

Bagabigna [550 B.C.]
|
Hydarnes I, 521
|
Hydarnes II, 480
|
Aroandes (Orontes) I
|
Artasyras, satrap of Hyrcania
|
Aroandes (Orontes) II ╤ Rhodogune, dau.of
satrap of Armenia 401, | Artaxerxes II, K.of
Mysia 360 d.344 | Persia (Ped. 6)
|
Aroandes (Orontes) III, fl.331, satrap of
Armenia c.344-331 K.of Armenia 331
|
Mithranes I, K.of Armenia
331-before 317
|
Aroandes K.of Armenia
before 317-c.260
|
Samos I, K.of Armenia c.260
|
Arsames I, K.of Armenia 260+-228+
|
Xerxes, K.of Armenia ╤ Antiochis, dau.of Antiochus III,
228+-212+ | K.of Syria (Ped. 12)
|
Ptolemy I
K.of Commagene c.163
|
Isias ╤ Samus I Theosebes Dikaios,
Philostorgos | K.of Commagene c.140
↓
(Ped. 15)

See note pp.254-5

PEDIGREE 15   COMMAGENE (II)

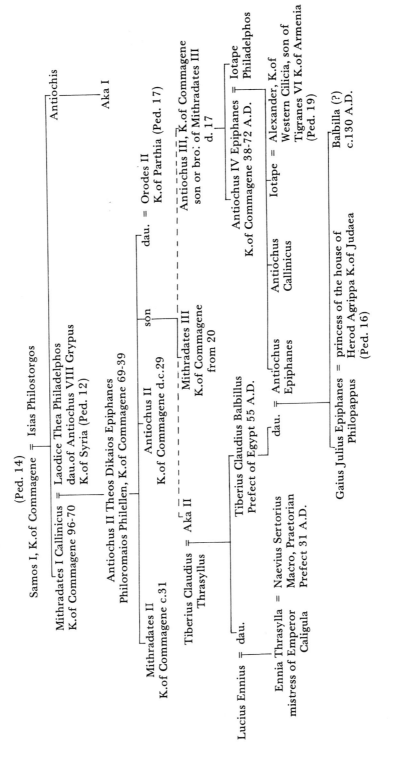

PEDIGREE 16   JUDAEA, COMANA

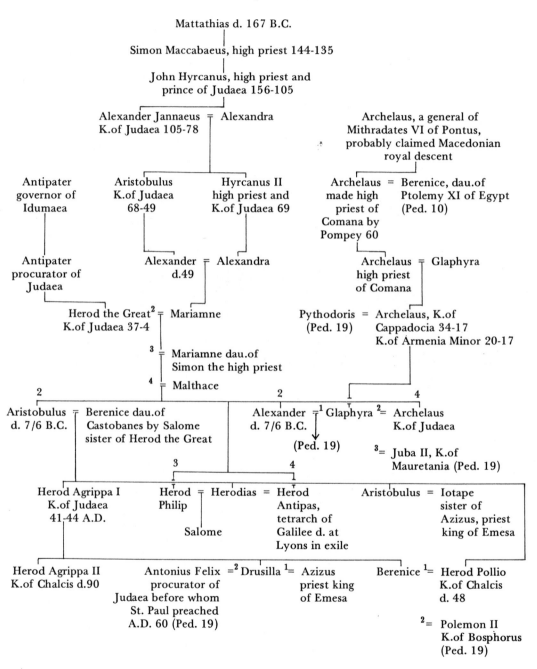

Mattathias d. 167 B.C.

Simon Maccabaeus, high priest 144-135

John Hyrcanus, high priest and
prince of Judaea 156-105

Alexander Jannaeus = Alexandra
K.of Judaea 105-78

Archelaus, a general of
Mithradates VI of Pontus,
probably claimed Macedonian
royal descent

Antipater
governor of
Idumaea

Aristobulus
K.of Judaea
68-49

Hyrcanus II
high priest and
K.of Judaea 69

Archelaus =
made high
priest of
Comana by
Pompey 60

Berenice, dau.of
Ptolemy XI of Egypt
(Ped. 10)

Antipater
procurator of
Judaea

Alexander = Alexandra
d.49

Archelaus = Glaphyra
high priest
of Comana

Herod the Great² = Mariamne
K.of Judaea 37-4

Pythodoris = Archelaus, K.of
(Ped. 19)   Cappadocia 34-17
            K.of Armenia Minor 20-17

³ = Mariamne dau.of
Simon the high priest

⁴ = Malthace

2
Aristobulus = Berenice dau.of
d. 7/6 B.C.   Castobanes by Salome
              sister of Herod the Great

2
Alexander =¹ Glaphyra ²= Archelaus
d. 7/6 B.C.   K.of Judaea

(Ped. 19)

³= Juba II, K.of
Mauretania (Ped. 19)

4

3
Herod Agrippa I
K.of Judaea
41-44 A.D.

Herod = Herodias = Herod
Philip   Antipas,
                   tetrarch of
Salome   Galilee d. at
                   Lyons in exile

Aristobulus = Iotape
              sister of
              Azizus, priest
              king of Emesa

Herod Agrippa II
K.of Chalcis d.90

Antonius Felix =² Drusilla ¹= Azizus
procurator of   priest king
Judaea before whom   of Emesa
St. Paul preached
A.D. 60 (Ped. 19)

Berenice ¹= Herod Pollio
            K.of Chalcis
            d. 48

²= Polemon II
   K.of Bosphorus
   (Ped. 19)

See note p.255

PEDIGREE 17   EARLY ARSACIDS OF PARTHIA

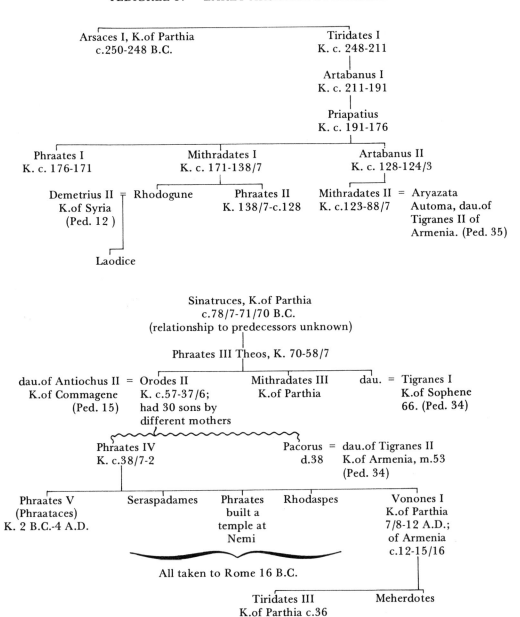

Arsaces I, K.of Parthia
c.250-248 B.C.

Tiridates I
K. c. 248-211

Artabanus I
K. c. 211-191

Priapatius
K. c. 191-176

Phraates I
K. c. 176-171

Mithradates I
K. c. 171-138/7

Artabanus II
K. c. 128-124/3

Demetrius II ┬ Rhodogune
K.of Syria
(Ped. 12)

Phraates II
K. 138/7-c.128

Mithradates II = Aryazata
K. c.123-88/7   Automa, dau.of
                 Tigranes II of
                 Armenia. (Ped. 35)

Laodice

Sinatruces, K.of Parthia
c.78/7-71/70 B.C.
(relationship to predecessors unknown)

Phraates III Theos, K. 70-58/7

dau.of Antiochus II = Orodes II
K.of Commagene   K. c.57-37/6;
(Ped. 15)   had 30 sons by
                     different mothers

Mithradates III
K.of Parthia

dau. = Tigranes I
       K.of Sophene
       66. (Ped. 34)

Phraates IV
K. c.38/7-2

Pacorus = dau.of Tigranes II
d.38   K.of Armenia, m.53
          (Ped. 34)

Phraates V
(Phraataces)
K. 2 B.C.-4 A.D.

Seraspadames

Phraates
built a
temple at
Nemi

Rhodaspes

Vonones I
K.of Parthia
7/8-12 A.D.;
of Armenia
c.12-15/16

All taken to Rome 16 B.C.

Tiridates III
K.of Parthia c.36

Meherdotes

See note p.255

PEDIGREE 18   THE CAESARS

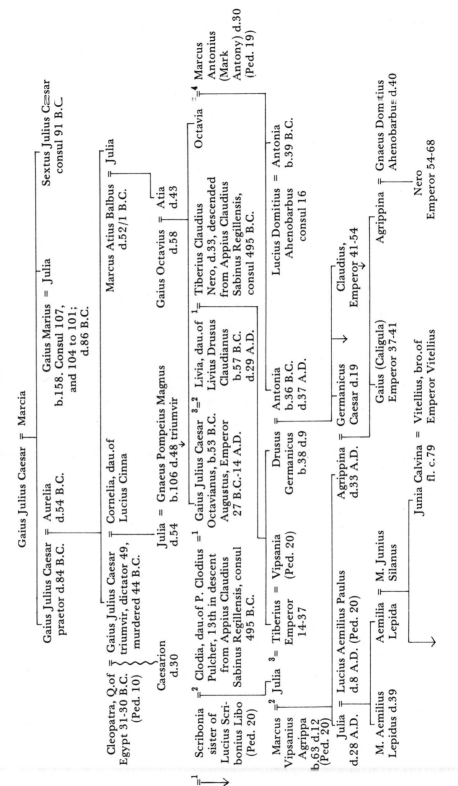

See note p.255

PEDIGREE 19   MARK ANTONY

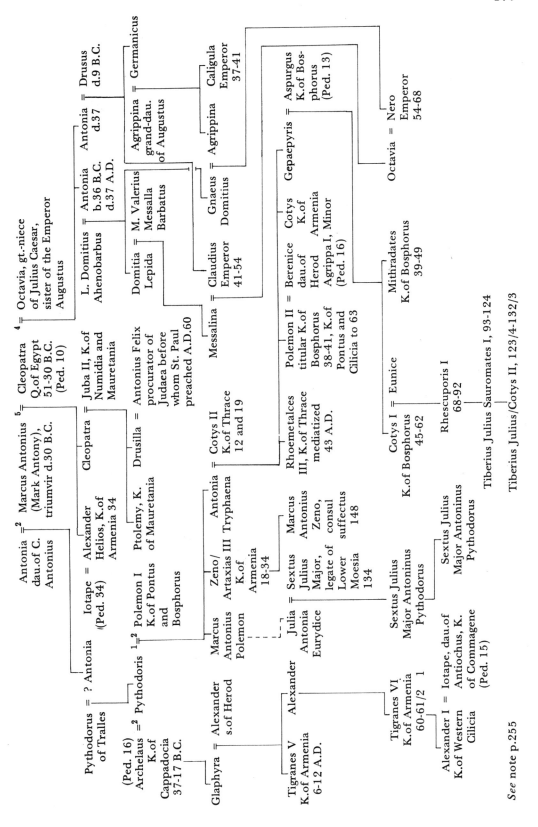

See note p.255

PEDIGREE 20   SCRIBONIA TO PAULA

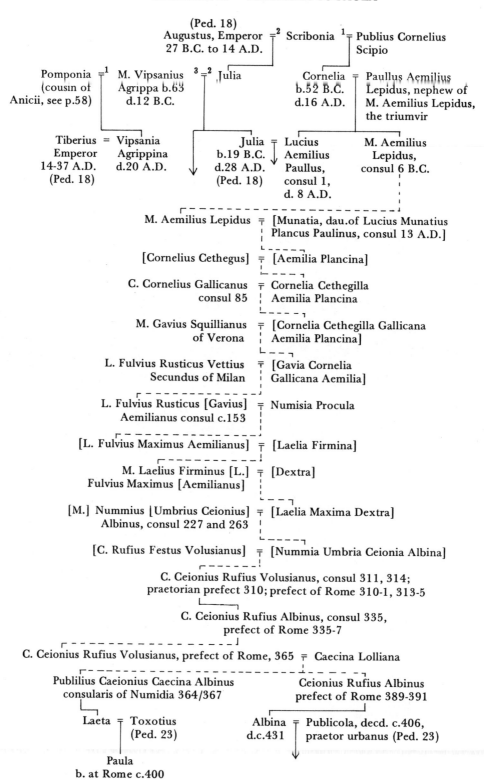

(Ped. 18)
Augustus, Emperor =² Scribonia ¹= Publius Cornelius
27 B.C. to 14 A.D.   Scipio

Pomponia =¹ M. Vipsanius ³=² Julia   Cornelia = Paullus Aemilius
(cousin of   Agrippa b.63   b.52 B.C.   Lepidus, nephew of
Anicii, see p.58) d.12 B.C.   d.16 A.D.   M. Aemilius Lepidus,
                                                        the triumvir

Tiberius = Vipsania   Julia = Lucius   M. Aemilius
Emperor   Agrippina   b.19 B.C. Aemilius   Lepidus,
14-37 A.D. d.20 A.D.   d.28 A.D. Paullus,   consul 6 B.C.
(Ped. 18)   (Ped. 18) consul 1,
                                         d. 8 A.D.

M. Aemilius Lepidus = [Munatia, dau.of Lucius Munatius
                       Plancus Paulinus, consul 13 A.D.]

[Cornelius Cethegus] = [Aemilia Plancina]

C. Cornelius Gallicanus = Cornelia Cethegilla
           consul 85   Aemilia Plancina

M. Gavius Squillianus = [Cornelia Cethegilla Gallicana
       of Verona   Aemilia Plancina]

L. Fulvius Rusticus Vettius = [Gavia Cornelia
   Secundus of Milan   Gallicana Aemilia]

L. Fulvius Rusticus [Gavius] = Numisia Procula
Aemilianus consul c.153

[L. Fulvius Maximus Aemilianus] = [Laelia Firmina]

M. Laelius Firminus [L.] = [Dextra]
Fulvius Maximus [Aemilianus]

[M.] Nummius [Umbrius Ceionius] = [Laelia Maxima Dextra]
Albinus, consul 227 and 263

[C. Rufius Festus Volusianus] = [Nummia Umbria Ceionia Albina]

C. Ceionius Rufius Volusianus, consul 311, 314;
praetorian prefect 310; prefect of Rome 310-1, 313-5

C. Ceionius Rufius Albinus, consul 335,
prefect of Rome 335-7

C. Ceionius Rufius Volusianus, prefect of Rome, 365 = Caecina Lolliana

Publilius Caeionius Caecina Albinus   Ceionius Rufius Albinus
consularis of Numidia 364/367   prefect of Rome 389-391

Laeta = Toxotius   Albina = Publicola, decd. c.406,
        (Ped. 23)   d.c.431 praetor urbanus (Ped. 23)

Paula
b. at Rome c.400

See note p.255

179

PEDIGREE 21   THE ANICII (I)

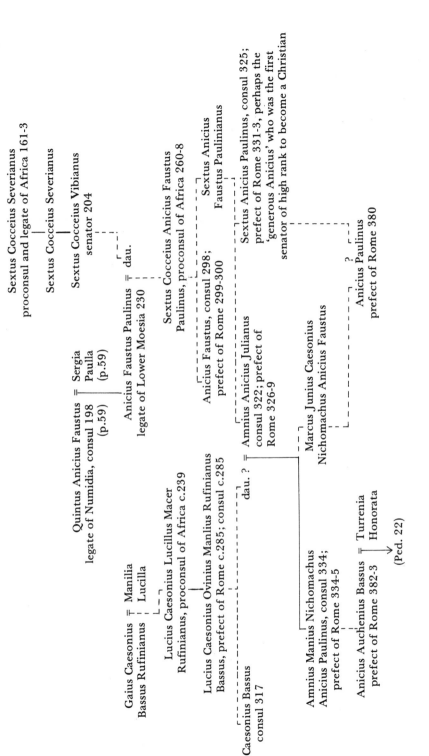

See note p.255

PEDIGREE 22   THE ANICII (II)

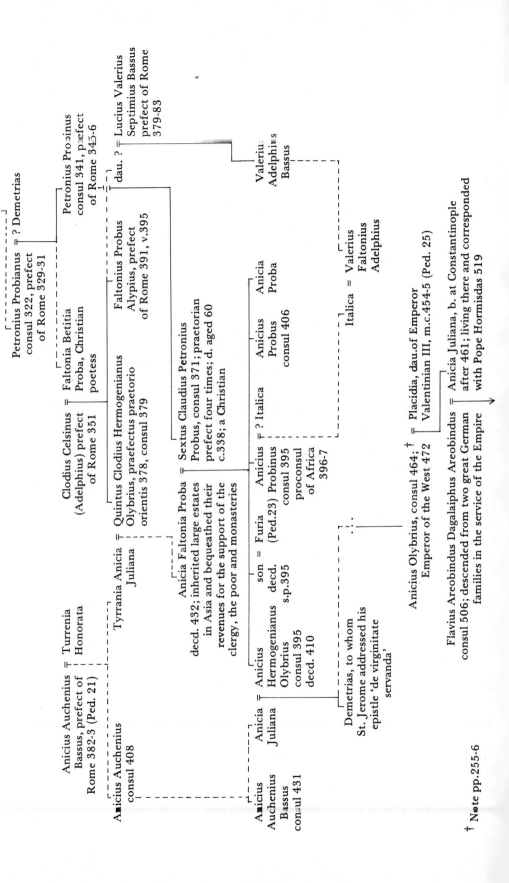

† Note pp.255-6

181

PEDIGREE 23   LINKS OF FOURTH CENTURY ROMAN EMPERORS TO ANCIENT FAMILIES

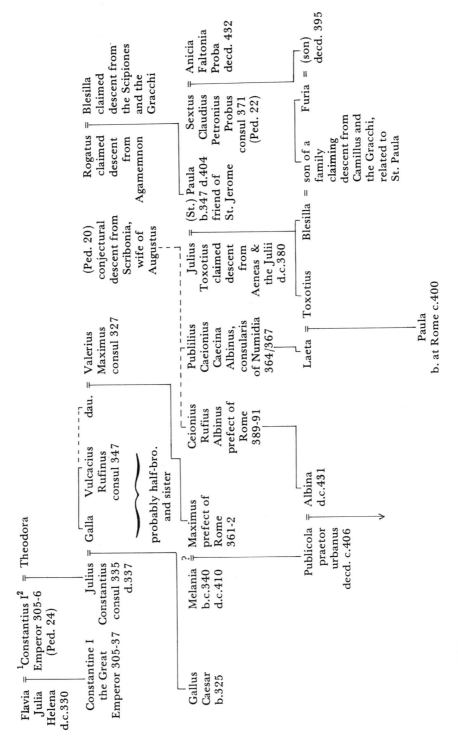

See note p.256

182

PEDIGREE 24   ROMAN EMPERORS: DIOCLETIAN TO THEODOSIUS I

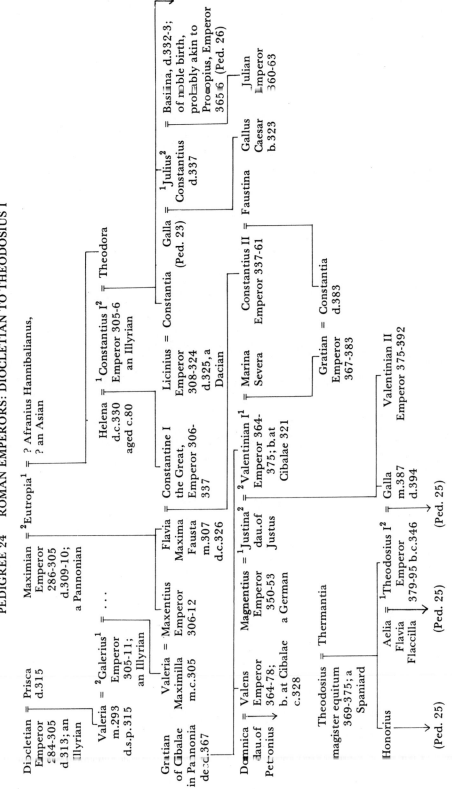

See note p.256

PEDIGREE 25   ROMAN EMPERORS: THEODOSIUS I TO OLYBRIUS

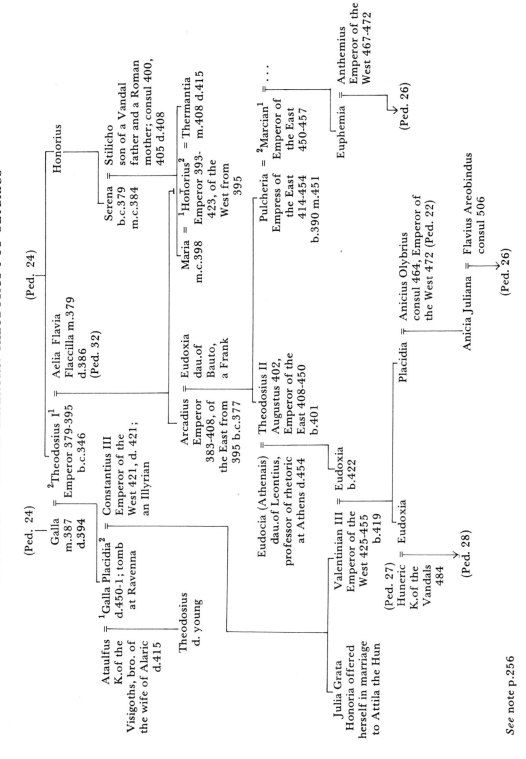

See note p.256

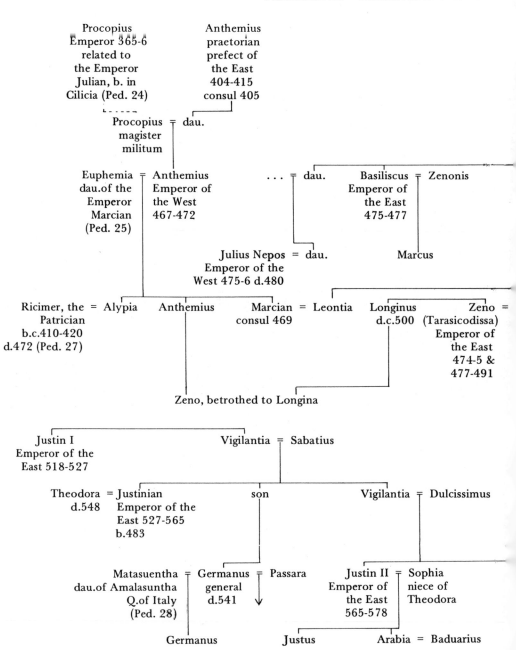

See note p.256

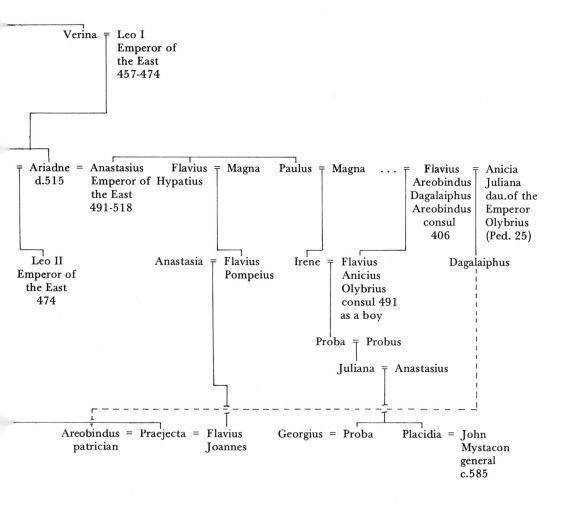

EMPERORS: PROCOPIUS TO JUSTIN II

PEDIGREE 27   BURGUNDIANS, VISIGOTHS, FRANKS AND LOMBARDS

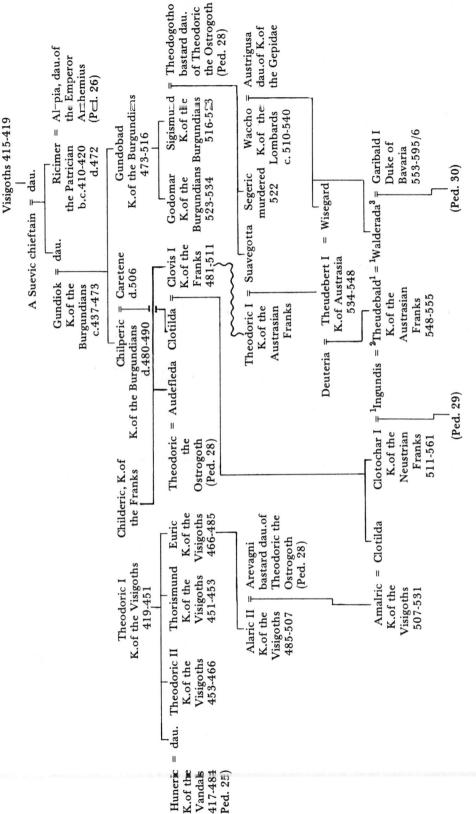

See note p.256

PEDIGREE 28   OSTROGOTHS AND VANDALS

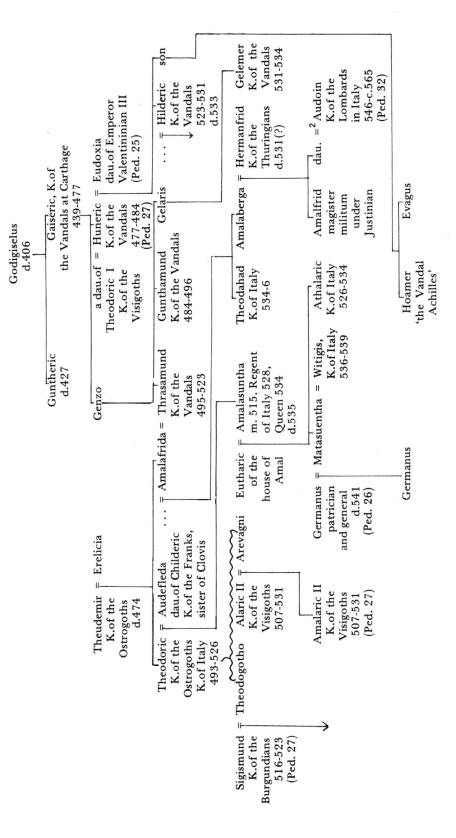

See note p.256

PEDIGREE 29   FRANKS, JUTES AND WEST SAXONS

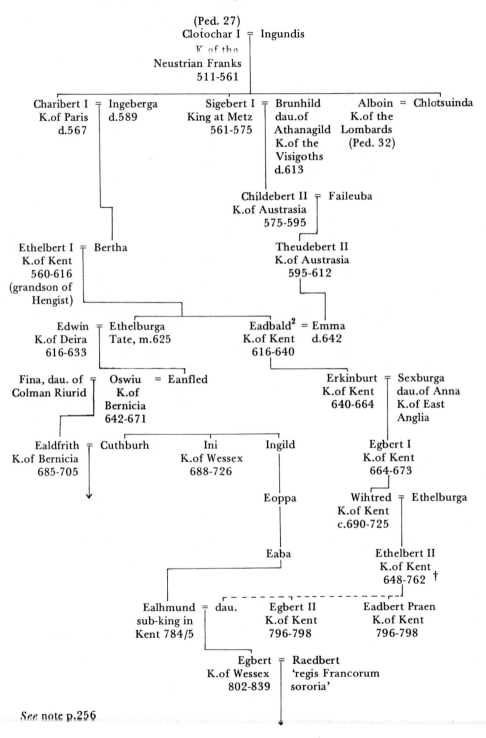

See note p.256

PEDIGREE 30 LOMBARDS, BAVARIA, CHARLEMAGNE

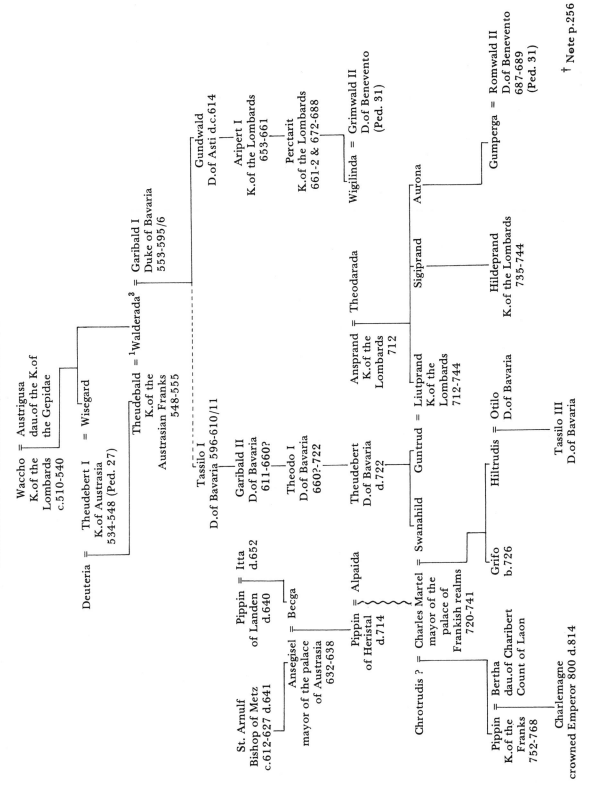

† Note p.256

PEDIGREE 31 LOMBARDS

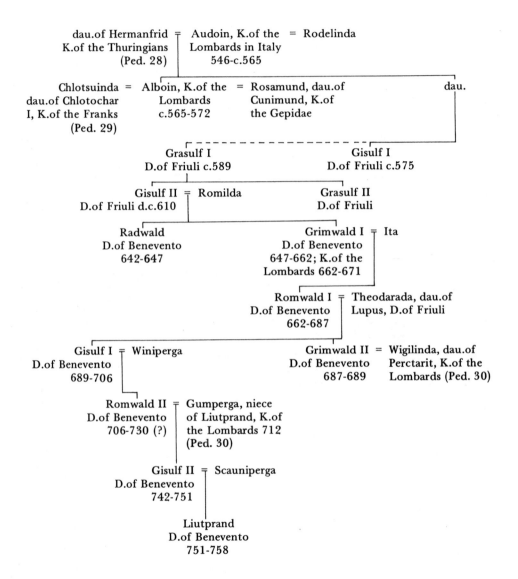

See note p.256

PEDIGREE 32   ROME TO ARMENIA, FOURTH CENTURY

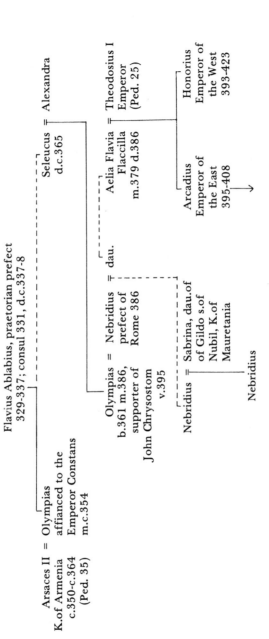

See note p.256

PEDIGREE 33   IBERIA

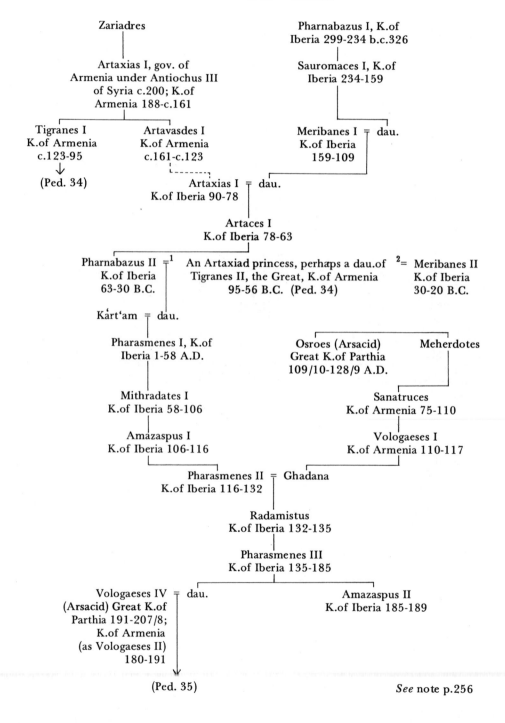

Zariadres

Artaxias I, gov. of
Armenia under Antiochus III
of Syria c.200; K.of
Armenia 188-c.161

Pharnabazus I, K.of
Iberia 299-234 b.c.326

Sauromaces I, K.of
Iberia 234-159

Tigranes I
K.of Armenia
c.123-95
↓
(Ped. 34)

Artavasdes I
K.of Armenia
c.161-c.123

Meribanes I = dau.
K.of Iberia
159-109

Artaxias I = dau.
K.of Iberia 90-78

Artaces I
K.of Iberia 78-63

Pharnabazus II =¹
K.of Iberia
63-30 B.C.

An Artaxiad princess, perhaps a dau.of ²=
Tigranes II, the Great, K.of Armenia
95-56 B.C. (Ped. 34)

Meribanes II
K.of Iberia
30-20 B.C.

Kártʻam = dau.

Pharasmenes I, K.of
Iberia 1-58 A.D.

Osroes (Arsacid)
Great K.of Parthia
109/10-128/9 A.D.

Meherdotes

Mithradates I
K.of Iberia 58-106

Sanatruces
K.of Armenia 75-110

Amazaspus I
K.of Iberia 106-116

Vologaeses I
K.of Armenia 110-117

Pharasmenes II = Ghadana
K.of Iberia 116-132

Radamistus
K.of Iberia 132-135

Pharasmenes III
K.of Iberia 135-185

Vologaeses IV = dau.
(Arsacid) Great K.of
Parthia 191-207/8;
K.of Armenia
(as Vologaeses II)
180-191

Amazaspus II
K.of Iberia 185-189

(Ped. 35)

See note p.256

PEDIGREE 34   ARTAXIADS OF ARMENIA: MEDIA ATROPATENE

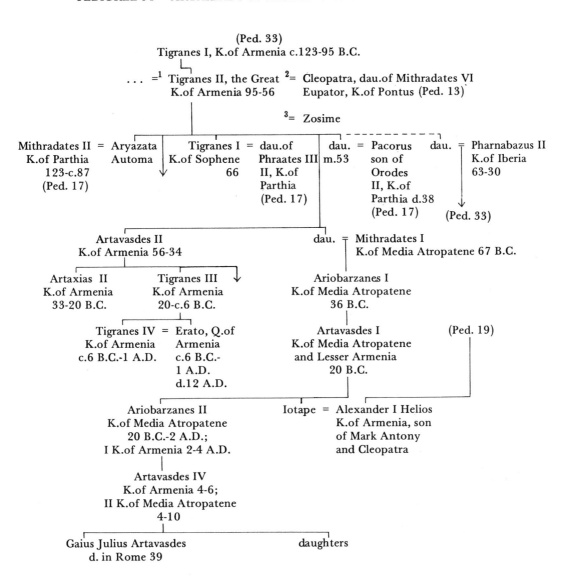

(Ped. 33)
Tigranes I, K.of Armenia c.123-95 B.C.

... =¹ Tigranes II, the Great ²= Cleopatra, dau.of Mithradates VI
K.of Armenia 95-56   Eupator, K.of Pontus (Ped. 13)

³= Zosime

Mithradates II = Aryazata   Tigranes I = dau.of   dau. = Pacorus   dau. = Pharnabazus II
K.of Parthia   Automa   K.of Sophene Phraates III m.53 son of   K.of Iberia
123-c.87   66   II, K.of   Orodes   63-30
(Ped. 17)   Parthia   II, K.of
                                          (Ped. 17)   Parthia d.38
                                                          (Ped. 17)   (Ped. 33)

Artavasdes II   dau. = Mithradates I
K.of Armenia 56-34   K.of Media Atropatene 67 B.C.

Artaxias II   Tigranes III   Ariobarzanes I
K.of Armenia   K.of Armenia   K.of Media Atropatene
33-20 B.C.   20-c.6 B.C.   36 B.C.

Tigranes IV = Erato, Q.of   Artavasdes I   (Ped. 19)
K.of Armenia Armenia   K.of Media Atropatene
c.6 B.C.-1 A.D. c.6 B.C.-   and Lesser Armenia
              1 A.D.   20 B.C.
              d.12 A.D.

Ariobarzanes II   Iotape = Alexander I Helios
K.of Media Atropatene   K.of Armenia, son
20 B.C.-2 A.D.;   of Mark Antony
I K.of Armenia 2-4 A.D.   and Cleopatra

Artavasdes IV
K.of Armenia 4-6;
II K.of Media Atropatene
4-10

Gaius Julius Artavasdes   daughters
d. in Rome 39

See note p.256

PEDIGREE 35   ARSACIDS OF ARMENIA

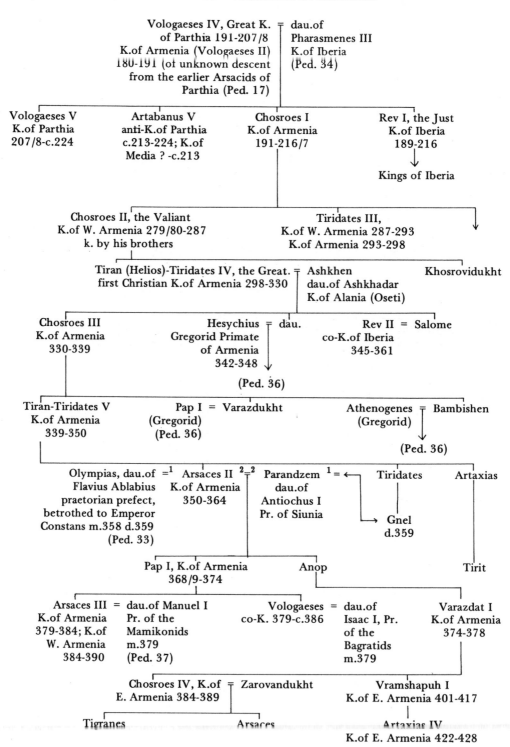

Vologaeses IV, Great K. ⊤ dau.of
of Parthia 191-207/8 │ Pharasmenes III
K.of Armenia (Vologaeses II) │ K.of Iberia
180-191 (of unknown descent │ (Ped. 34)
from the earlier Arsacids of
Parthia (Ped. 17)

Vologaeses V   Artabanus V   Chosroes I   Rev I, the Just
K.of Parthia   anti-K.of Parthia   K.of Armenia   K.of Iberia
207/8-c.224   c.213-224; K.of   191-216/7   189-216
                      Media ? -c.213

                                                                Kings of Iberia

Chosroes II, the Valiant   Tiridates III,
K.of W. Armenia 279/80-287   K.of W. Armenia 287-293
k. by his brothers   K.of Armenia 293-298

Tiran (Helios)-Tiridates IV, the Great. ⊤ Ashkhen   Khosrovidukht
first Christian K.of Armenia 298-330   │ dau.of Ashkhadar
                                         │ K.of Alania (Oseti)

Chosroes III   Hesychius ⊤ dau.   Rev II = Salome
K.of Armenia   Gregorid Primate   co-K.of Iberia
330-339   of Armenia   345-361
                          342-348 ↓

                          (Ped. 36)

Tiran-Tiridates V   Pap I = Varazdukht   Athenogenes ⊤ Bambishen
K.of Armenia   (Gregorid)   (Gregorid)
339-350   (Ped. 36)   ↓

                                                                (Ped. 36)

Olympias, dau.of =¹ Arsaces II ²⊤² Parandzem ¹= ← Tiridates   Artaxias
Flavius Ablabius   K.of Armenia   dau.of
praetorian prefect, 350-364   Antiochus I
betrothed to Emperor   Pr. of Siunia   Gnel
Constans m.358 d.359   d.359
(Ped. 33)

Pap I, K.of Armenia   Anop   Tirit
368/9-374

Arsaces III = dau.of Manuel I   Vologaeses = dau.of   Varazdat I
K.of Armenia   Pr. of the   co-K. 379-c.386 Isaac I, Pr.   K.of Armenia
379-384; K.of Mamikonids   of the   374-378
W. Armenia   m.379   Bagratids
384-390   (Ped. 37)   m.379

Chosroes IV, K.of ⊤ Zarovandukht   Vramshapuh I
E. Armenia 384-389   K.of E. Armenia 401-417

Tigranes   Arsaces   Artaxias IV
                                         K.of E. Armenia 422-428

See note p.257

PEDIGREE 36   ARMENIA: SUREN-PAHLAVIDS/GREGORIDS

Anak, of the Iranian house of
Suren-Pahlav

St. Gregory I, the Illuminator, Primate of Armenia = Maria
314-328; Prince of Acilisene, Taraun-Ashtishot, Bagravandene | dau.of David

St. Vrtanes I
Primate of Armenia
Pr. of A., T.-A., B.
327-342

St. Aristakes
Primate of Armenia
Pr. of A., T.-A., B.
320-327

Hesychius/Yusik I = dau.of Tiridates IV
Primate of Armenia | the Great, K.of
Pr. of A., T.-A., B. | Armenia m.317
342-348 b.c.305 | (Ped. 35)

Pap I, Pr. of the = Varazdukht, dau.of   Athenogenes = Bambishen, dau.
Gregorid domain   Chosroes III, K.of   of Chosroes III,
348- ?   Armenia (Ped. 35)   K.of Armenia
                                                             (Ped. 35)

St. Narses I, the Great = Sandukht, dau.of
Primate of Armenia;   Vardan I, Pr. of the
Pr. of the Gregorid   Mamikonids (Ped. 37)
domain 355-373

St. Isaac I, the Great, Primate of Armenia
Pr. of the Gregorid domain 378-438

Hamazasp I, Pr. of the = Sahakanoysh
Mamikonids 387-432

(Ped. 37)

See note p.257

PEDIGREE 37   ARMENIA: MAMIKONIDS

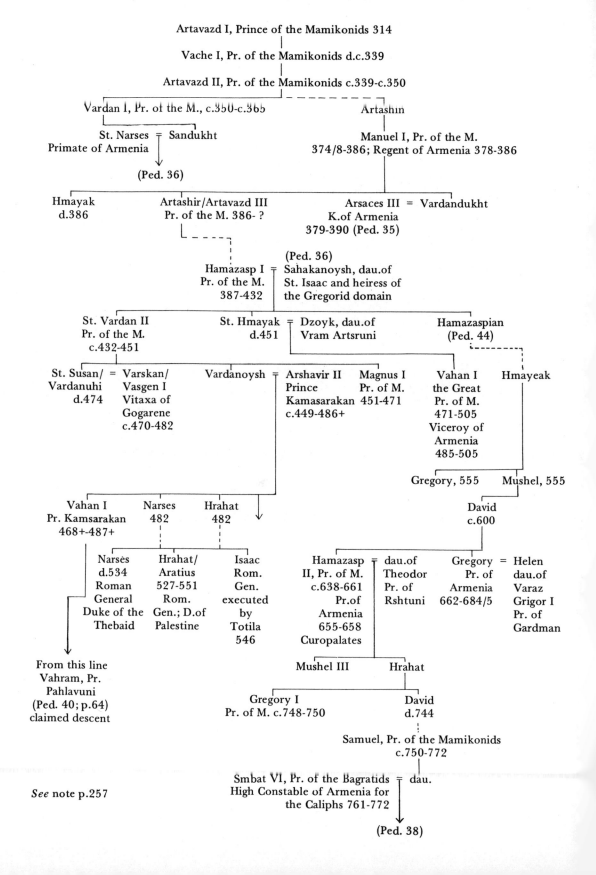

Artavazd I, Prince of the Mamikonids 314

Vache I, Pr. of the Mamikonids d.c.339

Artavazd II, Pr. of the Mamikonids c.339-c.350

Vardan I, Pr. of the M., c.350-c.365   Artashin

St. Narses ⊤ Sandukht   Manuel I, Pr. of the M.
Primate of Armenia   374/8-386; Regent of Armenia 378-386

(Ped. 36)

Hmayak   Artashir/Artavazd III   Arsaces III = Vardandukht
d.386   Pr. of the M. 386- ?   K.of Armenia
                                              379-390 (Ped. 35)

(Ped. 36)
Hamazasp I ⊤ Sahakanoysh, dau.of
Pr. of the M.   St. Isaac and heiress of
387-432   the Gregorid domain

St. Vardan II   St. Hmayak ⊤ Dzoyk, dau.of   Hamazaspian
Pr. of the M.   d.451   Vram Artsruni   (Ped. 44)
c.432-451

St. Susan/ = Varskan/   Vardanoysh ⊤ Arshavir II   Magnus I   Vahan I   Hmayeak
Vardanuhi   Vasgen I   Prince   Pr. of M.   the Great
d.474   Vitaxa of   Kamasarakan 451-471   Pr. of M.
            Gogarene   c.449-486+   471-505
            c.470-482   Viceroy of
                                                                          Armenia
                                                                          485-505

                                                           Gregory, 555   Mushel, 555

Vahan I   Narses   Hrahat   David
Pr. Kamsarakan   482   482   c.600
468+-487+

Narses   Hrahat/   Isaac   Hamazasp ⊤ dau.of   Gregory = Helen
d.534   Aratius   Rom.   II, Pr. of M. Theodor Pr. of   dau.of
Roman   527-551   Gen.   c.638-661   Pr. of   Armenia   Varaz
General   Rom.   executed   Pr.of   Rshtuni 662-684/5 Grigor I
Duke of the Gen.; D.of by   Armenia   Pr. of
Thebaid   Palestine Totila   655-658   Gardman
                      546   Curopalates

From this line   Mushel III   Hrahat
Vahram, Pr.
Pahlavuni   Gregory I   David
(Ped. 40; p.64)   Pr. of M. c.748-750   d.744
claimed descent

                              Samuel, Pr. of the Mamikonids
                                        c.750-772

See note p.257

Smbat VI, Pr. of the Bagratids ⊤ dau.
High Constable of Armenia for
the Caliphs 761-772

(Ped. 38)

PEDIGREE 38   ARMENIA: BAGRATIDS

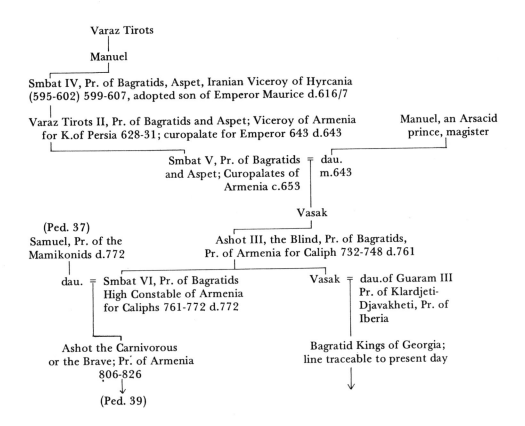

Varaz Tirots

Manuel

Smbat IV, Pr. of Bagratids, Aspet, Iranian Viceroy of Hyrcania
(595-602) 599-607, adopted son of Emperor Maurice d.616/7

Varaz Tirots II, Pr. of Bagratids and Aspet; Viceroy of Armenia   Manuel, an Arsacid
for K.of Persia 628-31; curopalate for Emperor 643 d.643   prince, magister

Smbat V, Pr. of Bagratids = dau.
and Aspet; Curopalates of   m.643
Armenia c.653

Vasak

(Ped. 37)
Samuel, Pr. of the   Ashot III, the Blind, Pr. of Bagratids,
Mamikonids d.772   Pr. of Armenia for Caliph 732-748 d.761

dau. = Smbat VI, Pr. of Bagratids   Vasak = dau.of Guaram III
       High Constable of Armenia   Pr. of Klardjeti-
       for Caliphs 761-772 d.772   Djavakheti, Pr. of
                                                    Iberia

Ashot the Carnivorous   Bagratid Kings of Georgia;
or the Brave; Pr. of Armenia   line traceable to present day
806-826

(Ped. 39)

See note p.257

PEDIGREE 39   ARMENIA: BAGRATIDS AND ARTSRUNI

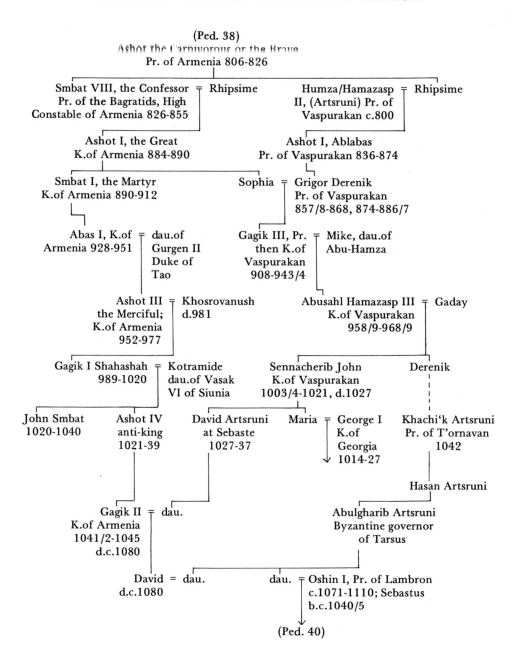

(Ped. 38)

Ashot the Carnivorous or the Brave
Pr. of Armenia 806-826

Smbat VIII, the Confessor = Rhipsime
Pr. of the Bagratids, High
Constable of Armenia 826-855

Humza/Hamazasp = Rhipsime
II, (Artsruni) Pr. of
Vaspurakan c.800

Ashot I, the Great
K.of Armenia 884-890

Ashot I, Ablabas
Pr. of Vaspurakan 836-874

Smbat I, the Martyr
K.of Armenia 890-912

Sophia = Grigor Derenik
Pr. of Vaspurakan
857/8-868, 874-886/7

Abas I, K.of = dau.of
Armenia 928-951   Gurgen II
Duke of
Tao

Gagik III, Pr. = Mike, dau.of
then K.of   Abu-Hamza
Vaspurakan
908-943/4

Ashot III = Khosrovanush
the Merciful;   d.981
K.of Armenia
952-977

Abusahl Hamazasp III = Gaday
K.of Vaspurakan
958/9-968/9

Gagik I Shahashah = Kotramide
989-1020   dau.of Vasak
VI of Siunia

Sennacherib John
K.of Vaspurakan
1003/4-1021, d.1027

Derenik

John Smbat
1020-1040

Ashot IV
anti-king
1021-39

David Artsruni
at Sebaste
1027-37

Maria = George I
K.of
Georgia
1014-27

Khachi'k Artsruni
Pr. of T'ornavan
1042

Hasan Artsruni

Gagik II = dau.
K.of Armenia
1041/2-1045
d.c.1080

Abulgharib Artsruni
Byzantine governor
of Tarsus

David = dau.
d.c.1080

dau. = Oshin I, Pr. of Lambron
c.1071-1110; Sebastus
b.c.1040/5

(Ped. 40)

See note p.257

PEDIGREE 40   ARMENIA: KARIN-PAHLAVIDS (KAMSARAKAN) / PAHLAVUNI

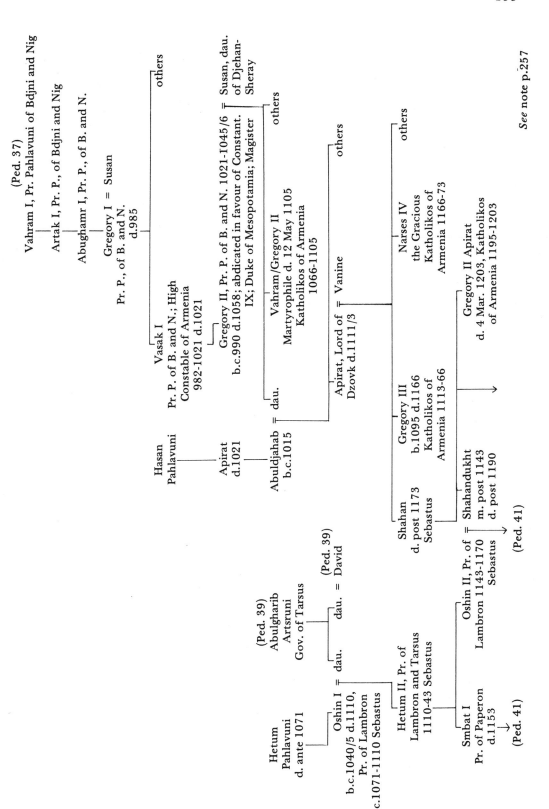

See note p.257

PEDIGREE 41   ARMENO-CILICIA AND OUTRE MER

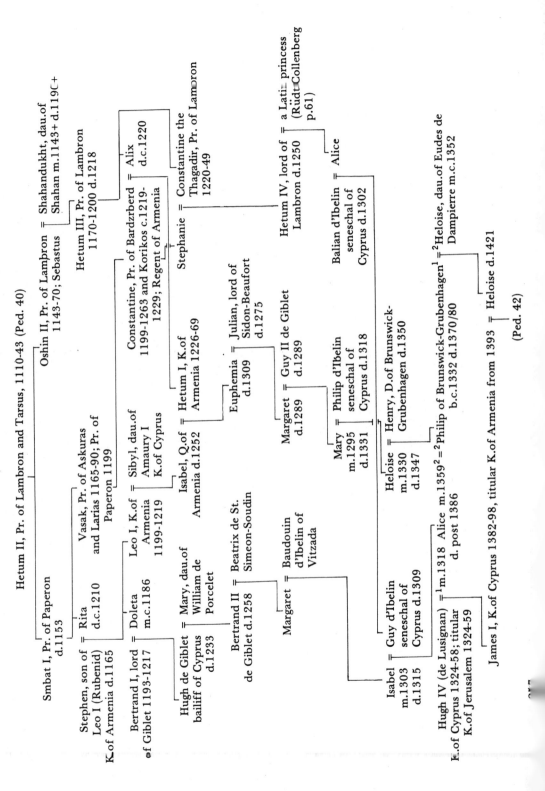

(Ped. 42)

PEDIGREE 42   OUTRE MER TO ENGLAND

(Ped. 41) James I, K.of Cyprus 1382-98, K.of Armenia from 1393 ╤ Heloise, d.1421 (Ped. 41)

Janus, K.of Cyprus 1398-1432 ╤ Charlotte, dau.of Jean II of Bourbon-Vendôme
Ct. of La Marche

Louis, D.of Savoy d.1468 ╤ Anne, m.1433

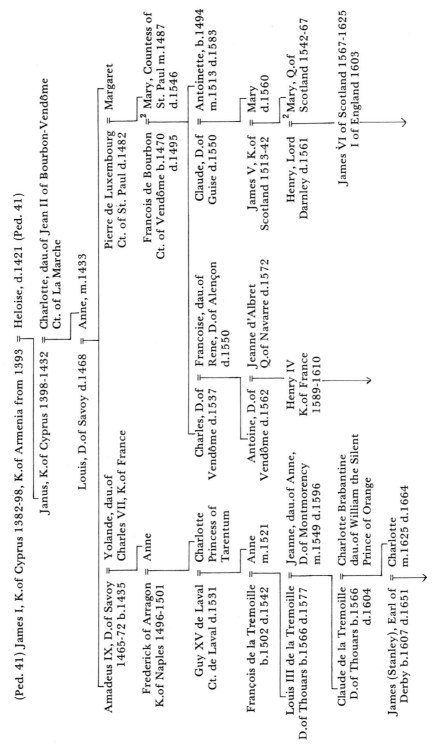

Pierre de Luxembourg ╤ Margaret
Ct. of St. Paul d.1482

Francois de Bourbon ╤² Mary, Countess of
Ct. of Vendôme b.1470   St. Paul m.1487
d.1495   d.1546

Claude, D.of ╤ Antoinette, b.1494
Guise d.1550   m.1513 d.1583

James V, K.of ╤ Mary
Scotland 1513-42   d.1560

Henry, Lord ╤² Mary, Q.of
Darnley d.1561   Scotland 1542-67

James VI of Scotland 1567-1625
I of England 1603

Amadeus IX, D.of Savoy ╤ Yolande, dau.of
1465-72 b.1435   Charles VII, K.of France

Frederick of Arragon ╤ Anne
K.of Naples 1496-1501

Guy XV de Laval ╤ Charlotte
Ct. de Laval d.1531   Princess of
                      Tarentum

Charles, D.of ╤ Francoise, dau.of
Vendôme d.1537   Rene, D.of Alençon
                  d.1550

Antoine, D.of ╤ Jeanne d'Albret
Vendôme d.1562   Q.of Navarre d.1572

Henry IV
K.of France
1589-1610

François de la Tremoille ╤ Anne
b.1502 d.1542   m.1521

Louis III de la Tremoille ╤ Jeanne, dau.of Anne,
D.of Thouars b.1566 d.1577   D.of Montmorency
                             m.1549 d.1596

Claude de la Tremoille ╤ Charlotte Brabantine
D.of Thouars b.1566   dau.of William the Silent
d.1604   Prince of Orange

James (Stanley), Earl of ╤ Charlotte
Derby b.1607 d.1651   m.1625 d.1664

See note p.258

PEDIGREE 43   MAMIKONIDS, BASILID EMPERORS OF THE EAST, EDWARD I

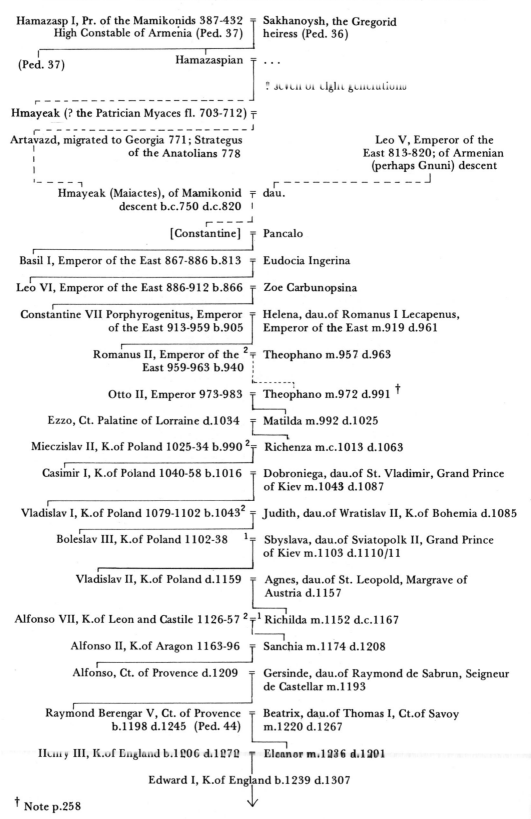

Hamazasp I, Pr. of the Mamikonids 387-432 ⊤ Sakhanoysh, the Gregorid
High Constable of Armenia (Ped. 37) heiress (Ped. 36)

(Ped. 37)   Hamazaspian ⊤ ...

? seven or eight generations

Hmayeak (? the Patrician Myaces fl. 703-712) ⊤

Artavazd, migrated to Georgia 771; Strategus   Leo V, Emperor of the
of the Anatolians 778   East 813-820; of Armenian
(perhaps Gnuni) descent

Hmayeak (Maiactes), of Mamikonid ⊤ dau.
descent b.c.750 d.c.820

[Constantine] ⊤ Pancalo

Basil I, Emperor of the East 867-886 b.813 ⊤ Eudocia Ingerina

Leo VI, Emperor of the East 886-912 b.866 ⊤ Zoe Carbunopsina

Constantine VII Porphyrogenitus, Emperor ⊤ Helena, dau.of Romanus I Lecapenus,
of the East 913-959 b.905 Emperor of the East m.919 d.961

Romanus II, Emperor of the ^{2}⊤ Theophano m.957 d.963
East 959-963 b.940

Otto II, Emperor 973-983 ⊤ Theophano m.972 d.991 †

Ezzo, Ct. Palatine of Lorraine d.1034 ⊤ Matilda m.992 d.1025

Mieczislav II, K.of Poland 1025-34 b.990 ^{2}⊤ Richenza m.c.1013 d.1063

Casimir I, K.of Poland 1040-58 b.1016 ⊤ Dobroniega, dau.of St. Vladimir, Grand Prince
of Kiev m.1043 d.1087

Vladislav I, K.of Poland 1079-1102 b.1043^2 ⊤ Judith, dau.of Wratislav II, K.of Bohemia d.1085

Boleslav III, K.of Poland 1102-38 ^{1}⊤ Sbyslava, dau.of Sviatopolk II, Grand Prince
of Kiev m.1103 d.1110/11

Vladislav II, K.of Poland d.1159 ⊤ Agnes, dau.of St. Leopold, Margrave of
Austria d.1157

Alfonso VII, K.of Leon and Castile 1126-57 ^{2}⊤^{1} Richilda m.1152 d.c.1167

Alfonso II, K.of Aragon 1163-96 ⊤ Sanchia m.1174 d.1208

Alfonso, Ct. of Provence d.1209 ⊤ Gersinde, dau.of Raymond de Sabrun, Seigneur
de Castellar m.1193

Raymond Berengar V, Ct. of Provence ⊤ Beatrix, dau.of Thomas I, Ct.of Savoy
b.1198 d.1245 (Ped. 44) m.1220 d.1267

Henry III, K.of England b.1206 d.1272 ⊤ Eleanor m.1236 d.1291

Edward I, K.of England b.1239 d.1307

† Note p.258

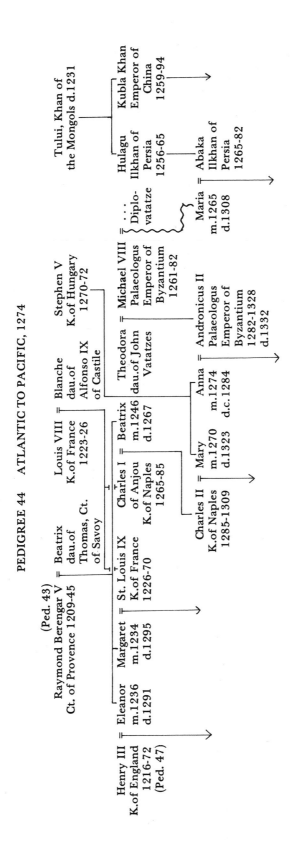

PEDIGREE 44   ATLANTIC TO PACIFIC, 1274

See note p.258

PEDIGREE 45   THE CONQUEROR'S KIN (I)

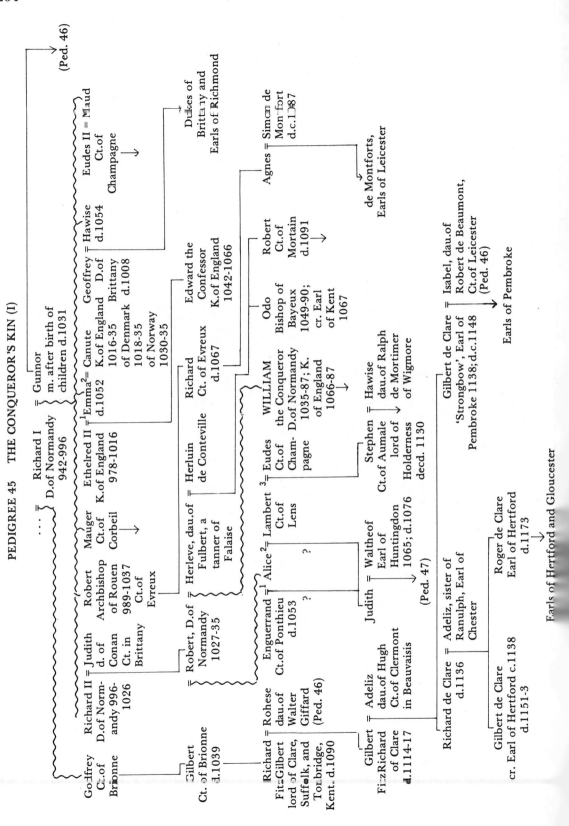

Earls of Hertford and Gloucester

PEDIGREE 46   THE CONQUEROR'S KIN (II)

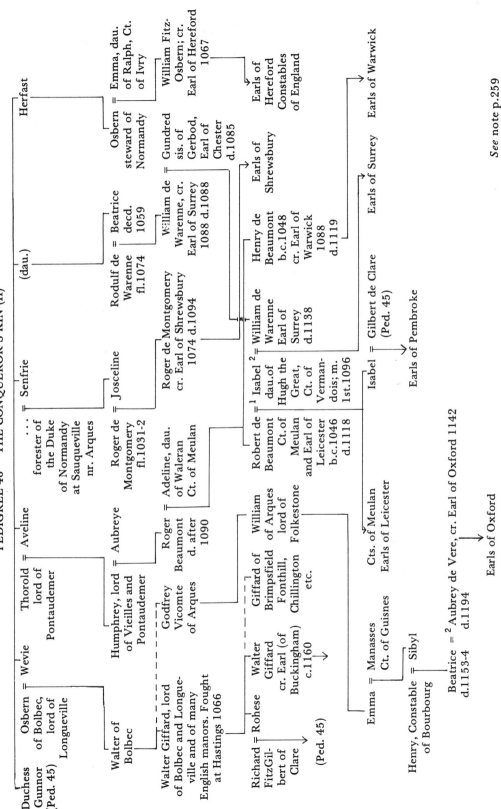

See note p.259

PEDIGREE 47   ENGLISH ANCESTORS OF KING EDWARD IV (I)

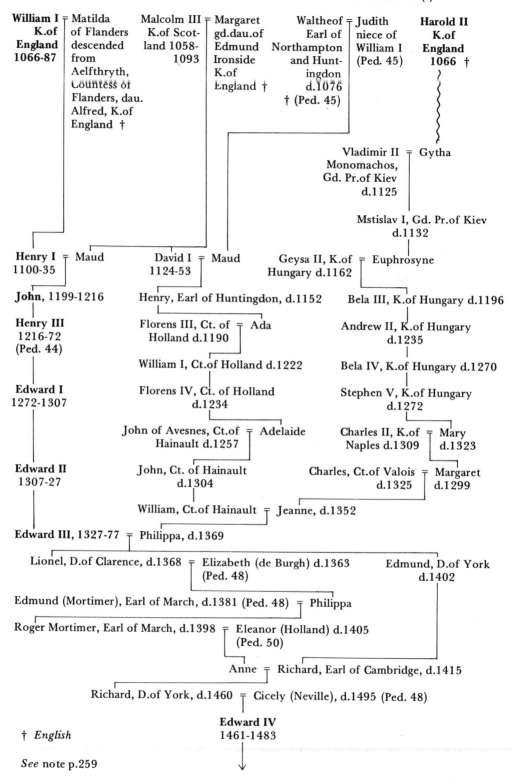

† *English*

See note p.259

PEDIGREE 48   ENGLISH ANCESTORS OF EDWARD IV (II)

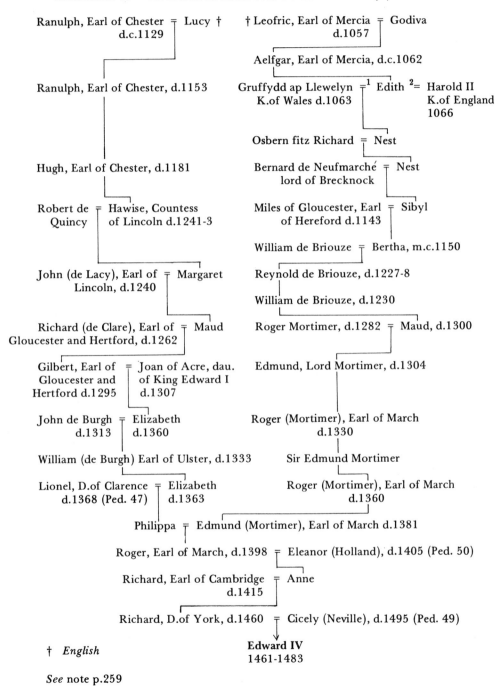

† *English*

See note p.259

PEDIGREE 49   ENGLISH ANCESTORS OF EDWARD IV (III)

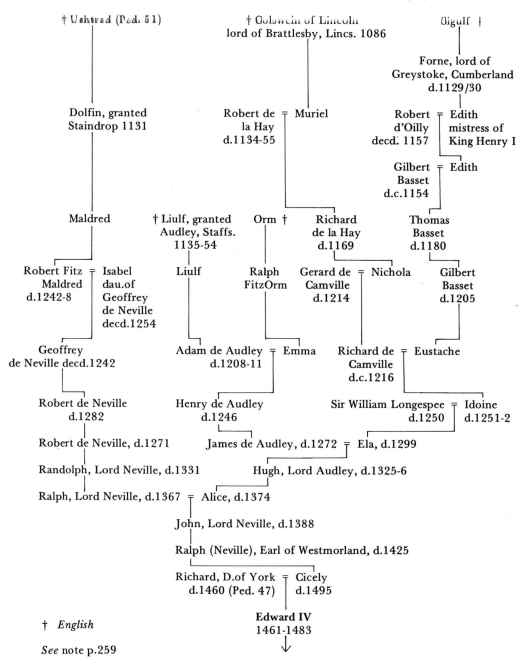

† Uhtred (Ped. 51)

† Colswein of Lincoln
lord of Brattlesby, Lincs. 1086

Oigulf |

Forne, lord of
Greystoke, Cumberland
d.1129/30

Dolfin, granted
Staindrop 1131

Robert de = Muriel
la Hay
d.1134-55

Robert = Edith
d'Oilly   mistress of
decd. 1157 King Henry I

Gilbert = Edith
Basset
d.c.1154

Maldred

† Liulf, granted
Audley, Staffs.
1135-54

Orm †

Richard
de la Hay
d.1169

Thomas
Basset
d.1180

Robert Fitz = Isabel
Maldred   dau.of
d.1242-8   Geoffrey
de Neville
decd.1254

Liulf

Ralph
FitzOrm

Gerard de = Nichola
Camville
d.1214

Gilbert
Basset
d.1205

Geoffrey
de Neville decd.1242

Adam de Audley = Emma
d.1208-11

Richard de = Eustache
Camville
d.c.1216

Robert de Neville
d.1282

Henry de Audley
d.1246

Sir William Longespee = Idoine
d.1250   d.1251-2

Robert de Neville, d.1271

James de Audley, d.1272 = Ela, d.1299

Randolph, Lord Neville, d.1331

Hugh, Lord Audley, d.1325-6

Ralph, Lord Neville, d.1367 = Alice, d.1374

John, Lord Neville, d.1388

Ralph (Neville), Earl of Westmorland, d.1425

Richard, D.of York = Cicely
d.1460 (Ped. 47) d.1495

Edward IV
1461-1483

† *English*

See note p.259

PEDIGREE 50   ENGLISH ANCESTORS OF EDWARD IV (IV)

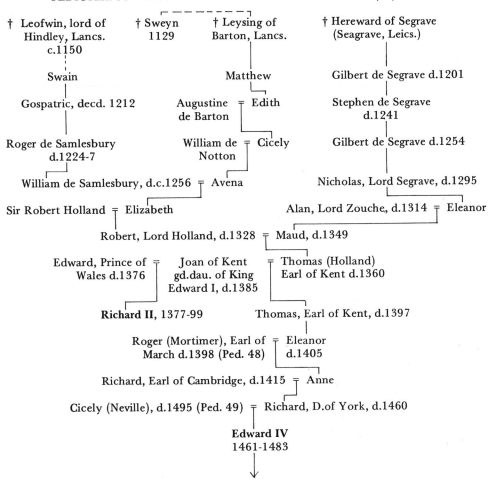

† *English*

See note p.259

210

PEDIGREE 51   ENGLISH EARLS OF NORTHUMBERLAND

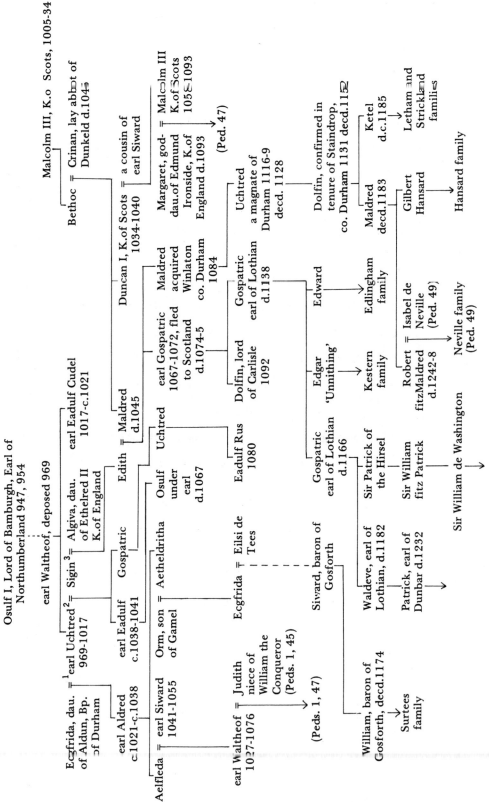

See note p.260

PEDIGREE 52   THE LONDON PATRICIATE: FITZAILWIN, BARROW, LE RUS, LE VIEL

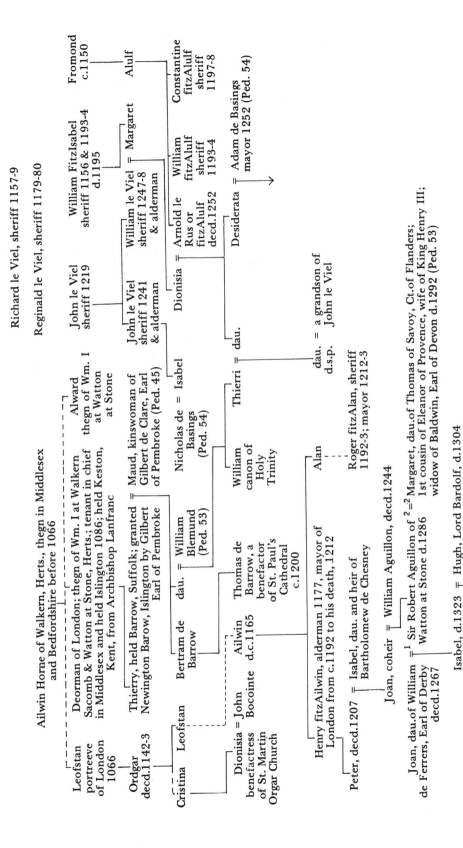

See note p.260

PEDIGREE 53   THE LONDON PATRICIATE: FITZALGAR, FITZHERLWIN, CORNHILL

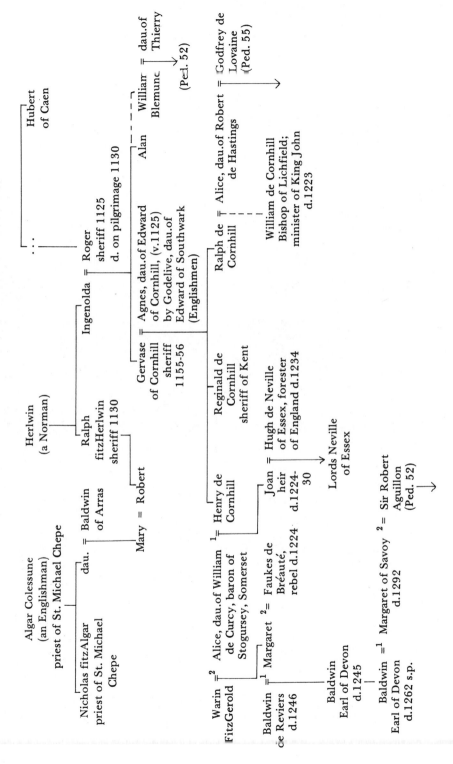

See note p.260

FIGURE 54 THE LONDON PATRICIATE: BASINGS, ASWY

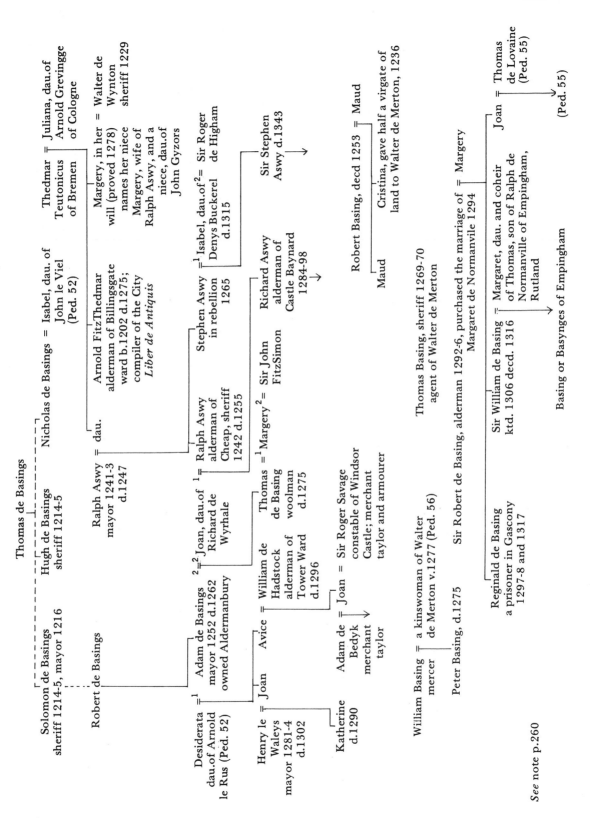

Thomas de Basings

See note p.260

PEDIGREE 55   LOVAINE

Godfrey I, the Bearded, D.of Lower Lorraine,
Ct.of Louvain d.1139; 10th in descent from Charlemagne (Ped.1)

Godfrey II,
D.of Lower Lorraine
d.1142

Henry I[2] = [1]Adeliz[2] ⊤ William d'Aubigny
K.of England   d.1151   Earl of Arundel
1100-35   d.1176

(Ped. 57)

Margaret, dau.of ⊤ Godfrey III, D.of Lower ⊤ Imaine, dau.of
Henry II, Ct. of   Lorraine and Ct. of   Louis, Ct. of Loos
Limburg d.1172   Louvain d.1190

Maud, dau.of Matthew ⊤ Henry I
of Flanders by Mary,   D.of Brabant
dau.of Stephen, K.of   d.1235
England
(Ped. 2)

Godfrey de ⊤ Alice, dau.of = Ralph de
Lovaine,   Robert de   Cornhill
custodian of Hastings, lord (Ped. 53)
the Honor of of Little Easton
Eye, Suffolk Essex m. 2ndly
d.1226   c.1199

Muriel ⊤ Matthew de Lovaine, custodian of the Honor of Eye;
v.1275   lord of the Honor of Little Easton decd. 1258

Helesant = Matthew de Lovaine, lord ⊤ Maud Poyntz, mentioned
a kinswoman of   of Little Easton; steward of   apparently as her niece, in
Henry III,   of Eye, d.1302   the will of Maud Walraunt of
K.of England   London 1289, decd. 1306
m.1268

Joan, probably ⊤ Sir Thomas de Lovaine, whose marriage
dau.of Sir Robert   (as a minor) was acquired in 1305 by
de Basing, alderman Margery, widow of Sir Robert de Basing,
of London (Ped. 54), alderman of London, so that she might
d.1318   marry him to one of her daus. d.1345

Margaret, dau. and coheir ⊤ John de Lovaine of Little
of Sir Thomas de Weston, 1349 | Easton d.s.p.m.1347

Eleanor ⊤ Sir William Bourchier
coheir d.1397 | d.1375

Edmund, Earl = [1]Anne, Countess of Buckingham,[2] ⊤ Sir William Bourchier, pardoned
of Stafford   Hereford and Northampton, dau.   1405 for marrying without royal
d.1403   of Thomas of Woodstock, D.of   licence; granted County of Eu in
                Gloucester, son of Edward III,   Normandy 1419. d.1420
                K.of England d.1438

Bourchier, Earl of Essex
and Earls of Bath

See note p.261

PEDIGREE 56   WALTER DE MERTON

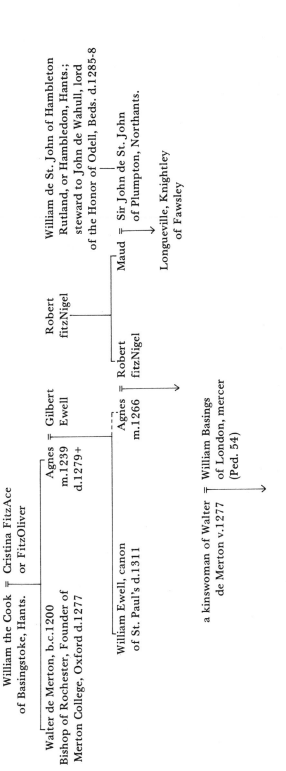

William the Cook = Cristina FitzAce
of Basingstoke, Hants. | or FitzOliver

Walter de Merton, b.c.1200
Bishop of Rochester, Founder of
Merton College, Oxford d.1277

Agnes = Gilbert
m.1239   Ewell
d.1279+

William Ewell, canon
of St. Paul's d.1311

Agnes = Robert
m.1266   fitzNigel

Robert
fitzNigel

William de St. John of Hambleton
Rutland, or Hambledon, Hants.;
steward to John de Wahull, lord
of the Honor of Odell, Beds. d.1285-8

Maud = Sir John de St. John
of Plumpton, Northants.

Longueville, Knightley
of Fawsley

a kinswoman of Walter = William Basings
de Merton v.1277   of London, mercer
                        (Ped. 54)

See note p.261

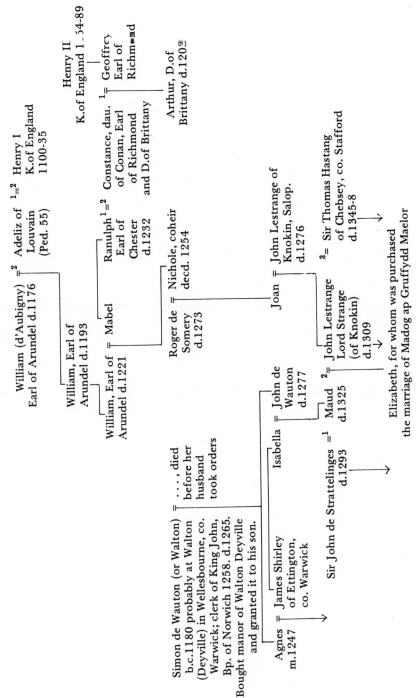

PEDIGREE 57   SIMON DE WAUTON

See note p.261

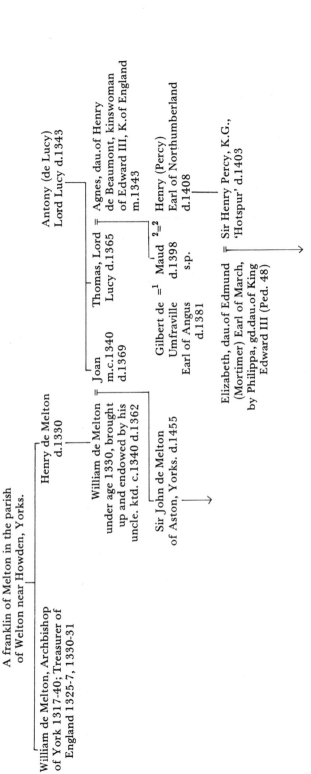

PEDIGREE 58 WILLIAM DE MELTON

A franklin of Melton in the parish
of Welton near Howden, Yorks.

William de Melton, Archbishop
of York 1317-40; Treasurer of
England 1325-7, 1330-31

Henry de Melton
d.1330

William de Melton =
under age 1330, brought
up and endowed by his
uncle. ktd. c.1340 d.1362

Joan
m.c.1340
d.1369

Antony (de Lucy)
Lord Lucy d.1343

Thomas, Lord
Lucy d.1365

= Agnes, dau.of Henry
de Beaumont, kinswoman
of Edward III, K.of England
m.1343

Sir John de Melton
of Aston, Yorks. d.1455

Gilbert de =¹ Maud ²=²
Umfraville   d.1398
Earl of Angus   s.p.
d.1381

Henry (Percy)
Earl of Northumberland
d.1408

Elizabeth, dau.of Edmund
(Mortimer) Earl of March,
by Philippa, gd.dau.of King
Edward III (Ped. 48)

= Sir Henry Percy, K.G.,
'Hotspur' d.1403

218

PEDIGREE 59   HENRY DE BRAY

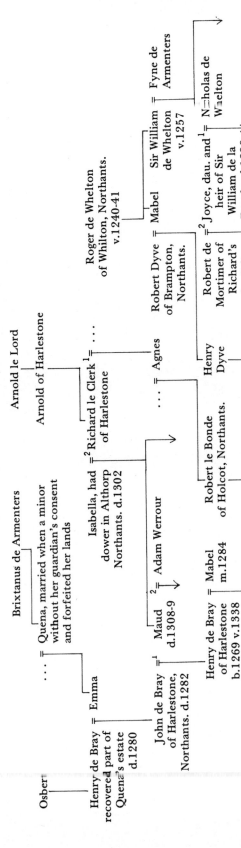

See note p.261

PEDIGREE 60   HENRY CHICHELE

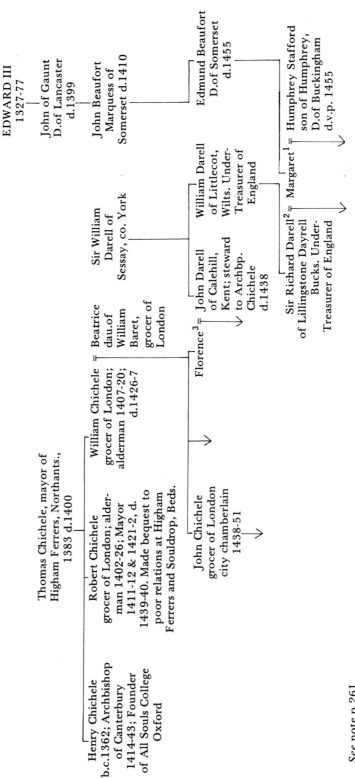

Thomas Chichele, mayor of
Higham Ferrers, Northants.,
1383 d.1400

Henry Chichele
b.c.1362; Archbishop
of Canterbury
1414-43; Founder
of All Souls College
Oxford

Robert Chichele
grocer of London; alder-
man 1402-26; Mayor
1411-12 & 1421-2, d.
1439-40. Made bequest to
poor relations at Higham
Ferrers and Souldrop, Beds.

William Chichele
grocer of London;
alderman 1407-20;
d.1426-7

= Beatrice
dau. of
William
Baret,
grocer of
London

John Chichele
grocer of London
city chamberlain
1438-51

Florence[3] =

Sir William
Darell of
Sessay, co. York

William Darell
of Littlecot,
Wilts. Under-
Treasurer of
England

John Darell
of Calehill,
Kent; steward
to Archbp.
Chichele
d.1438

Sir Richard Darell[2]
of Lillingstone Dayrell
Bucks. Under-
Treasurer of England

Margaret[1] =

EDWARD III
1327-77

John of Gaunt
D.of Lancaster
d.1399

John Beaufort
Marquess of
Somerset d.1410

Edmund Beaufort
D.of Somerset
d.1455

Humphrey Stafford
son of Humphrey,
D.of Buckingham
d.v.p. 1455

See note p.261

PEDIGREE 61   DRAKE OF ESSEX

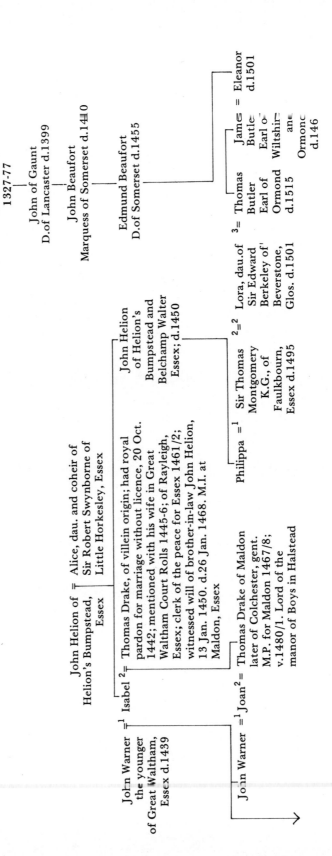

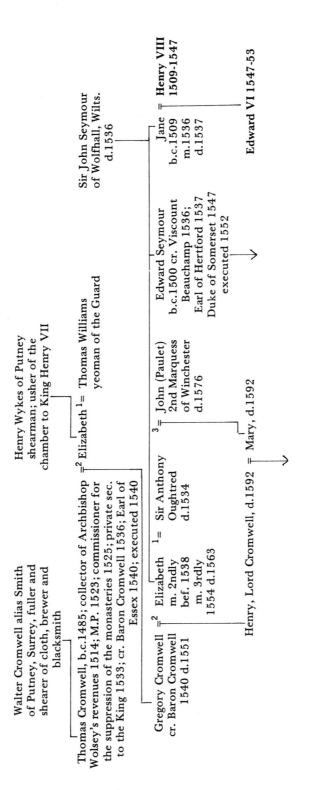

PEDIGREE 62   THOMAS CROMWELL

Walter Cromwell alias Smith
of Putney, Surrey; fuller and
shearer of cloth, brewer and
blacksmith

Henry Wykes of Putney
shearman; usher of the
chamber to King Henry VII

Thomas Cromwell, b.c.1485; collector of Archbishop
Wolsey's revenues 1514; M.P. 1523; commissioner for
the suppression of the monasteries 1525; private sec.
to the King 1533; cr. Baron Cromwell 1536; Earl of
Essex 1540; executed 1540

[2] Elizabeth [1]= Thomas Williams
yeoman of the Guard

Sir John Seymour
of Wolfhall, Wilts.
d.1536

Gregory Cromwell [2]=
cr. Baron Cromwell
1540 d.1551

Elizabeth [1]= Sir Anthony
m. 2ndly   Oughtred
bef. 1538   d.1534
m. 3rdly
1554 d.1563

[3]= John (Paulet)
2nd Marquess
of Winchester
d.1576

Edward Seymour
b.c.1500 cr. Viscount
Beauchamp 1536;
Earl of Hertford 1537
Duke of Somerset 1547
executed 1552

Jane = Henry VIII
b.c.1509   1509-1547
m.1536
d.1537

Henry, Lord Cromwell, d.1592 = Mary, d.1592

Edward VI 1547-53

See note p.261

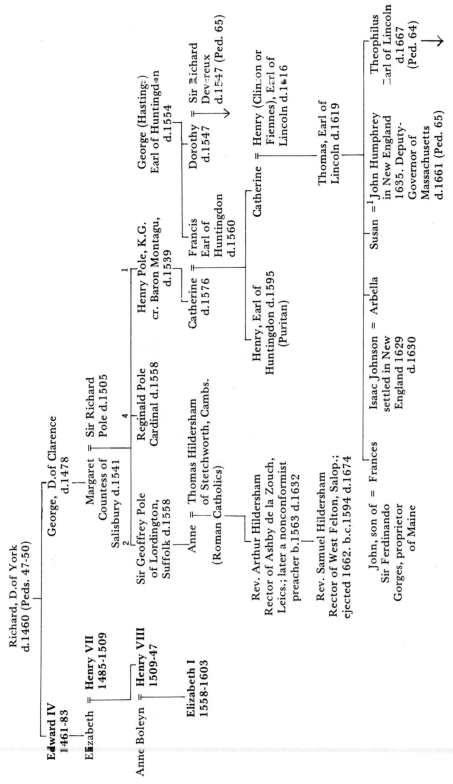

PEDIGREE 63   PURITANS AND COLONISTS (I)

Richard, D.of York
d.1460 (Peds. 47-50)

George, D.of Clarence
d.1478

Edward IV
1461-83

Elizabeth = Henry VII
1485-1509

Anne Boleyn = Henry VIII
1509-47

Elizabeth I
1558-1603

Margaret = Sir Richard
Countess of   Pole d.1505
Salisbury d.1541

Sir Geoffrey Pole   Reginald Pole   Henry Pole, K.G.
of Lordington,   Cardinal d.1558   cr. Baron Montagu,
Suffolk d.1558   d.1539

Anne = Thomas Hildersham
of Stetchworth, Cambs.
(Roman Catholics)

Catherine = Francis
d.1576   Earl of
            Huntingdon
            d.1560

George (Hastings =
Earl of Huntingdon
d.1554

Dorothy = Sir Richard
d.1547   Devereux
          d.1547 (Ped. 65)

Rev. Arthur Hildersham
Rector of Ashby de la Zouch,
Leics.; later a nonconformist
preacher b.1563 d.1632

Rev. Samuel Hildersham
Rector of West Felton, Salop.;
ejected 1662. b.c.1594 d.1674

Henry, Earl of
Huntingdon d.1595
(Puritan)

Catherine = Henry (Clinton or
Fiennes), Earl of
Lincoln d.1616

Thomas, Earl of
Lincoln d.1619

Theophilus
Earl of Lincoln
d.1667
(Ped. 64)

John, son of = Frances
Sir Ferdinando
Gorges, proprietor
of Maine

Isaac Johnson = Arbella
settled in New
England 1629
d.1630

Susan =[1]John Humphrey
in New England
1635. Deputy-
Governor of
Massachusetts
d.1661 (Ped. 65)

See note p.262

223

PEDIGREE 64   PURITANS AND COLONISTS (II)

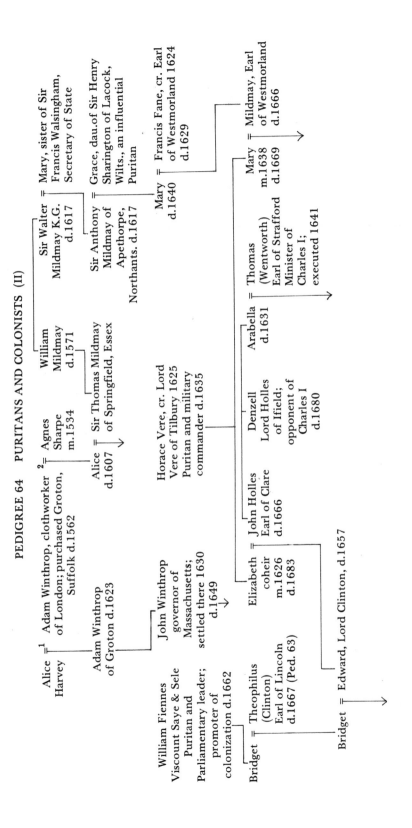

See note p.262

PEDIGREE 65   PURITANS AND COLONISTS (III)

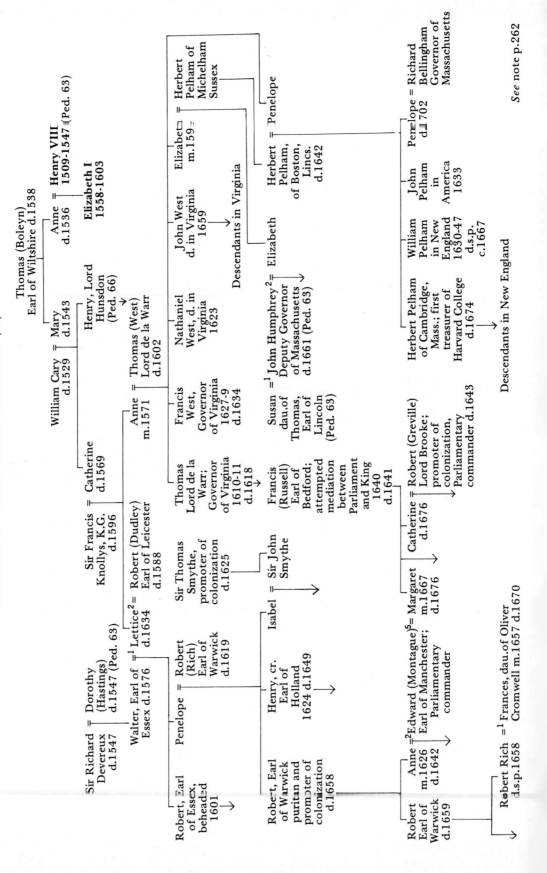

See note p.262

PEDIGREE 66 QUEEN ELIZABETH I TO WILLIAM SHAKESPEARE

Thomas (Boleyn), Earl of Wiltshire and Ormond d.1538 (Ped. 65)

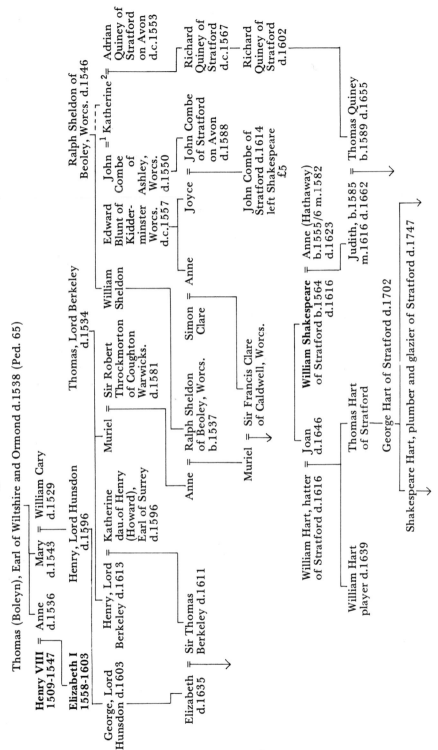

See note p.262

PEDIGREE 67   BURLEIGH AND ROBERT BROWNE

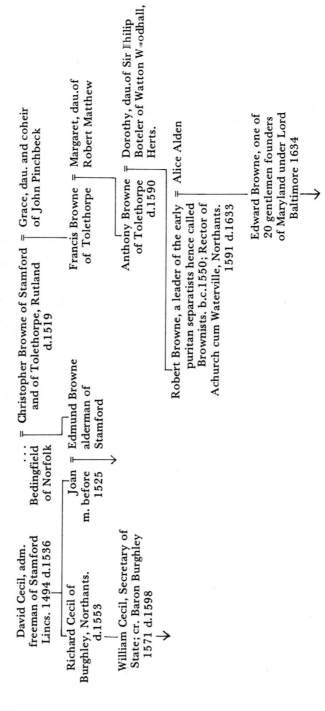

See note p.262

PEDIGREE 68   QUAKERS: CROWLEY AND LLOYD

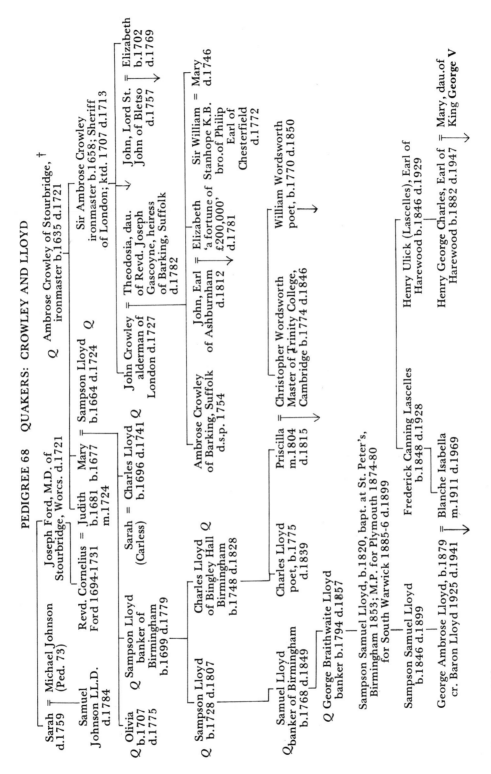

See note p.263

228

PEDIGREE 69   BIRMINGHAM UNITARIANS

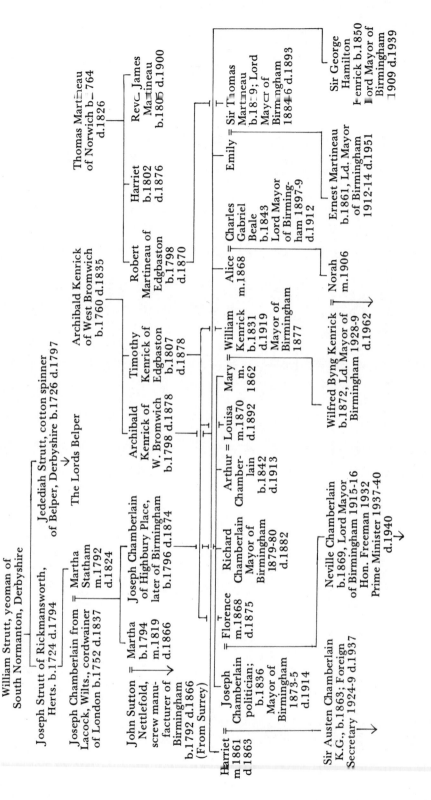

See note p.263

PEDIGREE 70   PIGOT

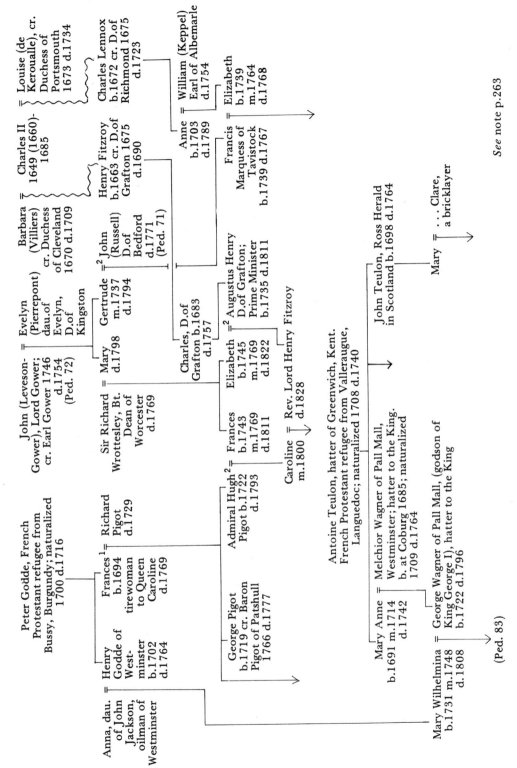

Peter Godde, French
Protestant refugee from
Bussy, Burgundy; naturalized
1700 d.1716

Anna, dau.
of John
Jackson,
oilman of
Westminster

Henry
Godde of West-
minster
b.1702
d.1764

Frances[1]
b.1694
tirewoman
to Queen
Caroline
d.1769

Richard
Pigot
d.1729

John (Leveson-
Gower), Lord Gower;
cr. Earl Gower 1746
d.1754
(Ped. 72)

Evelyn
(Pierrepont)
dau.of
Evelyn,
D.of
Kingston

Charles II
1649 (1660)-
1685

Louise (de
Keroualle), cr.
Duchess of
Portsmouth
1673 d.1734

Barbara
(Villiers)
cr. Duchess
of Cleveland
1670 d.1709

Charles Lennox
b.1672 cr. D.of
Richmond 1675
d.1723

Henry Fitzroy
b.1663 cr. D.of
Grafton 1675
d.1690

Sir Richard
Wrottesley, Bt.
Dean of
Worcester
d.1769

Mary
d.1798

Gertrude
m.1737
d.1794

[2]John
(Russell)
D.of
Bedford
d.1771
(Ped. 71)

Charles, D.of
Grafton b.1683
d.1757

Anne
b.1703
d.1789

William (Keppel)
Earl of Albemarle
d.1754

Elizabeth
b.1739
m.1764
d.1768

Francis
Marquess of
Tavistock
b.1739 d.1767

George Pigot
b.1719 cr. Baron
Pigot of Patshull
1766 d.1777

Admiral Hugh[2]
Pigot b.1722
d.1793

Frances
b.1743
m.1769
d.1811

Elizabeth
b.1745
m.1769
d.1822

[2]Augustus Henry
D.of Grafton;
Prime Minister
b.1735 d.1811

Caroline
m.1800

Rev. Lord Henry Fitzroy
d.1828

Antoine Teulon, hatter of Greenwich, Kent.
French Protestant refugee from Valleraugue,
Languedoc; naturalized 1708 d.1740

John Teulon, Ross Herald
in Scotland b.1698 d.1764

Mary
. . . Clare,
a bricklayer

Melchior Wagner of Pall Mall,
Westminster; hatter to the King.
b. at Coburg 1685; naturalized
1709 d.1764

Mary Anne
b.1691 m.1714
d.1742

George Wagner of Pall Mall, (godson of
King George I), hatter to the King
b.1722 d.1796

Mary Wilhelmina
b.1731 m.1748
d.1808

(Ped. 83)

See note p.263

230

PEDIGREE 71 WHIGS (I)

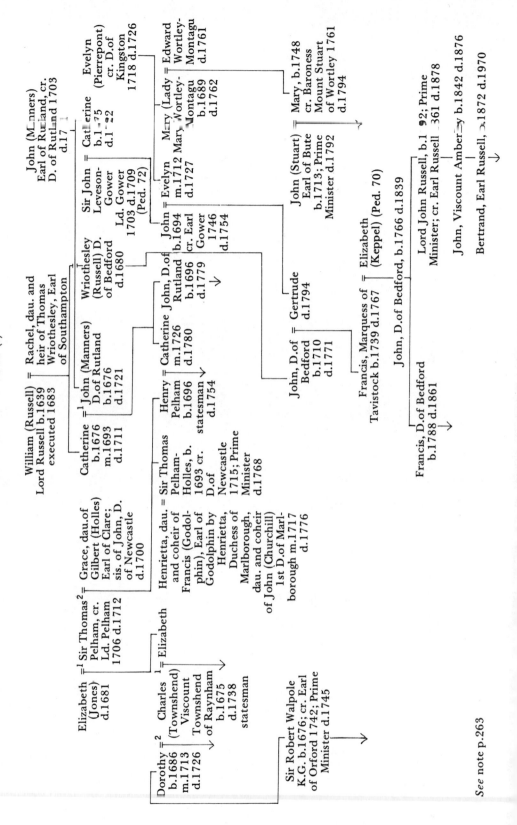

See note p.263

PEDIGREE 72   WHIGS (II)

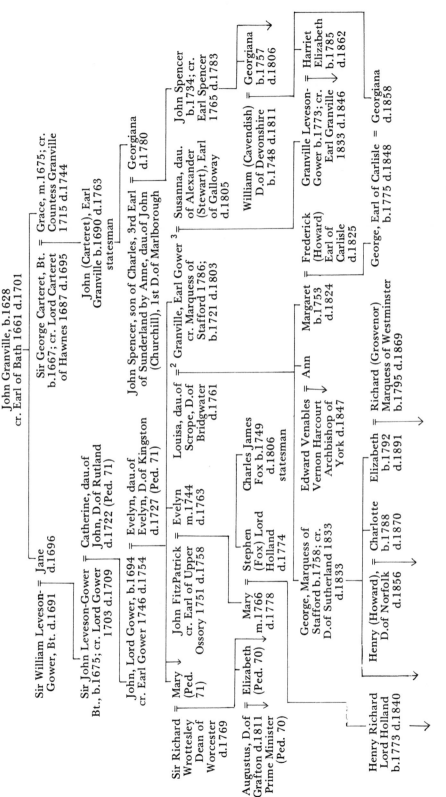

John Granville, b.1628
cr. Earl of Bath 1661 d.1701

Sir George Carteret, Bt.
b.1667; cr. Lord Carteret
of Hawnes 1687 d.1695

Grace, m.1675; cr.
Countess Granville
1715 d.1744

John (Carteret), Earl
Granville b.1690 d.1763
statesman

Georgiana
d.1780

John Spencer, son of Charles, 3rd Earl
of Sunderland by Anne, dau.of John
(Churchill), 1st D.of Marlborough

Susanna, dau.
of Alexander
(Stewart), Earl
of Galloway
d.1805

John Spencer
b.1734; cr.
Earl Spencer
1765 d.1783

William (Cavendish)
D.of Devonshire
b.1748 d.1811

Georgiana
b.1757
d.1806

Granville Leveson-
Gower b.1773; cr.
Earl Granville
1833 d.1846

Harriet
Elizabeth
b.1785
d.1862

George, Earl of Carlisle = Georgiana
b.1775 d.1848   d.1858

Sir William Leveson- = Jane
Gower, Bt.   d.1696

Sir John Leveson-Gower = Catherine, dau.of
Bt., b.1675; cr. Lord Gower   John, D.of Rutland
1703 d.1709   d.1722 (Ped. 71)

John, Lord Gower, b.1694 = Evelyn, dau.of
cr. Earl Gower 1746 d.1754   Evelyn, D.of Kingston
                             d.1727 (Ped. 71)

Sir Richard = Mary   John FitzPatrick = Evelyn
Wrottesley   (Ped.   cr. Earl of Upper   m.1744
Dean of   71)   Ossory 1751 d.1758 d.1763
Worcester
d.1769

Augustus, D.of = Elizabeth   Mary = Stephen
Grafton d.1811   (Ped. 70)   m.1766 (Fox) Lord
Prime Minister   d.1778 Holland
(Ped. 70)   d.1774

Charles James
Fox b.1749
d.1806
statesman

²Granville, Earl Gower ³
cr. Marquess of
Stafford 1786;
b.1721 d.1803

Louisa, dau.of
Scrope, D.of
Bridgwater
d.1761

= Ann

Margaret
b.1753
d.1824

Frederick
(Howard)
Earl of
Carlisle
d.1825

George, Marquess of
Stafford b.1758; cr.
D.of Sutherland 1833
d.1833

Edward Venables
Vernon Harcourt
Archbishop of
York d.1847

Elizabeth
b.1792
d.1891

Richard (Grosvenor)
Marquess of Westminster
b.1795 d.1869

Henry (Howard), = Charlotte
D.of Norfolk   b.1788
d.1856   d.1870

Henry Richard
Lord Holland
b.1773 d.1840

See note p.263

232

Thomas Egerton, b.1540; Lord Keeper 1596;
Lord Chancellor 1603; cr. Viscount Brackley 1616 d.1617

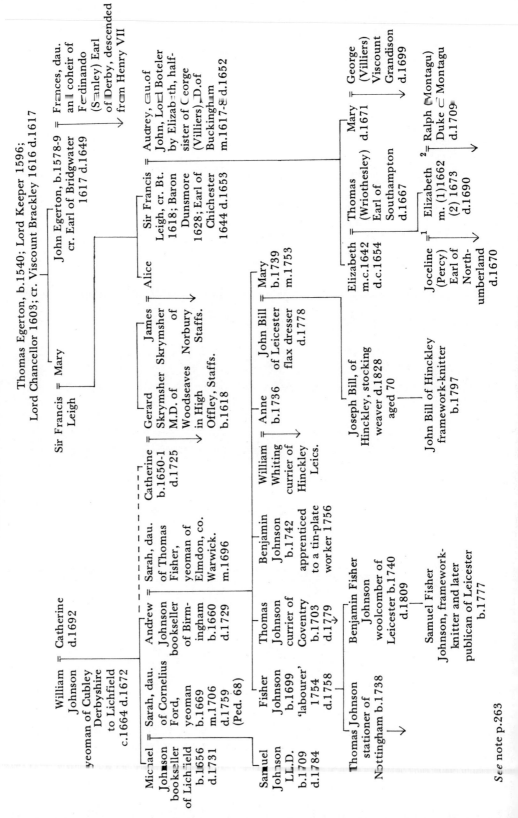

See note p.263

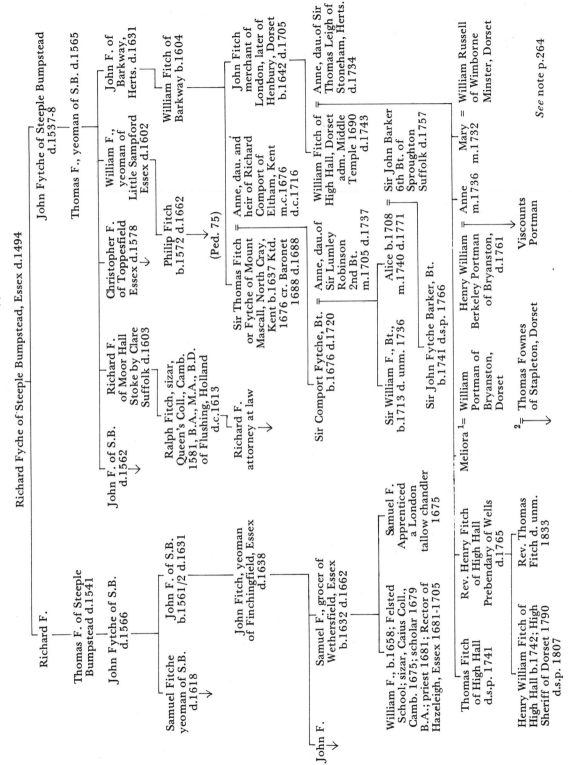

PEDIGREE 74   FITCH (I)

See note p.264

PEDIGREE 75   FITCH (II)

(Ped. 74)
Philip Fitch b.1572 d.1662

Samuel Fitch, yeoman of Great Dunmow, Essex
b.1630 d.1695

George F., of Gt. D. d.1727

William F., farmer of Writtle, Essex;
an Independent. b.1706 d.1758

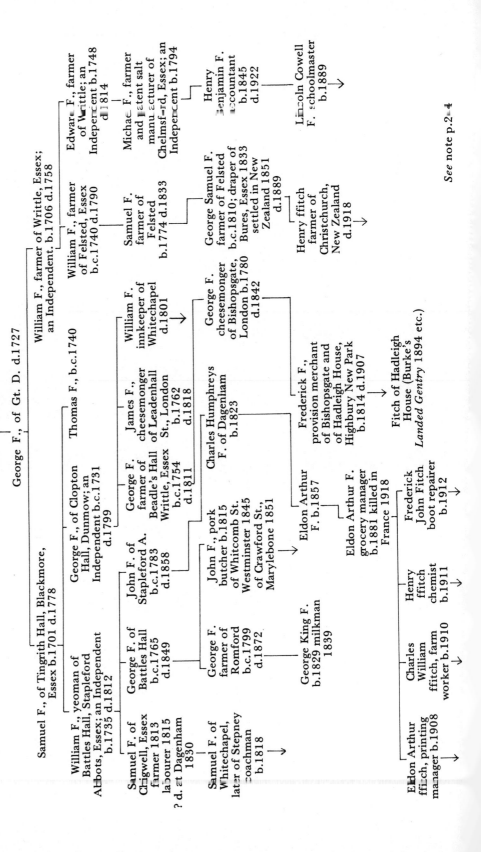

Samuel F., of Tingrith Hall, Blackmore,
Essex b.1701 d.1778

William F., yeoman of
Battles Hall, Stapleford
Abbots, Essex; an Independent
b.1735 d.1812

Samuel F. of
Chigwell, Essex
farmer 1813
labourer 1815
? d. at Dagenham
1830

Samuel F. of
Whitechapel,
later of Stepney
coachman
b.1818

George F., of Clopton
Hall, Dunmow; an
Independent b.c.1731
d.1799

George F. of Battles Hall
b.c.1765
d.1849

George F.
farmer of
Romford
b.c.1799
d.1872

George King F.
b.1829 milkman
1839

Thomas F., b.c.1740

George F., farmer of
Beadle's Hall
Writtle, Essex
b.c.1754
d.1811

John F. of Stapleford A.
b.c.1783
d.1858

John F., pork
butcher b.1815
of Whitcomb St.
Westminster 1845
of Crawford St.,
Marylebone 1851

William F.,
farmer of Felsted, Essex
b.c.1740 d.1790

Samuel F.
farmer of
Felsted
b.1774 d.1833

James F.,
cheesemonger
of Leadenhall
St., London
b.1762
d.1818

Charles Humphreys
F. of Dagenham
b.1823

Eldon Arthur
F. b.1857

Eldon Arthur F.
grocery manager
b.1881 killed in
France 1918

Eldon Arthur
ffitch, printing
manager b.1908

Edward F., farmer
of Writtle; an
Independent b.1748
d.1814

Michael F., farmer
and patent salt
manufacturer of
Chelmsford, Essex; an
Independent b.1794

William F.,
innkeeper of
Whitechapel
d.1801

George F.
cheesemonger
of Bishopsgate,
London b.1780
d.1842

Frederick F.,
provision merchant
of Bishopsgate and
of Hadleigh House,
Highbury New Park
b.1814 d.1907

Fitch of Hadleigh
House (Burke's
Landed Gentry 1894 etc.)

Frederick
John Fitch
boot repairer
b.1912

Charles
William
ffitch, farm
worker b.1910

Henry
ffitch
chemist
b.1911

George Samuel F.
farmer of Felsted
b.c.1810; draper of
Bures, Essex 1833
settled in New
Zealand 1851
d.1889

Henry ffitch
farmer of
Christchurch,
New Zealand
d.1918

Henry
Benjamin F.
accountant
b.1845
d.1922

Lincoln Cowell
F. schoolmaster
b.1889

See note p.244

William Dee, tailor at Eton
(Will 1638) (? of the Day family, Ped. 77)

Robert Montague (or Mountague)† = Margaret, dau.
of Boveney, Bucks.   of Roger Coton

Margaret dau.of John
Malthouse
of Benfield

Peter
Montague

William
Montague
of Bove-
ney d.
1593

William
Montague
of Boveney
b.c.1563
KS c.1563
81.SK 1581
FK 1584-95
v.1634

Joan
Rad-
cliffe
of Wy-
combe

Laurence
Montague
Vicar of
Dorney,
Bucks.

Peter Montague
1604-59, settled
in Virginia 1621
→

Richard Montague
b.1575.KS c.1590-4
SK 1594.FK 1597-
1604.assisted Sir
Henry Savile (PE)
with his edition of
Chrysostom.R.of
Wootton Courtney
(EL) 1610-13.FE
1613.Dean of Hereford
1616-7.CW 1617-28
Bp.of Chichester
1628-38.Bp.of
Norwich 1638-41
D.N.B.

Charles Elizabeth = Matthew
Stokes   Day
KS c.1657-   (Ped.77)
62.SK
1661
d.1665

Thomas
Dee conduct
of Eton
d.1683

Sarah =² William Dee, tailor
Atlee

Jane
m.1621

David
Stevens
conduct
of Eton

Jonas Mountague† b.c.1586; KS
1598-1604.Merton Coll. Ox.
1604.assisted Sir Henry Savile
(PE) with ed. of Chrysostom) on
Coll. business c.1606-18; LME
1618-31 d.c.1633

Eleanor
m.at Eton
1612

Thomas Mountague
2nd son b.Eton 1615
KS c.1626-31; SK
1631.FK 1634-51
LM 1648-60.HM
1660-71.FE 1671-91
R.of Everdon (EL)
1683

= David Stokes D.D. Fellow of
Peterhouse, Camb. 1618-24
FE 1624.CW 1628-43 and
1660-9.Precentor of Chichester
1629-31. R.of Everdon (EL)
1638.d.1669 bur. St. George's
Windsor

Richard Stokes
b.at Aldingbourne
Sussex (a residence
of the Bp. of Chi-
chester) c.1635.KS
c.1646-50. SK 1650
FK 1653-7.M.D.
1653 v.at Eton 1661
d.in Newgate a pri-
soner for debt 1681

Thomas
Dee
b.1666
E 1678-9

William
Stevens
b.Eton
1632.KS
c.1646-51
SK 1651
FK 1654-99
bursar of
King's

Mary

Daniel
Stevens
b.Eton
1634-41
d.1641

Jonas Mountague
5th son, b.Eton
1632.KS c.1643-50
SK 1650.FK 1653-6
R.of Wootton
Courtney, Somerset
(EL) 1661-86 d.
Eton and there bur.

Dorothy
m.at Wexham
Bucks. 1674

dau.

Charles Young
b.Eton c.1686
KS 1701-4

Robert Young
b. Kingston on
Thames 1643.KS
c.1656-62.SK
1662.FK 1665-73
LM 1669/72
domestic chaplain
to Prince Rupert
CW 1673-1716
R. Everdon (EL)
1674-1716.FE
1694-1716

Edward Young
b.Eton 1678
Eton c.1690-4

Jonas
Mountague
b.c.1671
KS 1682-9
SK 1689
FK 1692-
1720.bursar
of King's

William
Mountague
b.1670.KS
1685-90
SK 1690
FK 1694-
1701.R.of
Hitcham
1701-2.V.of
Sturminster
Marshall (EL)
Dorset 1702-45

Jane dau.
of Dr.
George
Evans CW
and R.of
Hitcham

William Mountague b.1708.KS 1722.SK
1727. FK 1730-4

Philip Mountague
b.1705.KS 1720
SK 1725.FK 1728-
42.R. Piddlehinton
Dorset (EL) 1751-82

† Note p.264

† Note p.264

PEDIGREE 77   ETON FAMILIES: DAY, WICKHAM

Nicholas Day of Wrockwardine, Shropshire

William Barlow
Bp.of Chichester
d.1563 (*D.N.B.*)

Agnes, dau.of Henry =[1] Richard Day (or Dee) =[2] Joan, dau.of
Osborne of Gnossall   of Newport, Shropshire   Roger Selytoe
Shropshire

Roger Day of
Newport, Shropshire

George Day, b.c.1501
PK 1538-47 Bp.of Chichester
1543-56 (*D.N.B.*)

William Day of Windsor
and Eton; bought manor of
Sunninghill, Berks. 1583 d.1615
aet.82 bur. Eton: M.I.

Ann = Herbert   Margaret = William   Frances = Toby   William Wickham KS 1552-6   Antonina = William Day L. Newport
       Westfaling   Overton   Matthew   SK 1556. FK 1559-69.FE   1529.KS c.1541.SK 1545
       Bp.of   Bp.of   Archbp.   1568.VPE 1570.CW 1571-84   FK 1548-59. IE 1561
       Hereford   Lichfield   of York   Bp.of Lincoln 1584-95, Bp.of   PE 1561-96.CW 1563-72
       d.1628   d.1609   d.1628   Winchester 1595 d.1595   DW 1572-95. Bp.of Win-
                                                                                        chester 1595 d.1596

Elizabeth = Richard Day   Matthew Day, 5 times   Mary, dau.
            KS c.1586-90.FK   mayor of Windsor, Ld.of   of George
            SK 1590.FK   the manor of Sunninghill   Lowdeswell
            1593-4; gave   d.1661 aet.87 M.I.   of Eton
            advowson of   St. John's Windsor
            Weedon Pinkney
            Northants to
            King's

Toby Matthew   Henry Wickham   William Day of   William Day, b.Windsor 1605 = Mary
E. 1588-9   KS c.1604-8.FK   Ockholt Manor   KS c.1618-24.FK 1627-37   Collins
                1611-6.Archdeacon   Bray, Berks.   V.of Mapledurham (EL) 1637-84   (Ped. 78)
                of Yorkshire   prob. E.c.1582-9   divinity reader St. George's
                1624-41   d.1628   Windsor 1660 d.1684 bur.at
                                        Mapledurham

Elizabeth Stokes = Matthew Day, b.Windsor 1611
m.at Windsor 1645   KS c.1624-30.SK 1630.FK 1633-43
(Ped. 76)   DD 1661, R.of Everdon (EL)
                    1642-4.Master of Lewisham Sch.
                    1652-60.V.of Staines, Mdx. 1660-3
                    Preb.of St. Paul's 1660-3 d.1663

Ellen, dau. of
Paul Wentworth
of Burnham,
Bucks. had 4
brothers at Eton

Richard Day
E. 1514-22 KS.
SK 1622.FK 1625-44
V.of Prescot
Lancs. d.1650

See note p.264

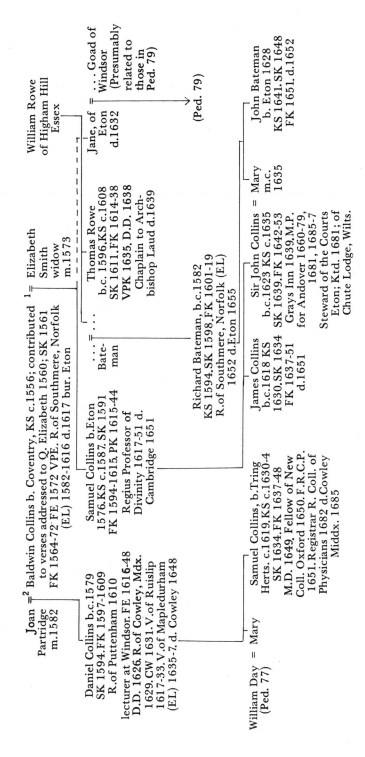

PEDIGREE 78   ETON FAMILIES: COLLINS, BATEMAN, ROWE

See note p.264

PEDIGREE 79   ETON FAMILIES: GOAD, WOODHALL

Thomas Goad, mayor of Windsor & M.P. for Windsor 1553 = ... dau.of Symonde Aley, yeoman of the Queen's Chamber

Christopher Goad, b.at Windsor 1552, KS c.1564   Roger Goad b.1567 at Stretham, Cambs. KS
SK 1569.FK 1572-7; Gray's Inn 1577, probably d.1596   c.1580.SK 1585.FK 1588-94. Went to Ireland d.1634

Roger Goad, b.Horton, Bucks., c.1538.KS c.1550.SK 1555. FK 1558-70; Master of = Katherine, dau.of
Guildford Grammar School to 1570.PK 1570-1610; Vice-Chancellor. M.I. King's   Richard Hill of London

Matthew Goad b.1575 | Thomas Goad b.1576 | Robert Goad | Roger Goad | Christopher Goad | Richard Goad
KS c.1587.SK 1591.FK | KS 1588.SK 1592.FK | b.1577.KS | b.1585.KS | KS 1598.SK 1607 | KS c.1606.SK
1591-1600.Gray's Inn | 1595-1611.D.D.1615 | c.1590.SK | c.1597.SK | FK 1610-3.d.1613 | 1610.K 1613-15
1600; of Hadleigh, Suffolk | R.of Hadleigh 1618-30 | 1594.d.1596 | 1601.FK 1604-9 | | of Milton, Cambs.
and the Court of Chancery | Prebendary of Canterbury | | | | d.London 1625
d.1638 | 1638 d.1638 (D.N.B.)

Edmund Woodhall of Saffron Walden, Essex b.c.1582
KS c.1592.SK 1597.FK 1600-3; Principal Registrar of
Prerogative Court of Canterbury; Lord of manor of Little
Munden, Herts. d.1638

Jane Collins = ... Goad of Windsor (Presumably
of Eton | related to those above)
d.1632 | (Ped. 78)

Thomas Goad b.Windsor = Mary   John Woodhall
1595.KS c.1607.SK 1611   KS c.1632.SK 1636
FK 1614-34.Ll.D.1630   FK 1639-49
Regius Professor of Civil
Law 1635-66.d.Cambridge
1666 (D.N.B.)

Jane
d.1656

Christopher Goad b.Windsor | George Goad, bp. at | George Goad, KS c.1659 | Thomas Goad b.Eton c.1653
1601.KS c.1609.SK 1613.FK | Windsor 1603.KS c.1616 | SK 1662.FK 1666-78 | KS 1662.SK 1668.FK 1671-84
1616-37; Chaplain to 1st Visct. | SK 1620.FK 1623-47 |
Saye and Sele d.1652 | HME 1647-9.FE 1648-
 | 58.R. Southmere (EL)
 | 1655-71.d.Eton 1671

Christopher Goad b. Eton
KS 1664.SK 1670.FK 1673-82

See note p.264

PEDIGREE 80   ETON FAMILIES: HAWTREY

Ralph Hawtrey of Ruislip, Middlesex d.1637

Edward Hawtrey b.c.1605,KS c.1617 = Margaret (Sigmore) widow of John Wright
SK 1622.FK 1625-43.V.of Burnham   V.of Burnham (EL) perhaps akin to other
(EL) 1643,d.1669   Eton Wrights

John Hawtrey b.1645,KS c.1658.SK 1665,FK 1668-80.FE 1680-1715
V.of Mapledurham (EL) 1684-1715,d.Eton bur. Mapledurham

John Hawtrey of Ruislip
eldest son

John Hawtrey 2nd son KS 1638.SK 1647
FK 1650-55; Barrister-at-law 1654.d.1682

Charles Hawtrey b.1687 E. 1698 = Anne
KS 1700.SK 1707.FK 1710-20   Sleech
R.of Wootton Courtney (EL)   d.1751
1729-70,sub-dean of Exeter 1731-70 (Ped. 81)

William Hawtrey
b.1693.KS 1706
SK 1712.d.1714

John Hawtrey
b.c.1686 E. 1698-
1705

Henry Foster
bricklayer and
alderman of
Windsor

Charles Hawtrey
b.1732.KS 1745
V.of Bampton

John Hawtrey
b.1737.KS 1749
SK 1755.FK 1758-79
VPK 1776-9
Preb. Winchester
1803-17

Stephen Hawtrey
b.1738 Recorder of
Exeter; Registrar of
Eton 1795

Edward Hawtrey
b.1741.KS 1754
SK 1761.FK 1764-80
AME 1766-82.V.of
Burnham (EL)
1783.FE 1792
d.1803

= Elizabeth

John Foster   William Foster
b.1731.KS   b.1749.KS 1762
1743.SK 1748   SK 1768.FK
FK 1751-8   1771-88.AME
AME 1754-65   1753-90; chaplain
HME 1765-73   to the King
CW 1772-4   1793-1827.R.of
                 Clewer (EL) d.1827

Stephen Hurnard Hawtrey E. 1793
KS 1796.SK 1798.FK 1802-13,V.of
Broadchalke, Wilts. d.1838

John Hawtrey b.1779.KS 1796
d.1853.Wesleyan Minister and
later R.of Kingston Seymour, Som.

Edward Craven Hawtrey b.1789
E. 1799.KS 1805.SK 1807, FK 1810
AME 1814-34,HME 1834-52,PE 1853-62

Stephen Thomas Hawtrey b.1808; Manchester
Grammar and Sherborne Schools and Trin. Coll.,
Cambridge; Mathematical AME 1836-72; Founded
St. Mark's School, Windsor d.1886

John William Hawtrey b.1818
KS 1832.SK 1857. AME 1842-69
HM St. Michael's School, West-
gate on Sea 1869-89 d.1891

Henry Courtenay Hawtrey
b.c.1820 E. 1835,Emmanuel
Coll., Camb. 1839. R.of Holy
Trinity, Windsor d.1906

Montague John
Grey Hawtrey
b.c.1802.R.of
Rimpton, Som.
d.1886

Edward Montague Hawtrey b.1847
KS.St. John's, Camb. HM St. Michael's
Preparatory School, Westgate on Sea d.1916

Sir Charles Henry Hawtrey
actor b.1858.E. 1866-9.d.1923

Edmond Charles Hawtrey
b.1861.E. 1875-80.d.1942

George Procter Hawtrey
b.1846. KS. d.1910

Sir Ralph George Hawtrey b.1879,KS 1893
d.1975

Stephen Charles Hawtrey b.1907,KS 1921-6

Ralph Stephen Wilmot Hawtrey b.1941. KS 1953-9.

See note p.264

PEDIGREE 81   ETON FAMILIES: SLEECH, DAMPIER, COOKE

William Cooke of
St. James's
Westminster

Stephen Sleech b.1705
KS 1720.SK 1723.FK
1726-30.FE 1730-46.PE
1746-65.R.of Farnham
Royal (EL) 1729-52.R.of
Worplesdon (EL) 1752-65

Frances Cooke
Captain 3d
Dragoon
Guards
d.1816
aet.93

= [2] Anna
Dupuis
b.1723
m.1st
1746
(Ped. 83)

Frances
dame at
Eton d.
1779

= ... Yonge

Frances
dame at
Eton d.
17-?

Catherine
dame at
Eton d.
1804

George Harris
(Ped. 82)

= Elizabeth
dame at
Eton c.
1758-92

Edward Sleech
b.1715.KS 1729
Dep. clerk of the
pells d.1779

John Sleech b.1711
KS 1726.SK 1730.AME
Archdeacon of Cornwall
d.1788; schoolfellow
and friend of 1st Lord
Camden

William Cooke b.1711
Harrow 1718.KS 1721
SK 1731.FK 1730-46
AME c.1733-43.HME
1743-5.FE 1747-72.PK
1772-97.R.of Sturminster
Marshall (EL),Dean of
Ely 1780.d.1797

Catherine
m.1746

Anne = Charles
d.1751   Hawtrey
(Ped. 79)

Thomas Dampier b.1749 E. 1753
KS 1763.SK 1766.FK 1769-73
private tutor to Earl of Guilford's
sons at Eton; Dean of Rochester
1782.Bp.of Rochester 1802-8.d.1812

= Elizabeth

of Ely 1808.d.1812

Arabella
m.1755
d.1758

Henry Sleech b.c.1723
KS 1737.SK 1741.FK
1744-55.AME 1747-67
LME 1767-75.FE 1775-84
R.of Hitcham (EL) tutor
to Lord Bowmont

John Dampier
b.c.1750,E. 1756
R.of Wylye, Wilts.
Preb. of Ely
d.1826

Thomas Dampier
b.1713.KS 1728.SK
1732.FK 1735-47
Usher to Earl of
Guilford AME,LME
1745-67. FE 1767
CW 1769-74.Dean of
Durham 1774-77

Sir Henry Dampier
b.1758.KS 1773.SK
1776.FK 1779-90
Judge 1813.d.1816

See note p.265

PEDIGREE 82   ETON FAMILIES: WISE, POTE, HARRIS

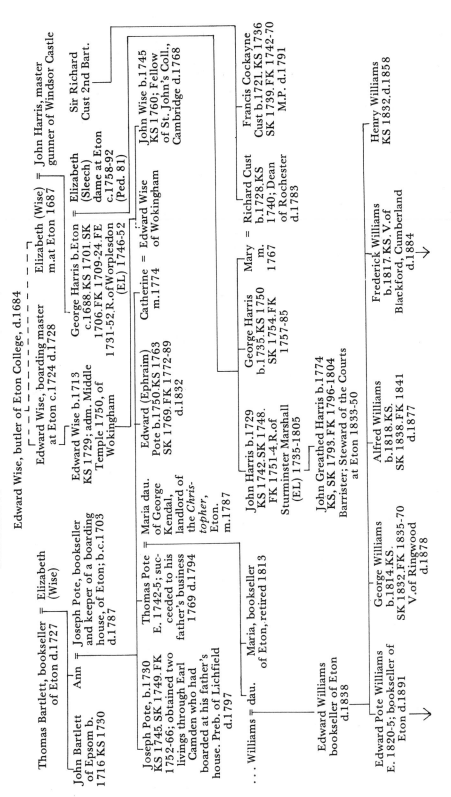

See note p.264

PEDIGREE 83   ETON FAMILIES: DUPUIS, CHAMBERLAYNE, ROBERTS

See note p.265

Abraham Dupuis of Pall Mall, St. James's, Westminster
Court Milliner to the Dowager Princess of Wales d.1737

Richard Roberts of Gloucester

Edward Chamberlayne, R.of Great Cressingham, Norfolk

Anthony Dupuis American merchant of Gracechurch Street and Fulham d.1777

Francis Cooke (Ped. 81) =[2] Anna b.1723 m. 1st 1746 =[1] Anthony Wagner of Pall Mall, hatter to King George II d.1761 (son of Geo. W., Ped. 70)

Edward Chamberlayne b.1741.KS 1751.SK 1758.FK 1761-76.Jt. Secretary to the Treasury d.1782

Thomas Chamberlayne b.1743.KS 1754.SK 1762 FK 1765; tutor to Lord Middleton FE 1772.VPE 1791-1801. R.of Worplesdon (EL) 1790

George Chamberlayne b.1739.KS 1750.SK 1755.FK 17 8-81; tutor to Lord Lincoln; R.C. priest c.1815 = Jane d.1776

Charlotte =[2] William Hayward Roberts b.1734, KS 1744.SK 175 FK 1756-61.AME 1760-71.FE 1771.PE 1781-91.R. f Farnham Royal (EL) 1779

Richard Rober s b.1764 KS 1777.SK 373.FK 1786-93.V.of S orle (EL) 1794-1831; ha a school at Mitch m

William Roberts b.1762 KS 1777.SK 1781.FK 1784-6.FE 1786.VPE 1818-33. R.of Clewer, Farnham Royal and Worplesdon (EL)

John Roberts b.1763 KS 1777. SK 1781.tutor to Lord Morpeth.AME 1791-1800.FE 1800.R.of Creeting.V.of Burnham (EL) d.1822

J n Ch v all r Co b d d.18 2 =[2] Lucy (Patteson)

Richard Arthur Roberts b.1797 KS 1814.V.of Christchurch Mon. (EL) 1824-39 d.1854

Thomas Roberts b.1798 KS 1814 SK 1817 FK 1820-3

Adela Harriette b.1837 m.1858 d.1917 = John Pattesor Cobbold M.P. for Ipswich b.1831 E. 1844.KS d 1875

George Dupuis b.1757 E. 1771-6 (Francis Yonge's house) Merton Coll., Oxford 1776.Christ Church 1777. R.of Wendlebury, Oxon. 1779-1839

George John Dupuis b.1795 KS 1808.SK 1815.FK 1818-31 AME 1819-34.LME 1834-40 FE 1838.VPE.R.of Creeting (EL) 1840-62.R.of Worplesdon (EL) 1862-78.d.1884 =[Julia Maria

William Henry Roberts b.1795 KS 1811.SK 1815 FK 1818-28 R.of Clewer (EL) 1827-43

Edward John Gore Dupuis KS 1855-62.Conduct of Eton 1875

Olive m.1894 d.1952 = Wilfrid Dallas, Earl Cairns b.1965 d.1946

Descendants at Eton

Hester Margaret b.1895.m.1917 = Robert Croft Bourne P.C., M.P.

Henry Dupuis b.1808 KS 1820.SK 1827.FK 1330-52.AME 1835-52 V.of Richmond, Surrey 1852-67

Descendants at Eton

George Richard Dupuis b.1835 KS 1850.SK 1854.FK 1857.AME 1858-75.R.of Sturminster Marshall (EL) 1875-7. d.1912 =[Annette Laetitia (Lloyd) (Ped. 86)

(Ped. 84)

Margaret Rose (Lyttelton) m.1949 = Robert Morice Antony Bourne b.1918 AM

Alice Jane b.1862 m.1886 = Henry Broadbent b.1852 AME 1876-1919 d.1935

Cicely b.1890 d.1952 = Patrick Arthur Macindoe b.1878 (nephew of H.C. Hollway Calthrop, Bursar of Eton 1896-1917) Junior Bursar of Eton 1902, Bursar 1917-1942.d.1963

David Henry Macindoe b.1917 AME

PEDIGREE 84   ETON FAMILIES: LYTTELTON, COLERIDGE

James Coleridge, J.P. of Ottery
St. Mary, Devon b.1759 d.1836

Rev. Henry Patteson
E. 1770-4 d.1824

Sir Stephen
Glynne, Bt.
E. 1793

John Chevallier = Lucy
Cobbold b.1797 m.1827
d.1882.M.P. for ↓ d.1879
Ipswich   (Ped. 83)

Sir John Patteson = Frances
Judge, b.1790 d. Duke b.
1861.KS 1808.SK 1796
1808 d.1842

Many descendants
at Eton

Francis John
Coleridge b.1794
d.1854

Edward Coleridge = Mary
b.1800 E. 1814 Keate
AME 1825.LME (Ped.
1850 d.1883 85)
↓

Mary b.1813 =¹ George William, 4th Lord   Catherine
m.1839 d.1857   Lyttelton b.1817.E. 1827
FE 1871.d.1876

=² Sybella Harriet
dau.of George
Clive M.P.

William Ewart
Gladstone, Prime
Minister b.1809.
Eton.d.1898

John Coleridge
Patteson Bp.of
Melanesia.b.1821
Eton.d.1871

Nehemiah
John
Coleridge

Charles George
5th Ld. Lyttelton
8th Vsct. Cobham
b.1842.FE 1891-
1918.d.1922

Edward Lyttelton
b.1855.AME 1802-90
HME 1905-16.d.
1942

Lavinia
m.1870
d.1939

Edward Stuart
Talbot, Bp.of
Winchester
d.1934

Hester Margaret =
b.1874 m.1904
d.1958

Cyril Argentine
Alington b.1872
AME 1899-1908
HME 1916-33
Dean of Durham

Rev. Stephen
Edward Glad-
stone b.1844
d.1920

Hugh For-
tescue
Coleridge
b.1859
d.1928

George William
Lyttelton b.1883
AME 1908-44
d.1962

Richard Glynne
Lyttelton b.1893

Mary Catherine
b.1875 m.1904
d.1957

Lionel George Bridges,
Justice Ford b.1865
AME 1888-1901.HM
of Harrow 1910-25
Dean of York d.1932

Joan = John Comyn
m.   Vaughan Wilkes
1940 KS, AME 1925-37
↓ Warden of Radley
1937-54

Sir Charles
Andrew Glad-
stone, 6th Bt.
b.1888.AME
1912-46 d.1968

Frederick John
Randolph Coleridge
KS 1921.AME.LME
VPE
↓

Robert Morice = Margaret
Antony Bourne Rose m.
b.1918 AME 1949
(Ped. 85)

Thomas Glynne
Lyttelton b.1940
AME

Peter Stafford Hayden = Helena Frances
Lawrence b.1913 AME m.1940
1936- ↓

Sir Erskine William
Gladstone, 7th Bt.
b.1925 AME 1951-61
HM of Lancing 1961-9

See note p.264

PEDIGREE 85   ETON FAMILIES: KEATE, DURNFORD

William Keate, b. Wells, Somerset 1739.KS 1753.FK 1759.FK 1762-8
Master of Stamford Grammar School; R.of Laverton, Somerset d.1795

John Keate b.1773.KS 1784.SK 1792.FK 1795-1803 = Frances, dau.of Sir Charles Brown
AME 1795-1803.LME 1803-9.HME 1809-34.D.D. 1810   who was said to be a natural son of
CW 1820-52.d.1852   the Young Pretender

Francis Edward Durnford b.1816.KS 829.SK 1835
FK 1838-44.AME 1839-64.LME 1864-77.FE 1877-81
R.of Creeting, Suffolk (EL),d.1881

Sir Walter Durnford b.1847.KS, SK 1865.F = 1869
AME 1870-99.VPK 1909-18.PK 1918-26.G.E.E. 1919

William Burland Keate b.1770
KS 1783.R.of Winfrith Newburgh,
Dorset d.1817

Edward Coleridge = Mary
(Ped. 84)

Emma = Richard Durnford
b.1802, Eton; Bp.of
Chichester d.1895

Richard Durnford b.1844 KS, SK 1861
FK 1866-85. d.1934

Violet Mary = Ven. John Chaloner Chute, son of Chaloner William Chute
m.1922   of the Vyne, Hants. Auditor of Eton; b.1881 KS 1895.AME

See note p.264

PEDIGREE 86   ETON FAMILIES: CARTER, STONE, BALSTON

Richard Carter b.1751 d.1843; Secretary to the Earl of Suffolk
From Purton, Wilts., then of London, then of Foxley, Wilts.

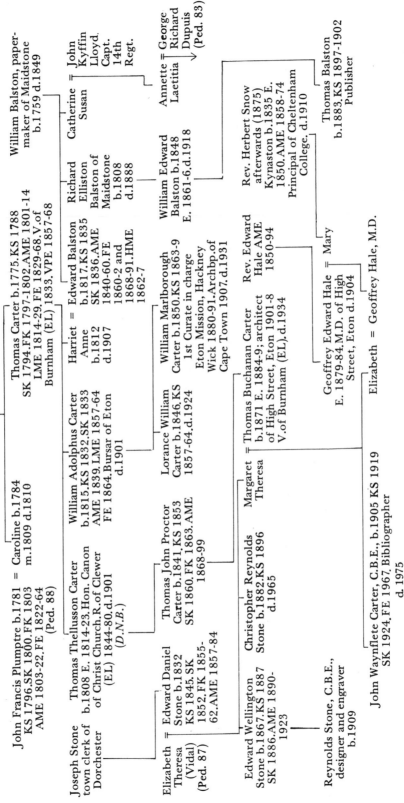

See note p.265

PEDIGREE 87   ETON FAMILIES: REYNOLDS, FURSE, CORY, VIDAL, ABRAHAM

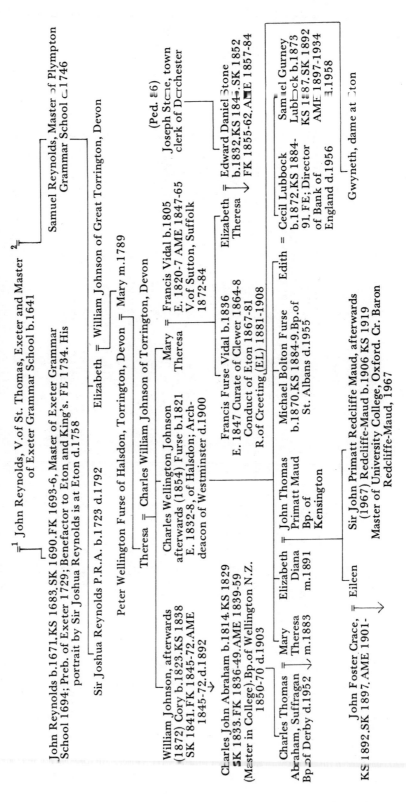

=¹ John Reynolds, V.of St. Thomas, Exeter and Master
of Exeter Grammar School b.1641

Samuel Reynolds, Master of Plympton
Grammar School c.1746

John Reynolds b.1671.KS 1683.FK 1693-6, Master of Exeter Grammar
School 1694; Preb. of Exeter 1729; Benefactor to Eton and King's. FE 1734. His
portrait by Sir Joshua Reynolds is at Eton d.1758

Sir Joshua Reynolds P.R.A. b.1723 d.1792

Elizabeth ╤ William Johnson of Great Torrington, Devon

Peter Wellington Furse of Halsdon, Torrington, Devon ╤ Mary m.1789

Theresa ╤ Charles William Johnson of Torrington, Devon

(Ped. 86)
Joseph Stone, town
clerk of Dorchester

Francis Vidal b.1805
E. 1820-7 AME 1847-65
V.of Sutton, Suffolk
1872-84

Mary ╤
Theresa

Charles Wellington Johnson
afterwards (1854) Furse b.1821
E. 1832-8, of Halsdon; Archdeacon of Westminster d.1900

Elizabeth ╤ Edward Daniel Stone
Theresa   b.1832.KS 1846-.SK 1852
              FK 1855-62.AME 1857-84

William Johnson, afterwards
(1872) Cory b.1823.KS 1838
SK 1841.FK 1845-72.AME
1845-72.d.1892

Francis Furse Vidal b.1836
E. 1847 Curate of Clewer 1864-8
Conduct of Eton 1867-81
R.of Creeting (EL) 1881-1908

Edith = Cecil Lubbock
         b.1872.KS 1884-
         91. FE; Director
         of Bank of
         England d.1956

Samuel Gurney
Lubbock b.1873
KS 1887.SK 1892
AME 1897-1934

Charles John Abraham b.1814.KS 1829
SK 1833.FK 1836-49. AME 1839-59
(Master in College).Bp.of Wellington N.Z.
1850-70 d.1903

Michael Bolton Furse
b.1870.KS 1884-9.Bp.of
St. Albans d.1955

Gwyneth, dame at Eton

Charles Thomas ╤ Mary
Abraham, Suffragan Theresa
Bp.of Derby d.1952   m.1883

Elizabeth ╤ John Thomas
Diana   Primatt Maud
m.1891   Bp. of
             Kensington

Sir John Primatt Redcliffe Maud, afterwards
(1967) Redcliffe-Maud b.1906 KS 1919
Master of University College, Oxford. Cr. Baron
Redcliffe-Maud, 1967

John Foster Crace, ╤ Eileen
KS 1892.SK 1897. AME 1901-

See note p.265

PEDIGREE 88   ETON FAMILIES: NAYLOR, HANSON, YOUNG, PLUMPTRE

Oliver Naylor, R.of Tavistock, Devon

John Hanson, Registrar of Eton College d.1714

Fermor Naylor b.c.1675.KS 1687.SK 1692 FK 1695-1701; private tutor to Sir Bourchier Wrey at Eton 1698 d.1714
= Mary, m.1702 dame at Eton d.1723

John Hanson, Registrar of Eton College b.1681.KS 1696 d.1741

Arthur Young b.1693 d.1759 Chaplain to the House of Commons (*D.N.B.*)

Arthur Young agriculturist and author b.1761 d.1820 of Bradfield, Suffolk

Bartholomew Young b.c.1698.KS 1709 SK 1717. FK 1720-5.AME c.1720-32
= Mary, boarding dame of the Manor House, Eton m.1725 d.1775

Rachel, dame at the Manor House c.1775-94 d.1797

Edward Young b.1726 KS 1738.SK 1743.FK 1746-60.AME c.1746-63 Dean of Clogher 1761 Bp.of Dromore 1763 Bp.of Ferns 1765 d.1772
= Anne Newcome (Ped. 89)

John Young b.1728 KS 1747.FK 1750-3 FE 1776-86 Private tutor to the Duke of Grafton; Preb. of Worcester
= Alicia (Cooper) nat. dau.of Henry (Fox) 1st Lord Holland m. 1760

Arthur Young b.1769 E. 1785-9 d.1827

Catherine m.1753
= Septimius Plumptre b.1717.KS 1731.SK 1737.FK 1740-52. AME c.1742-8; tutor to Lord Lisburne's son d.1782

Robert Plumptre Master of Queen's Coll, Cambridge d.1782

Ped. 91

John Plumptre b.1764.KS 1767.SK 1773 FK 1776-8; tutor at Eton to 3rd Earl Bathurst; Dean of Gloucester d.1825
= Diana m.1781

John Francis Plumptre b.1781 KS 1796.SK 1800.FK 1803 AME 1803-22.FE 1822-64
= Caroline (Carter) b.1784 m.1809 d.1810 (Ped. 86)

See note p.264

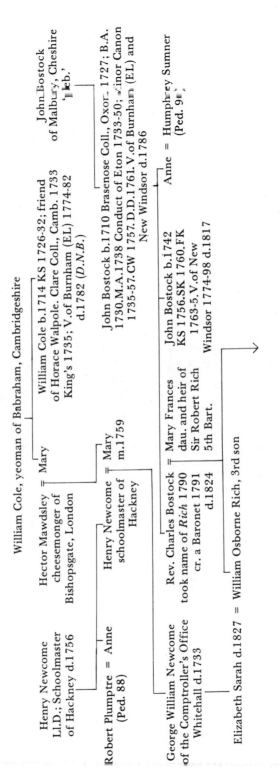

248

PEDIGREE 89   ETON FAMILIES: COLE, BOSTOCK

William Cole, yeoman of Babraham, Cambridgeshire

Hector Mawdsley = Mary
cheesemonger of
Bishopsgate, London

Henry Newcome
Ll.D.; Schoolmaster
of Hackney d.1756

Henry Newcome = Mary
schoolmaster of   m.1759
Hackney

Robert Plumptre = Anne
(Ped. 88)

William Cole b.1714 KS 1726-32; friend
of Horace Walpole. Clare Coll., Camb. 1733
King's 1735; V. of Burnham (EL) 1774-82
d.1782 (D.N.B.)

John Bostock b.1710 Brasenose Coll., Oxon. 1727; B.A.
1730,M.A.1738 Conduct of Eton 1733-50; Minor Canon
1735-57.CW 1757.D.D.1761.V.of Burnham (EL) and
New Windsor d.1786

John Bostock
of Malbury, Cheshire
'Feb.'

John Bostock b.1742
KS 1756.SK 1760.FK
1763-5.V.of New
Windsor 1774-98 d.1817

Anne = Humphrey Sumner
(Ped. 9)

Rev. Charles Bostock = Mary Frances
took name of Rich 1790   dau. and heir of
cr. a Baronet 1791   Sir Robert Rich
d.1824   5th Bart.

George William Newcome
of the Comptroller's Office
Whitehall d.1733

Elizabeth Sarah d.1827 = William Osborne Rich, 3rd son

See note p.264

PEDIGREE 90   ETON FAMILIES: SUMNER

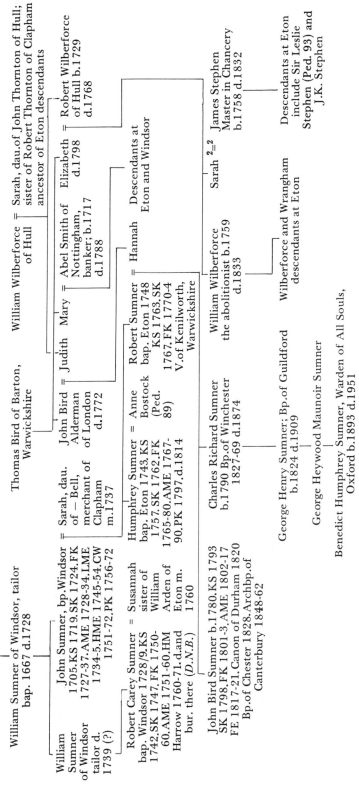

Thomas Sumner of Windsor, tailor; signed loyal address 1683 d.1698

Thomas Bird of Barton, Warwickshire

William Wilberforce = Sarah, dau. of John Thornton of Hull; of Hull   sister of Robert Thornton of Clapham   ancestor of Eton descendants

William Sumner of Windsor, tailor bap. 1667 d.1728

John Sumner, bp.Windsor 1705.KS 1719.SK 1724.FK 1727-37.AME 1728-34.LME 1734-5.HME 1745-54.CW 1751-72.PK 1756-72

Robert Wilberforce of Hull b.1729 d.1768

Elizabeth d.1798

Abel Smith of Nottingham, banker; b.1717 d.1788

Mary = Judith = John Bird Alderman of London d.1772

Robert Sumner bap. Eton 1748 KS 1763.SK 1767.FK 1770-4 V.of Kenilworth, Warwickshire

= Hannah

Descendants at Eton and Windsor

Sarah 2=2 James Stephen Master in Chancery b.1758 d.1832

William Wilberforce the abolitionist b.1759 d.1833

Wilberforce and Wrangham descendants at Eton

Descendants at Eton include Sir Leslie Stephen (Ped. 93) and J.K. Stephen

William Sumner of Windsor tailor d. 1739 (?)

Robert Carey Sumner bap. Windsor 1728/9.KS 1742.SK 1747.FK 1750-60.AME 1751-60.HM Harrow 1760-71.d.and bur. there (D.N.B.)

= Susannah sister of William Arden of Eton m. 1760

Humphrey Sumner = Anne bap. Eton 1743.KS   Bostock 1757.SK 1762.FK   (Ped. 1765-80.AME 1767-   89) 90.PK 1797.d.1814

= Sarah, dau. of — Bell, merchant of Clapham m.1737

Charles Richard Sumner b.1790 Bp.of Winchester 1827-69 d.1874

John Bird Sumner b.1780.KS 1793 SK 1798.FK 1801-3.AME 1802-17 FE 1817-21.Canon of Durham 1820 Bp.of Chester 1828.Archbp.of Canterbury 1848-62

George Henry Sumner; Bp.of Guildford b.1824 d.1909

George Heywood Maunoir Sumner

Benedict Humphrey Sumner, Warden of All Souls, Oxford b.1893 d.1951

See note p.265

250

PEDIGREE 91   ETON FAMILIES: PRIOR, GOODALL, THACKERAY

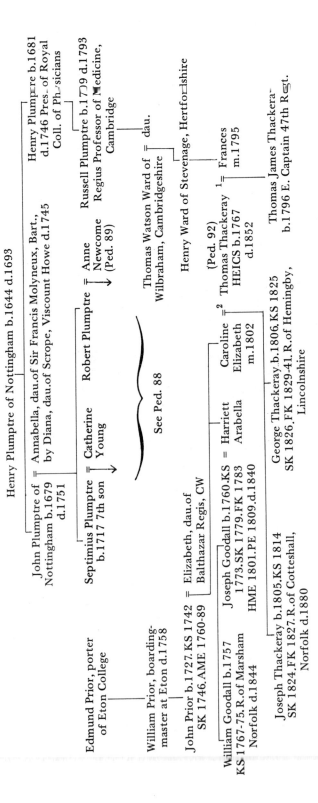

See note p.265

PEDIGREE 92 ETON FAMILIES: THACKERAY, WOODWARD

Thomas Thackeray of Hampsthwaite, Yorkshire, yeoman b.1628 d.1670

Robert Woodward + butler of Eton College; granted a lease 1690

Thomas Woodward, brewer of Eton College d.1707

Rev. Thomas Woodward b.1666 E.1678 Chapel clerk of Eton 1691-1741

John Woodward butler of Eton College d.1717 = Anne dame at Eton d.1793(?)

Rev. Nicholas Boscawen, 18th child of 1st Viscount Falmouth b.1723 D.D. Camb. 1753; Preb. of Westminster

Jane = 1 ... Hatton, linen draper in Newgate
2 d.1797

Elias Thackeray, adm. sizar, Christ's Coll., Cambridge 1682 V.of Hauxwell, Yorkshire on presentation of Mary, Viscountess Preston 1711 d.1737

Timothy Thackeray Parish clerk of Hampsthwaite b.1664 d.1722

Yeomen and tradesmen in Yorkshire

William Makepeace Thackeray; Bengal Civil Service b.1749 d.1813 (Ped. 93)

Joseph Thackeray parish clerk of Hampsthwaite

Thomas Thackeray b.1693 KS 1706.SK 1712.FK 1715-29 AME.HM of Harrow 1746-60 (*D.N.B.*)

= Anne m.1729; as a widow kept a boarding house at Eton d.at Harrow 1797 aged 88

Frederick Thackeray b.1737 E.1745 physician at Windsor d.1782

Decima   Theodosia

Dames at Eton 1771-1809

Martin Thackeray b.1783.KS 1793 SK 1802.FK 1805 Dean 1815-26.VPK 1826-34 d.1864

George Thackeray b.1777 KS 1792.SK 1797.FK 1800-3.AME 1801-9.LME 1809-14.D.D.1814.PK 1814-50

Elias Thackeray b.1732.KS 1744 SK 1751.FK 1754-77.R.of Walkern d.1781

John Thackeray b.1735 KS 1747 Assistant Chaplain at St.Petersburg d.1770

Thomas Thackeray b.1736.E.1742 Surgeon at Cambridge d.1806

Elias Thackeray b.1771.KS 1784 SK 1791.FK 1794-8 V.of Dundalk d.1854

Frederick Thackeray M.D. of Cambridge b.1744

John Richard Thackeray b.1772.R.of Hadley, Middx. d.1846

Charles Thackeray b.1831 KS 1846-51 Major 28th Foot

Thomas Thackeray HEICS b.1767 d.1852 (See Ped. 91)

William Makepeace Thackeray b.1770 KS 1783.M.D. of Chester d.1849

Frederick Thackeray b.1817 KS 1831-5.V.of Shapland, Essex d.1892

Richard William Thackeray b.1815 KS 1830.R.of Hunsdon Herts. d.1861

+ Possible kinship with the Visitation family of Woodward of Upton, Bucks., some of whom were at Eton and intermarried with the (Harl. Soc. 58, 132) Eton family of Oxenbridge.

See note p.265

PEDIGREE 93   ETON FAMILIES: THACKERAY, WARRE-CORNISH

William Makepeace Thackeray, Bengal Civil Service b.1749 d.1813 (Ped. 92)

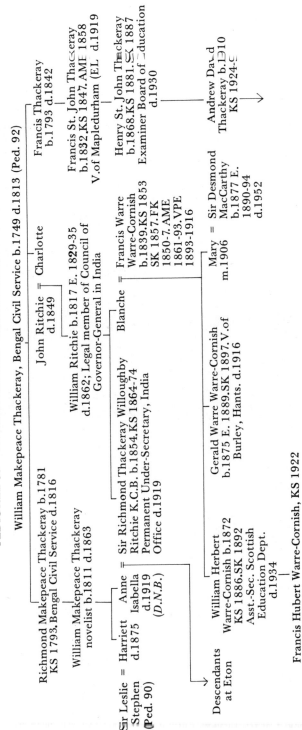

Richmond Makepeace Thackeray b.1781 KS 1793.Bengal Civil Service d.1816

William Makepeace Thackeray novelist b.1811 d.1863

Sir Leslie = Harriett   Anne   = Sir Richmond Thackeray Willoughby
Stephen   d.1875   Isabella   Ritchie K.C.B. b.1854.KS 1864-74
(Ped. 90)   d.1919   Permanent Under-Secretary, India
                      (D.N.B.)   Office d.1919

William Herbert
Warre-Cornish b.1872
KS 1886.SK 1892
Asst.-Sec. Scottish
Education Dept.
d.1934

Descendants
at Eton

Francis Hubert Warre-Cornish, KS 1922

John Ritchie = Charlotte   Francis Thackeray
d.1849   b.1793 d.1842

William Ritchie b.1817 E. 1829-35   Francis St. John Thackeray
d.1862; Legal member of Council of   b.1832.KS 1847. AME 1858
Governor-General in India   V.of Mapledurham (EL d.1919

Blanche   = Francis Warre   Henry St. John Thackeray
            Warre-Cornish   b.1868.KS 1881.SK 1887
            b.1839.KS 1853   Examiner Board of Education
            SK 1857.FK   d.1930
            1850-7. AME
            1861-93.VPE
            1893-1916

Gerald Warre Warre-Cornish   Mary = Sir Desmond   Andrew David
b.1875 E. 1889.SK 1897.V.of m.1906 MacCarthy   Thackeray b.1910
Burley, Hants. d.1916   b.1877 E.   KS 1924
                                     1890-94
                                     d.1952

See note.p. 65

NOTES TO THE PEDIGREES

Pedigrees 1 to 4 *The Swan Badge*

Pages 44-5, 159-162.   *S* signifies a bearer of a Swan Badge.

It has hitherto been supposed that Geoffrey, Domesday tenant of Carshalton, Surrey, brother of Eustace III, Count of Boulogne, was his *illegitimate* brother and he is so shown in Pedigree 1. Miss Catherine Morton, who gives some account of the House of Boulogne in her recent edition (with Miss Hope Muntz, Oxford, Clarendon Press, 1972), thinks it likelier (letter of 28 Sept. 1973) that at this date of the *Carmen de Hastingae Proelio of Guy Bishop of Amiens, Goisfridus* in Domesday represents *Godfrey* rather than *Geoffrey.* The two names, though etymologically distinct, were at this date liable to confusion and the House of Boulogne, so far as can be traced, chose its countesses from the 'German' rather than the 'French' part of the original Carolingian Empire. Sir Steven Runciman (letter, 30 Oct. 1973) is quite ready to accept that *Goisfridus* here could stand for Godfrey. Thus far Goisfridus of Carshalton could be Godfrey of Bouillon, rather than a bastard brother. Sir Steven, however, knows of no record of Godfrey marrying and points out that in the Crusader chronicles he appears as a man reputed to have led a completely chaste life. He adds, however, that he might have married in his youth some girl of lower rank—a sort of morganatic marriage. Miss Morton notes that Eustace *could* have had a legitimate and a bastard son of the same name.

Judith, niece of the Conqueror and wife of Waltheof has usually been thought her mother's daughter by her second husband, Lambert, Count of Lens, as stated in the *Vita et Passio Waldevi Comitis.* However, Catherine Morton and Hope Muntz, *The Carmen de Hastingae Proelio of Guy Bishop of Amiens,* (Oxford, 1972), p.127, give serious reasons for thinking that she may have been the daughter of her mother's first marriage to Enguerrand II, Count of Ponthieu.

Pedigrees 5 and 6 *Lydia, Media, Persia, Achaemenids*

Pages 68-9, 163-4.

Cambridge Ancient History, IV, pp.2-6.
Ferdinand Justi, *Iranisches Namenbuch*, (1895).
Information from Prince Toumanoff.

Between three versions of a story of a marriage of a Persian king (Ped. 5, Cyrus the Great or his son, Cambyses) to the daughter (Nitetis) of an Egyptian king, Pauly's *Real-Encyclopaedie der Classischen Alter-tumswissenschaft*, ed. Georg Wissowa, XVII, i, p.168, is unable to decide but thinks there is a substratum of truth.

Pedigrees 7 and 8 *Macedonia*

Pages 64, 165-6.

Pauly-Wissowa.
Herodotus VIII, 137-8, derives the Macedonian dynasty from Perdiccas I, whom he makes an Argive exile of the House of Temenus and thus a descendant of Heracles. The order of the wives and concubines of Philip II is unknown and the numbering therefore arbitrary.

Pedigree 9 *Epirus*

Page 167.

Pauly-Wissowa.
The Molossian kings were deduced from Neoptolemus, son of Achilles (Pindar, *Nemean Odes*, VI, 82; VII, 54).

Pedigree 10 *Ptolemies of Egypt*

Pages 69, 168.

Pauly-Wissowa.
Cambridge Ancient History.
A. Bouché-leclerq, *Histoire des Lagides.*

Pedigrees 11 and 12 *Seleucids of Syria and Bactria*

Pages 68, 169, 170.

W.W. Tarn, *The Greeks in Bactria and India*, 2nd ed., (1951).
Cambridge Ancient History.

Pedigree 13 *Pontus*

Pages 69, 171.

Cambridge Ancient History, IX, pp.216-233, 1023, Tab. II.
Pauly-Wissowa.
Henry Fynes-Clinton, *Fasti Hellenici*, (1830), III, pp.421-8.
F. Justi, *Iranisches Namenbuch*, (1895).
Ellis H. Minns, *Scythians and Greeks*, (1913).
Some problems of identity and dating remain to be solved.

Pedigrees 14 and 15 *Orontids of Armenia and Commagene*

Pages 69-71, 172-3.

C. Toumanoff, *Studies in Christian Caucasian History*, (Georgetown, 1963), pp.277-354.

Information from Prince Toumanoff.

Pauly-Wissowa, *Real-Encyclopaedie*, Supp. IV, (1924), pp.987-990.

Pedigree 16 *Judaea, Comana*

Pages 70-71, 175.

The Jewish Encyclopaedia, Vol. VI, p.361.

Pauly-Wissowa.

† It has been suggested that the wife of Archelaus, K.of Cappadocia, 34-17 B.C., may have been an Artaxiad princess (see Ped. 34 and p.70, n.80).

Pedigree 17 *Early Arsacids of Parthia*

Pages 67-8, 175.

Nelson C. Debevoise, *A Political History of Parthia*, (Chicago, 1938), pp. 25, 47, 52, 74, 76, 93, 140-157.

For later Arsacids whose descent from these is untraced, see Peds. 33, 35, 38 and pp. 62-3.

Pedigree 18 *The Caesars*

Pages 56-8, 71, 176.

Pauly-Wissowa.

Cambridge Ancient History.

Pedigree 19 *Mark Antony*

Pages 71, 177.

Pauly-Wissowa; Justi; Minns, *op. cit.*

The marriage of Pythodorus to Antonia has been disputed.

Pedigree 20 *Scribonia to Paula*

Pages 57, 178.

John Morris, 'Munatius Plancus Paulinus', in *Bonner Jahrbücher Band 165*, (1965), pp.88-96.

A.H.M. Jones, J.R. Martindale and John Morris, *The Prosopography of the Later Roman Empire*, (1971), pp.1138, 1142-3.

Names in [ ] and - - - - indicate conjectures.

Pedigrees 21 and 22 *The Anicii*

Pages 58-60, 179, 180

Jones, Martindale and Morris, *op. cit.* Dr. John Martindale writes that, though, to judge by his names (attested on his coins) and the names of his daughter, Anicius Olybrius was a descendant of Anicius Hermogenianus Olybrius (consul, 395) and his wife Anicia Juliana, there remains the difficulty that there is no hint that Demetrias, the daughter of this couple, to whom Jerome wrote on the subject of virginity, had a brother or sister. Other possibilities might be descent from Anicius Auchenius Bassus, consul 431, and Anicius Probus, consul 406.

Pedigrees 23 to 26 *Roman and Byzantine Emperors*

Pages 52, 56, 59, 60, 181-5.

Pauly-Wissowa; Jones, Martindale and Morris, *op. cit.*

See also: O. Seeck's article in Pauly-Wissowa, II, ii, (1894), pp. 2196-9.

Charles du Fresne, seigneur du Cange, *Familiae Augustae Byzantinae*, ed. Venice (1729), pp.32-70, 78-82.

Thomas Hodgkin, *Italy and her Invaders*, 2nd ed., (1892-5), Vol. I, pp.185, 276; II, pp.451, 474, 479; III, p.35; and

André Chastagnol, *Les Fastes de la Préfecture de Rome au Bas-Empire*, (Paris, 1962), pp.291-2.

Pedigrees 27 to 31 *Burgundians, Goths, Vandals, Franks, Lombards, Anglo-Saxons*

Pages 52-6, 186-190.

Hodgkin, *op. cit.*, II, p.389; III, pp.5, 320, 595; V, pp.48, 118, 121, 178, 251, 282; VI, pp.36, 62, 148, 337, 438; VII, pp.1, 24, 64, 85.

W.G. Searle, *Anglo-Saxon Bishops, Kings and Nobles*, (1899), pp.258-9, 303, 323, 334-5, 339.

† Pages 53, 188

Pedigree 32 *Rome to Armenia, Fourth Century*

Page 191.

Jones, Martindale and Morris, *op. cit.*

Toumanoff, *op. cit.*

Pedigree 33 *Iberia*

Pages 63, 192.

Traditio, Vol. XXV, (1969). C. Toumanoff, 'Chronology of the Early Kings of Iberia'.

Pedigree 34 *Artaxiads of Armenia*

Pages 62-3, 193.

Information from Prince Toumanoff.

Pedigree 35 *Arsacids of Armenia*

Pages 62-4, 194.

Revue des Études Arméniennes, N.S., Tome VI, (1969), pp.233-281. Cyrille Toumanoff, 'The Third-Century Armenian Arsacids, A Chronological and Genealogical Commentary'.

Pedigree 36 *Armenia: Suren-Pahlavids/Gregorids*

Pages 63-4, 195.

Information from Prince Toumanoff.

Pedigree 37 *Armenia: Mamikonids*

Pages 62, 64-5, 196.

Toumanoff, *Studies in Christian Caucasian History*, *supra cit.*
Information from Prince Toumanoff.
René Grousset, *Histoire de l'Arménie des origines à 1071*, (Paris, 1947).

Pedigree 38 *Armenia: Bagratids*

Pages 64, 197.

Toumanoff, *op. cit.*
Information from Prince Toumanoff.
Grousset, *op. cit.*
Jos. Markwart, *Südarmenien und die Tigrisquellen*, (Wien, 1930).

Pedigree 39 *Armenia: Bagratids and Artsruni*

Pages 64-7, 198.

Grousset, *op. cit.*; Markwart, *op. cit.*; Toumanoff, *op. cit.* and information.

Pedigree 40 *Armenia: Karin-Pahlavids (Kamsakaran)/Pahlavuni*

Pages 64-5, 199.

Information from Prince Toumanoff.

Pedigree 41 *Armeno-Cilicia and Outre Mer*

Pages 65-6, 200.

Markwart; Grousset, and Toumanoff, *op. cit.*
Count W.H. Rüdt-Collenberg, *The Rupenides, Hethumides and Lusignans, the structure of the Armeno-Cilician dynasties*, (Paris, 1963).

Pedigree 42 *Outre Mer to England*

Pages 66, 201.

W.K. Prinz von Isenburg, *Stammtafeln zur Geschichte der europäischen Staaten*, (1936).

Pedigree 43 *Mamikonids, Basilid Emperors of the East, Edward I*

Pages 66, 202.

For the supposed Mamikonid origin of the Emperor Basil I, accepted as almost certain by Prince Toumanoff, see Nicolas Adontz, *Études Arméno-Byzantines*, (Lisbon, 1965), pp. 47-109, 'L'Age et l'Origine de l'Emperor Basile I (867-886)', reprinted from *Byzantion*, (1933, 1934).

The parentage of Theophano, wife of the Emperor Otto II, has been much disputed. The evidence and arguments are summarized and discussed in a recent article by Count Rüdt-Collenberg, 'Wer war Theophano'.

Prince Toumanoff (in a letter of 5 Nov. 1972) comments that though this well sums up all the arguments, it fails, in his view to draw correct conclusions. 'That she is referred to as a niece of John Tsimisces, instead of as a daughter of Romanus II is no argument, because at the moment of her marriage she was indeed the niece of the then reigning Emperor, i.e. John I. Vasiliev has shown that Romanus and Theophano indeed had another child, so that there is room for Theophano in their family. Her name, rare enough, is that of Romanus II's low-born wife, assumed after her elevation. Finally, there is only one serious argument, cited by Rüdt-Collenberg, namely, that of affinity and no trace of dispensation, in connexion with the marriage, or just betrothal, of Romanus II's granddaughter Zoë to Theophano's son Otto III, i.e. her first cousin. But the situation is not as simple as that. On the Western side, the fact (adduced by Rüdt-Collenberg) that we have no trace of a dispensation for such a marriage is rather an argument from silence, and silence complicated by the presence of an anti-Pope; he was a Byzantine creature and it was he who, prior to becoming an anti-pope, carried on the negotiations for the marriage (*C.M.H.*, VI, (1966), p.184); he quite obviously would have acceded to the wishes of his Imperial protector at Constantinople. On the Byzantine side, one notices very often that the intransigence of the clergy withers before a forceful Emperor such as Basil II. Indeed, Zoë later married her second cousin (once removed) Romanus Argyrus and no questions were asked. In view of all this, I personally consider Theophano a daughter of Romanus II, unless stronger argument to the contrary is produced'.

Pedigree 44 *Atlantic to Pacific, 1274*

Pages 72, 203.

Pedigrees 45 and 46 *The Conqueror's Kin*

Pages 80-1, 204-5.

> *The Complete Peerage*, VII, p.520 and App. D. p.711; IX, App. A; X, p.204; XI, p.682; XII, i, App. K.
>
> G.H. White, 'The Sisters and Nieces of Gunnor, Duchess of Normandy', *The Genealogist*, N.S., Vol.37, (1921), pp.57-65, 128-132.
>
> G.A. Moriarty, 'The Early Giffards', *New England Historical and Genealogical Register*, Vol. 105, (1951), p.192; Vol. 106, p.76.
>
> D.C. Douglas, *Domesday Monachorum of Christ Church, Canterbury* (1944), p.43

For the paternity of Judith, wife of Waltheof, see note on Pedigrees 1 to 4, *supra.*, p.253.

Pedigree 47 *English Ancestors of King Edward IV (I)*

Pages 81, 82, 206.

> Isenburg, *op. cit.*
>
> E.A. Freeman, *The History of the Norman Conquest of England*, (1871), IV, p.654, n. R. 'The Children of Harold'.

Pedigree 48 *English Ancestors of King Edward IV (II)*

Pages 82, 207.

> *Complete Peerage, passim*, and Vol. VII, App. J, on 'The Countess Lucy', who was of English origin, perhaps descended from Leofric, Earl of Mercia, and related to Thorold the Sheriff.
>
> J.E. Lloyd, *A History of Wales*, (1911), Vol. II, p.395, n.123; p.347, n.135.
>
> *Dictionary of Welsh Biography*, p.312.

Pedigree 49 *English Ancestors of King Edward IV (III)*

Pages 82, 208.

On Colswein: I.J. Sanders, *English Baronies*, (1960), p.109.
On Edith, daughter of Forn: *Complete Peerage*, XI, App. D. p.10.
On Robert d'Oilly: Baker, *History of Northamptonshire*, I, pp.709-10.
On Gilbert Basset: *Victoria County History: Oxfordshire*, VI, p.325.
On Liulf, *Complete Peerage*, XII, i, p.243.
> *Complete Peerage, passim.*

Pedigree 50 *English Ancestors of King Edward IV (IV)*

Pages 82, 209.

On Leofwin: *Victoria County History: Lancashire*, VI, pp.303-4.
On Sir Robert Holland: *ibid.*, IV, p.92.
On Sweyn and Leysing of Barton: *ibid.*, IV, p.364n.
> *Complete Peerage, passim.*

Pedigree 51 *English Earls of Northumberland*

Pages 81, 210.

> W.G. Searle, *Anglo-Saxon Bishops, Kings and Nobles*, (1899), pp. 370-9.
>
> W. Percy Hedley, *Northumberland Families*, Vol. I, (1968), pp.8-12, 239.
>
> George S.H.L. Washington, *The Earliest Washingtons and their Anglo-Scottish connexions*, (1964), and 'The Origin of the Nevilles', in *The American Genealogist*, Vol. 46, No.3, (July 1970), pp.164-8.

On Crinan *see*: Wagner, *English Genealogy*, 2nd ed. (1972), p.26.

Pedigree 52 *The London Patriciate: FitzAilwin, Barrow, Le̜ Rus, Le Viel*

Pages 86-7, 93, 211.

Though some of the identifications and affiliations in this and Pedigrees 53 and 54 are open to discussion, it is believed that the uncertainties are not such as to affect the argument of pages 000-000.

> William Page, *London. Its Origin and early development*, (1923), pp.248-259.
>
> D.C. Douglas, *The Domesday Monachorum of Christ Church, Canterbury*, (1944), p.62.
>
> E. Williams, *Early Holborn*, (1927), p.1676.
>
> *Calendar of Charter Rolls*, II, p.71
>
> *Complete Peerage*, IV, pp.199, 321.

Pedigree 53 *The London Patriciate: Fitz Algar, Fitz Herlwin, Cornhill*

Pages 86-7, 93, 212.

> J.H. Round, *Geoffrey de Mandeville*, pp.304-12.
>
> William Page, *op. cit.*, pp.242-4.
>
> E. Williams, *op.cit.*, p.1663, identifies William Blemund (*a quo* Blemundisbury = Bloomsbury) as brother of Gervase of Cornhill, taking Blémund as a translation of Cornhill. However, Blémont is a French place name.

Pedigree 54 *The London Patriciate: Basings, Aswy*

Pages 86, 88, 213.

> William Page, *op.cit.*, pp.265-6.
>
> E. Williams, *op.cit.*, pp.706, 1034.
>
> London County Council, *Survey of London*, Vol. IX, *Old St. Pancras and Kentish Town*, (1938), App. VII, p.132.

For the Basings-Merton link, *The Early Rolls of Merton College*, ed., J.R.L. Highfield, *Oxford Hist. Soc.* N.S., XVIII, (1964), pp.6, 87, 110.

For Basings and Normanville, *Victoria County History: Rutland*, II, p.224, and Blore, *Rutland*, p.127.

Pedigree 55 *Lovaine*

Pages 87-8, 93, 214.

Complete Peerage, VIII, p.178; V, p.176.
I.J. Sanders, *English Baronies*, p.130.

Pedigree 56 *Walter de Merton*

Pages 84-6, 88, 215.

The Early Rolls of Merton College, supra cit., pp.40, 110.
Baker, *Northamptonshire*, II, p.96.

Pedigree 57 *Simon de Wauton*

Pages 84, 216.

Victoria County History: Warwickshire, V, pp.195, 78.
Nichols, *Leicestershire*, II, ii, p.715.
Complete Peerage, XII, i, p.153; VI, p.342.

Pedigree 58 *William de Melton*

Pages 89, 217.

L.H. Butler, 'Archbishop Melton, his Neighbours and his Kinsmen, 1317-1340', in *The Journal of Ecclesiastical History*, Vol. II, (1951), pp.54-67.
Complete Peerage, VIII, pp.250-5.

Pedigree 59 *Henry de Bray*

Pages 91-2, 218.

Notes [49] to [55], pp. 91-2.

Pedigree 60 *Henry Chichele*

Pages 95-6, 219.

Notes [65] to [67], p.96.

Pedigree 61 *Drake of Essex*

Pages 96-7, 220.

Notes [64] to [68], pp. 95-6.

Pedigree 62 *Thomas Cromwell*

Pages 100, 221.

Complete Peerage.

Pedigrees 63 to 65 *Puritans and Colonists*

Pages 98, 222-4; page 98, notes 76-7.

Wagner, *English Genealogy*, 2nd ed., (1972), Tab. IV.
Complete Peerage, XII, ii, p.409, note (c) quotes a letter from
Conway to Laud, 8 June 1640. 'The Earl of Warwick is the temporal
head of the Puritans, and the Earl of Holland is their spiritual head'.

Pedigree 66 *Queen Elizabeth I to William Shakespeare*

Pages 101, 225.

Complete Peerage.
Sheldon. College of Arms MSS. C27, fo.98, and Arundel I, 117.
Combe. E.K. Chambers, *William Shakespeare*, (1930), Vol. II, p.133,
    cites from J.H. Pollen, *Cathol ic Rec. Soc. Publ.* V, p.345. quoting
    English College at Rome Collectanea, F. f.90, an account   of the
    martyrdom of William Freeman, a Catholic priest, 13 Aug. 1595,
    which says that William Combe (second son of John Combe of Strat-
    ford by Katherine, widow of Adrian Quiney) was 'alied by marriage
    of their parents with Mistres Sheldon, with whom Mr. Freeman now
    conversed'. This, Chambers concludes, means Jane (Lewknor) wife
    of Anthony Sheldon of Broadway (d.1584), grandson of Ralph Shel-
    don of Beoley (d.1546). Hence he conjectures that Katherine
    (Quiney-Combe) was a sister or daughter of Ralph Sheldon (d.1546).
    As Ralph's grandson, Ralph II, was born in 1537 and Katherine's
    marriage to John Combe took place in 1534, it seems more likely
    that she was a daughter of Ralph I—unless, indeed, the kinship was
    on the Lewknor side.
    Ibid., p.128 on John Combe (d.1654) and 127, 139, on John
    Combe (d.1614), 'a notable usurer', whose epitaph Shakespeare is
    said to have written.
Quiney. Chambers, *op.cit.*, II, p.104.
Blunt. Chambers, *op.cit.*, II, p.137; Coll. Arm. MSS. Arundel I, p.117;
    2D14, p.197; 7D14, p.109.
Hathaway. Chambers, *op.cit.*, II, p.50. Richard Hathaway, nephew of
    Anne, was a baker of Stratford.
Hart. Chambers, *op.cit.*, II, p.xvi.
    Burke's Landed Gentry, (1952 ed.), pp.1175-6 (contributed by the
    present writer).

Pedigree 67 *Burleigh and Robert Browne*

Pages 102, 226.

Cecil. Victoria County History; Oswald Barron, *Northamptonshire
    Families*, (1906), pp.25-7.
Browne. Thomas Blore, *History of Rutland*, (1811), p.93.
    Dictionary of National Biography.

Pedigree 68 *Quakers: Crowley and Lloyd*

Pages 108-110, 227.

Q = Quaker

Crowley. A.L. Reade, *The Reades of Blackwood Hill*, (1906), pp.168-170; *East Anglian Notes and Queries*, N.S., Vol. IV, (1891-2), p.159.

Lloyd. The Dictionary of Welsh Biography, pp.590-1; Coll. Arm. Reg. Norfolk, XVIII, pp.132-5.

Pedigree 69 *Birmingham Unitarians*

Pages 110-112, 228.

Note [93].

Pedigree 70 *Pigot*

Pages 106-7, 229.

The Complete Peerage.

Pigot and Godde. Henry Wagner, 'Memoranda relating to the (?) French Refugee Family of Godde', in *Miscellanea Genealogica et Heraldica*, N.S., Vol. III, pp.221-2.

Wagner. A.R. Wagner, 'The Wagners of Brighton and their connections', in *Sussex Archaeological Collections*, Vol. 97, pp.35-57.

Teulon. Henry Wagner, 'Pedigree of the Huguenot Refugee Family of Teulon', in *Miscellanea Genealogica et Heraldica*, 4th Series, Vol. II, (1908), pp.202-5.

Anthony Wagner, 'The Teulon Ancestry in France', in *Proceedings of the Huguenot Society of London*, Vol. XXI, (1971), pp.569-98.

D.L. Teulon, *The Huguenot Refugee Family of Teulon*, (Newhaven, 1971).

Pedigrees 71 and 72 *Whigs*

Pages 103-4, 106-7, 230-1.

The Complete Peerage.

Pedigree 73 *Samuel Johnson*

Pages 107-110, 232.

Johnson. A.L. Reade, *Johnsonian Gleanings, X. Johnson's Early Life: The Final Narrative*, (1946), pp.10-11, 161-9.

Skrymsher. Ibid., Part IX, (1939), pp.112-8. 'Charles Skrymsher and his relationship to Johnson'.

Leigh. Coll. Arm. MSS. K3/83; 7D14/176; Benefactors, II, 19.

Pedigrees 74 and 75 *Fitch*

> *Pages 113-5, 233-4.*
>
> Pages 113 p. 108 and 114 p. 109

Pedigrees 76 to 93 *Eton Families*

> *Pages 123-133, 235-252.*

Abbreviations:

CW	=	Canon of Windsor
DW	=	Dean of Windsor
E	=	At Eton
EL	=	Eton Living
FE	=	Fellow of Eton
FK	=	Fellow of King's College, Cambridge
HME	=	Head Master of Eton
KS	=	King's Scholar at Eton
LME	=	Lower Master of Eton
PE	=	Provost of Eton
PK	=	Provost of King's College, Cambridge
SK	=	Scholar of King's College, Cambridge
VPE	=	Vice-Provost of Eton
VPK	=	Vice-Provost of King's.

The Pedigrees rest largely on Thomas Harwood, *Alumni Etonenses, 1797.*

> Sir Wasey Sterry, *Eton College Register, 1441-1698*, (1943).
> R.A. Austen Leigh, *Eton College Register, 1689-1752 & 1753-1790.*
> H.E.C. Stapylton, *Eton' School Lists, 1791-1850* and subsequent Eton Registers; the six volumes of *Etoniana* edited by R.A. Austen Leigh; and *Alumni Cantabrigienses*, ed. J. & J.A. Venn.

Pedigrees 76 and 77: Day: pp.235-6
College of Arms MSS., Vincent, Salop., fo. 292^b and F. 1, fo. 5^b; Harleian Society, Vol. 56, pp.83-4.

Montague (or Mountague)
Jonas (c.1586-c.1633) was probably related to the Boveney family, but Sterry's conjecture that he was a *son* of Thomas Montague of Winkfield, Yeoman of the Guard, who d. 1630, aet. 91 is chronologically difficult. On the probable Norman origin of these Montagues, *see* Wagner, *English Genealogy*, 2nd ed. (1972), p.62.

Pedigree 79: Goad: p.238
Etoniana, I, pp.149-151; G. Gyll, *History of Wraysbury*, p.284.

Pedigree 80: Hawtrey: p.239
F.M. Hawtrey, *The History of the Hawtrey Family*, (1903); Coll. Arm. Reg. Norfolk, 28, p.83. Information from Mr. S.C. Hawtrey.

The Norman origins (*De Alta Ripa*, *de Haute Rive*) and links of the one or more families of Hawtrey, Dealtry, Dawtrey etc. have still to be elucidated.

Pedigree 81: Sleech: p.240
F.M. Hawtrey, *The Hawtrey Family* (*supra cit.*) Ch. XII; *Burke's Landed Gentry*, ed. (1838), Vol. III, pp.571-2.
The parents of the four Sleech brothers (Stephen, b.1705, John, Edward, Henry and their sisters) and their previous Eton links have been accidentally omitted. The parents were the Rev. Richard Sleech, Fellow of Eton, prebendary of Windsor and Rector of Hitcham and Farnham, and his wife Elizabeth, daughter of the Rev. Mr. Upman, Fellow of Eton. The father of the Rev. Richard Sleech was Edward Sleech, said to have moved from Kent to Windsor, c.1660-70, whose widow Anne (Saunders) remarried after his death in 1681 the Rev. John Newborough (d.1712), Head Master of Eton. Edward and Anne Sleech had also a daughter Lucy, who married the Rev. Stephen Weston (1665-1742, *D.N.B.*), Eton, KS, FK, AME 1690, LME 1693-1707, FE 1707, D.D., Vicar of Mapledurham (EL) 1716, Bishop of Exeter 1724.

Pedigree 83: Dupuis: p.242
Henry Wagner, 'Hugenot Refugee Family of Dupuis', in *Miscellanea Genealogica et Heraldica*, N.S., Vol. III, pp.249-251.

Pedigrees 86 and 87: Carter, Stone, Balston, Kynastons, Hale, Johnson Cory, Furse, Vidal, Maud, Crace, Lubbock: pp.245-6
Faith Compton Mackenzie, *As much as I dare*, (1938), and information from Mr. J.W. Carter.
Balston: Information from the late Mr. Thomas Balston.

Pedigree 90: Sumner: p.249
Early generations: information from Mr. Jeremy Gibson.

Pedigrees 91 to 93: Thackeray: pp.250-252
Gordon N. Ray, *Thackeray: The Uses of Adversity, 1811-1846*, (1955), p.21; *The Herald and Genealogist*, Vol. II, (1865), pp.315-28. Coll. Arm. Reg., 17D14, fo. 228; information from Mr. A.D. Thackeray. *See also*, Belinda Norman-Butler, *Victorian Aspirations. The Life and Labour of Charles and Mary Booth*, (1972), pedigrees at end for links between the families of Macaulay, Trevelyan, Potter, Meinertzhagen, Cripps, Hobhouse, Fletcher, Llewelyn, Davies, Du Maurier, Booth, Ritchie, Thackeray and Norman-Butler.

INDEX

Notes

1. Word by word arrangement has been used
   e.g. West Felton
       Westfaling

2. Names with prefixes:
   Le, La, L', Du, De la — under prefix, with reference from name De, D' under name

3. Books and articles from which quotations are taken are indicated thus:
   Allegory of Love
   Names of periodicals or series are indicated thus:
   'Antiquaries Journal'